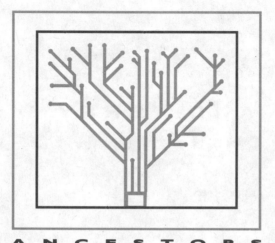

ANCESTORS

A BEGINNER'S GUIDE TO

FAMILY HISTORY AND

GENEALOGY

A COMPANION TO THE PBS TELEVISION SERIES

ANCESTORS

A TEN-PART SERIES CELEBRATING

THE SIGNIFICANCE OF FAMILY HISTORY

BY JIM AND TERRY WILLARD
WITH JANE WILSON

HOUGHTON MIFFLIN COMPANY   BOSTON   NEW YORK   1997

Ancestors

PRODUCED BY **KBYU** TELEVISION PROVO/SALT LAKE CITY UTAH

MAJOR FUNDING FOR THE ANCESTORS TELEVISION SERIES PROVIDED BY
BRIGHAM YOUNG UNIVERSITY AND KODAK IMAGE MAGIC SYSTEMS

The PBS logo is a registered trademark.

For information about permission to reproduce selections
from this book, write to Permissions, 215 Park Avenue
South, New York, NY 10003

For information about this and other Houghton Mifflin
trade and reference books and multimedia products, visit
The Bookstore at Houghton Mifflin on the World Wide
Web at http://www.hmco.com/trade/.

Library of Congress Cataloging-in-Publication Data
Willard, Jim.
Ancestors: a beginner's guide to family history and
genealogy/by Jim and Terry Willard with Jane Wilson.
    p.   cm.
"A companion to the PBS television series: Ancestors,
a ten-part series celebrating the significance
of family history."
Includes bibliographical references.
ISBN 0-395-85410-5
1. United States—Genealogy—Handbooks, manuals, etc.
2. Genealogy.   I. Willard, Terry.   II. Wilson, Jane. 1957—.
        CS16.W526   1997
    929'.1—dc21   96-39864

Design by Anne Chalmers
Typefaces: Linotype-Hell Fairfield Medium
and ITC Edwardian Script

Printed in the United States of America
QUM 10 9 8 7 6 5 4 3 2 1

Credits and permissions for illustrations on page 212.

Preface

THIS BOOK is a companion to the PBS television series *Ancestors*. It is the result of many years of development and research in bringing family history and genealogy to beginners.

Initially, development began with the cooperation of Alex Haley. In 1989, KBYU Television invited Mr. Haley to join the *Ancestors* project as coproducer and host of the series. He enthusiastically accepted. More than once, the *Ancestors* team went to Mr. Haley's farm in Tennessee where he offered insight, suggestions, and unbridled energy in moving the project forward. His death was a great loss to the project. Haley summed up the heart of the *Ancestors* project when he declared:

In all of us there is a hunger, marrow deep, to know our heritage
To know who we are and where we came from.
Without this enriching knowledge there is a hollow yearning.
No matter what our attainments in life,
there is still a vacuum, an emptiness
and the most disquieting loneliness.

The *Ancestors* project continued after Mr. Haley's death with a focus on creating a series that would help others find their roots. The content of this book is a result of much of the research and development from the television series. Brigham Young University caught the vision of *Ancestors* and contributed much of the funding and talent necessary to create the series. The Family History Library in Salt Lake City devoted the energies and resources of their staff over the years to help the *Ancestors* team with content. The National Genealogical Society and the Federation of Genealogical Societies were instrumental in introducing the *Ancestors* team to the many experts and resources within the genealogical community. When funding became an issue, Kodak Image Magic Systems stepped up to the plate and delivered the final run to bring the series home. To all of the individuals who have told their stories and opened their lives to share the impact of genealogy and family history with others, thank you.

Acknowledgments

ANCESTRY is pleased to have contributed to the creation of this book. Ancestry is a leading provider of high-quality books, magazines, software and Internet products to genealogists, historians, and libraries around the world. We celebrate the burgeoning interest in family history and recognize the positive impact that it has on individual lives. The *Ancestors* television series and this companion volume are a valuable introduction to the journey of a lifetime.

Loretto D. Szucs
Managing Editor
Ancestry, Incorporated
Salt Lake City, Utah

MANY CONTRIBUTIONS have been made to bring this book to you. Ancestry, Incorporated supplied reference material and content for the resources in the appendix. The following experts in genealogy have contributed material to chapters in the book. Each expert was part of the *Ancestors* series.

Desmond Walls Allen contributed content to chapter 1. Antonia Cottrell Martin helped with chapter 2 and Bill Zimmerman brought his warmth and knowledge to chapter 3. Chapter 4 was urged along with the help of John Philip Colleta and Sharon DeBartolo Carmack. The always cheerful Curt Witcher brought his expertise to chapter 6. Tony Burroughs gave clarity to chapter 7, Vickie Venne helped to iron out chapter 8, and Richard Eastman brought high-tech help to chapter 9. Each expert has brought a new dimension to the book. Their contributions provide a solid foundation for the beginner.

A final word of thanks goes to Johni Cerny of Lineages. Johni's vast experience in genealogical research was an invaluable touchstone for the book. She graciously fielded phone calls about large and small issues while the manuscript was being written.

TABLE OF CONTENTS

PREFACE   V

ACKNOWLEDGMENTS   VII

INTRODUCTION   1

ANCESTORS

A BEGINNER'S GUIDE TO
FAMILY HISTORY AND
GENEALOGY

INTRODUCTION

Getting Started

AMERICA IS EXPERIENCING a resurgence of interest in family history and genealogy. It has been estimated that more than 100 million Americans have started tracing their family histories.[1] The surge in interest began in the 1970s with Alex Haley's book *Roots* and the television miniseries that followed. Unfortunately, *Roots* left many Americans with the desire to trace their family history but with no clear idea of how to begin. The result was frustration and confusion for many well-intentioned beginners. This book is designed to ease that frustration and confusion. The information and stories in this book will inspire you to start your family history and help you meet with success.

An INSPIRING example of the value of family history and genealogy is Victor Edmundo Villasenor. He has been successful in his search for his roots. Of humble origins, his mother and father came to this country from Mexico and settled on a farm in Southern California. When Victor began his journey into family history, he was faced with common doubts:

"When I started my parents' story, I thought that the story of the family down the street was a better story. I didn't think much of my parents' story. But once you really start talking and getting to know people deep inside, an ordinary story can become great and wonderful. *Everyone is special.* I know we've all heard that cliché, but it's really not a cliché. Everyone is born with certain gifts and liabilities. As they live through life, they do heroic things and negative things. As you get to know them, they become heroic for doing the best that they can."

When Victor was a child, his father and grandmother filled Victor's soul with stories of Mexico and the culture from which he came. Victor's father once told him that everyone was Mexican, and if they were not, they wanted to be. In Victor's community everyone spoke Spanish. When Victor started school, his world was shattered. "I'll never forget it. The teacher put me in the back of the classroom with some other Mexican children. I started talking in Spanish and the teacher screamed, 'No Spanish!' It scared me so much I said, 'Bathroom, bathroom.' She said that I had to wait for recess. I was so scared that I peed in my pants. And within the first day of school, I began to see that everything I had been raised with was wrong."

Victor grew up angry and alienated, ashamed of his Mexican heritage. The stories of his village that he shared with other children were ridiculed. His teachers discounted his cultural heritage. "I didn't start resenting the teacher; she was the authority figure, she knew what was right. I started to hate my parents, I felt they had lied to me. All of the stories were lies."

In kindergarten, Victor had a friend, Howard, who was invited to play with Victor at his house. Although it happened forty years ago, Howard's response still hurts Victor: "I can't play with you, Mexicans are bad people." Victor replied, "Oh, I didn't know. I'm sorry." Victor remembered, "I wasn't even in first grade, and I already knew that my people are bad, are stupid, and that other people are frightened of them. That became my reality."

Victor's father told him of a big snake in his village in Mexico that had eaten children. "Everyone was terrified of it, and my grandfather, a great horseman, fought the serpent on horseback. The serpent was eight feet tall, and he took a tree branch, rammed it down the serpent's throat, and roped and dragged him, like Saint George. My father told me it was true. I thought it was a lie." It wasn't until a trip to the San Diego Zoo, when he was older, that Victor "went to the man that studies snakes and asked him, 'I hear that there is a snake who stands up eight feet tall and can attack a man on horseback. Is that possible?' He said, 'Oh yeah. That's the bushmaster.' And I said, 'What?' He said, 'Yeah, they're fourteen feet long and stand up seven feet. Half their length. And if they're sixteen feet, they stand up eight feet.' And he said, 'They were fearless. That's why they are basically extinct. They would attack a train, an automobile. So surely they'll attack a man on horseback.' I asked him, 'Can they eat a little kid, or a baby pig?' 'Well, a rattlesnake can eat a rabbit, and it's much smaller than the bushmaster, so sure.'" It was then that Victor realized he had been a doubting Thomas. "My father's stories were true."

Victor went to Mexico at age nineteen to see for himself the land of the stories of his youth. "When I went to Mexico, I could hear them speak Spanish, and then I could see the Indian cultures and the rich colors and the food. All of a sudden, I said, 'I am somebody, I come from somewhere.' It was like a great peace came over me. I just started crying. I started to understand that my parents were good people. I had been mad at them all these years, but they hadn't lied to me. The one thing that happened when I started researching my history is that now my parents are my greatest heroes. . . . Until you get to the roots of your family, you are absolutely lost. Just like a ship out at sea in storms, and you are helpless."

Victor found peace and identity in his family history. He spent sixteen years putting his family history together. He started with stories that he did not believe and an uncertain identity. He came away with a full understanding of himself and a gift for future generations.

$\mathcal{E}$VERYONE has an important history that makes them who they are. Your history and the history of your family are unique. You will treasure it and share it with others. But first you must begin to find it.

Anyone can research family history. If you can write a letter and talk on the telephone, you can do family history. No special skill or degree is needed. Family history and genealogy will help you reconnect with family members in a new way. You will be surprised and delighted with what you learn and with how willing people are to cooperate and help you.

Part of the excitement in genealogy comes from the discovery process. Think of yourself as a detective trying to solve a mystery. Learn to ask leading questions and make creative use of records you find. Take genealogy classes, read how-to books, join study groups, and attend conferences to increase your knowledge of sources. Eventually, you may want to travel in pursuit of your new hobby. You will want to go to libraries, archives and courthouses, and to the actual places where your great-grandparents and other family members lived. Some families plan vacations around family history and reunions.

The history that we learn in school is a record of great deeds by great men and women. What is neglected is the story of people who, step by step, and through quiet sacrifice helped to build a country. The story of your family is the story of a nation. What you will learn in researching your family history will go far beyond the walls of your home: you will find heroes and villains, saints and sinners. You will find yourself.

CHAPTER ONE

The Pedigree Chart

WHEN YOU BEGIN your search for ancestors you will find information about many of your relatives. Not every relative that you find information about will be an ancestor. An ancestor is someone from whom you are directly descended. Your parents, grandparents, and great-great-grandparents are your ancestors. Although you are related to aunts and great-aunts, uncles and great-uncles, they are not your ancestors because you are not descended *directly* from them. You will still gather information about these relatives, but they will not be the primary focus of your search. Understanding some basic principles and tools about genealogy and family history at the start will save you time and effort later on.

To begin with, there is a difference between family history and genealogy. The word *genealogy* comes from two Greek words, one meaning "race" or "family" and the other "theory" or "science." Therefore, genealogy is the science of tracing your ancestry.

Genealogy has been a practice among many different cultures over time. The older oral traditions focus primarily on royal lineages. From the Scottish bards who would recite the pedigree of the Scots King at inagurations to the Maori of New Zealand and the pre-Hispanic Peruvians, oral traditions of genealogy are found in many cultures on numerous continents. The surviving Chinese traditions of ancestor worship and long, detailed pedigrees are a marvel and show some claims to descent from Confucius.

The modern method of genealogy is descended from the western European tradition of tracing ancestry to prove royal succession to the throne. Genealogy was also used in lawsuits and court cases involving land transactions and taxation in western Europe. A more systematic method of genealogy evolved from the 1500s forward, and it is this tradition that has contributed to the standard practices that are followed

The word *genealogy* comes from two Greek words, one meaning "race" or "family," the other "theory" or "science." Therefore, genealogy is the science of tracing your ancestry. *Family history,* stories about your ancestors, can help you research your genealogy, and your genealogy proves your family history.

The word *pedigree* comes from two Latin words: *pes* meaning "foot," and *grus* meaning "crane." The standard pedigree chart that has been used for years does resemble a crane's foot. This form has become a well-known symbol and is synonymous with genealogy.

today. Current genealogy is based on exacting research that documents who your ancestors are.

If genealogy is the study of direct lineage and of proving one's ancestry, family history is the icing on the cake. Family history is the stories of the lives of your ancestors, the rich tapestry of their lives. Family history is the lore that has been passed down from generation to generation, the traditions that are heard in song or shared at the table over meals cooked from grandmother's recipes. It is your religion. It is the photos and the quilts, the diaries and the letters. Family history can help you research your genealogy, and your genealogy proves your family history.

In beginning your family history and genealogy, it is important to use the most common tools in genealogy for organizing the information you know about your ancestors, the *pedigree chart,* the *family group record,* and the *research log.* The pedigree chart is used to show your ancestry at a glance. The word *pedigree* comes from two Latin words: *pes* meaning "foot," and *grus* meaning "crane." The standard pedigree chart that has been used for years does resemble a crane's foot. This form has become a well-known symbol and is synonymous with genealogy.

As you gather information about your relatives and ancestors, the pedigree chart helps you keep track of the information you find. It is easy in the beginning when you write down the information about you and your parents—there are only three names and sets of dates to keep track of. But soon, this task will take on new proportions. With each generation back in time, you double your ancestors. You have two parents, four grandparents, eight great-grandparents, sixteen great-great-grandparents and thirty-two great-great-great-grandparents. Assuming that a generation averages thirty years, if you follow your ancestral lines through time to the thirteenth generation, around the founding of Jamestown, Virginia, in 1607, you will have as many as 4,096 ancestors in that one generation alone. The total number of your ancestors back to that time is an astounding 8,190 people. While you can remember the names and significant dates of your parents and grandparents, things are going to get confusing as early as your fourth generation when you have thirty-two names and sets of dates to keep track of in that generation alone.

A pedigree chart is like a road map of your ancestors. It will help you keep them organized. You can exchange pedi-

gree charts with relatives so you'll each be able to see how the other descends from a common ancestor. Some standard ways of recording information on pedigree charts have evolved in recent years:

You are in the number one position on the chart.

Your father is number two on the chart.

Your mother is number three.

Your father's father (your paternal grandfather) is number four.

Your father's mother is number five on the chart. Your maternal grandfather is number six and your maternal grandmother is number seven, and so on. A pattern develops in the numbering scheme that will help you keep track of the thousands of ancestors you are searching for.

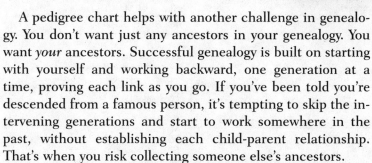

A pedigree chart helps with another challenge in genealogy. You don't want just any ancestors in your genealogy. You want *your* ancestors. Successful genealogy is built on starting with yourself and working backward, one generation at a time, proving each link as you go. If you've been told you're descended from a famous person, it's tempting to skip the intervening generations and start to work somewhere in the past, without establishing each child-parent relationship. That's when you risk collecting someone else's ancestors.

On page 8 is the pedigree chart of President John F. Kennedy. It clearly shows how much information can be understood about his ancestors at a glance. Birth, death, and marriage dates are right there for you to see. This pedigree chart shows four generations of the Kennedy family. You will notice information gaps in this pedigree in the fourth generation, which, in the Kennedy example, is the immigrant generation. It is common for Americans to find immigrant ancestors within three generations. Finding information about immigrant ancestors can be challenging, hence the missing information on JFK's pedigree chart. When you first fill out your pedigree chart there will be missing information. Don't let that discourage you. If a presidential pedigree can have some missing information, so can yours. After all, genealogy and family history is about filling in those gaps.

PEDIGREE CHART

ANCESTORS™

2 Joseph Patrick KENNEDY
FATHER (of no. 1)
Born 6 Sep 1888
Place East Boston, Suffolk Co, MA
Married 7 Oct 1914
Place Boston, Suffolk Co, MA
Died 18 Nov 1969
Place Hyannis Port, Barnstable Co, MA

1 John Fitzgerald KENNEDY

Born 29 May 1917
Place Brookline, Norfolk Co, MA
Married 12 Sep 1953
Place Newport, Newport Co, RI
Died 22 Nov 1963
Place Dallas, Dallas Co, TX

Jacqueline Lee BOUVIER
SPOUSE (of no. 1)

3 Rose Elizabeth FITZGERALD
MOTHER (of no. 1)
Born 22 Jul 1890
Place Boston, Suffolk Co, MA
Died 22 Jan 1995
Place Hyannis Port, Barnstable Co, MA

4 Patrick Joseph KENNEDY
FATHER (of no. 2)
Born 14 Jan 1858
Place East Boston, Suffolk Co, MA
Married 23 Nov 1887
Place Boston, Suffolk Co, MA
Died 18 May 1929
Place Boston, Suffolk Co, MA

5 Mary Augusta HICKEY
MOTHER (of no. 2)
Born 6 Dec 1857
Place Winthrop, Suffolk Co, MA
Died 18 May 1923
Place Boston, Suffolk Co, MA

6 John Francis "Honey Fitz" FITZGERALD
FATHER (of no. 3)
Born 11 Feb 1863
Place Boston, Suffolk Co, MA
Married 18 Sep 1889
Place Concord, Middlesex Co, MA
Died 3 Oct 1950
Place Boston, Suffolk Co, MA

7 Mary Josephine HANNON
MOTHER (of no. 3)
Born 31 Oct 1865
Place Acton, Middlesex Co, MA
Died 8 Aug 1964
Place Dorchester, Suffolk Co, MA

8 Patrick KENNEDY
FATHER (of no. 4)
Born ABT 1823
Place Dunganstown, Wexford Co, Ireland
Married 26 Sep 1849
Place Boston, Suffolk Co, MA
Died 22 Nov 1858
Place Boston, Suffolk Co, MA

9 Bridget MURPHY
MOTHER (of no. 4)
Born 1821
Place Dunganstown, Wexford Co, Ireland
Died 20 Dec 1888
Place Boston, Suffolk Co, MA

10 James HICKEY
FATHER (of no. 5)
Born 1836
Place Cork, Cork Co, Ireland
Married
Place
Died 22 Nov 1900
Place Boston, Suffolk Co, MA

11 Margaret M. FIELD
MOTHER (of no. 5)
Born ABT 1836
Place
Died 5 Jun 1911
Place Boston, Suffolk Co, MA

12 Thomas FITZGERALD
FATHER (of no. 6)
Born
Place
Married 15 Nov 1857
Place
Died 19 May 1885
Place Boston, Suffolk Co, MA

13 Rosanna COX
MOTHER (of no. 6)
Born ABT 1836
Place
Died 12 Mar 1879
Place Boston, Suffolk Co, MA

14 Michael HANNON
FATHER (of no. 7)
Born 30 Sep 1832
Place
Married 12 Feb 1854
Place
Died 1 Feb 1900
Place Acton, Middlesex Co, MA

15 Mary Ann FITZGERALD
MOTHER (of no. 7)
Born ABT 1832
Place
Died July 1 1904
Place Acton, Middlesex Co, MA

Through the ages, pedigree charts have taken many forms. The common ones we use today have been in general use since the mid-twentieth century. With all respect for individuality, there are some conventions in genealogy that will help you keep track of information effectively. Write names of women on our charts and forms with the names they were born with, their "maiden" names, rather than the names they acquired through marriage. If you look at JFK's pedigree chart you will notice that his mother is accounted for as Rose Elizabeth Fitzgerald, not Rose Fitzgerald Kennedy. Jacqueline Kennedy Onassis is accounted for by her maiden name, Jacqueline Lee Bouvier. Dates are written in a standard format as 25 July 1950, with the day of the month written first, then the month as a word, and the year as four digits. This format for dates keeps confusion to a minumum when jogging across the centuries in search of dates. If your ancestor had a common nickname, insert it in quotation marks as in JFK's pedigree chart where his maternal grandfather is listed as John Francis "Honey Fitz" Fitzgerald. If you choose to use a different format, it isn't techincally wrong, but it may lead to confusion. It will also be easier for genealogists to share with you information about research when standard formats are used.

Your pedigree chart lists all of your ancestors, that is your *direct* line, working back in time. There is no room to list all of the members of each family on this chart. So, where do you put that information? The family group record is used to place each person on the pedigree chart into family groups. On pages 10–11 is an example of a family group record for John F. Kennedy. This lists the president as a child in his parents' family group record. A second family group record could also be created that shows the president as a father in his own family group record. It is important to become familiar with family group records from the start. These records will help to keep your information straight and keep track of all of your relatives. One of the first mistakes that many beginners make in family history and genealogy is not keeping track of information in a systematic and organized fashion. Keeping good records from the start will save you time and frustration later.

A third record that you should be familiar with is the research log. The research log keeps track of what sources you have used to document your family history and genealogy.

THE FAMILY TREE AS AN IMAGE is a common frame of reference for many beginning family historians. If you rotate a pedigree chart 90 degrees counter-clockwise, you will see the image of a family tree with a trunk, two limbs, and branches coming off the two limbs. The trunk in this image could represent you. The two trunks would be your children and the next series of branches would be your grandchildren.

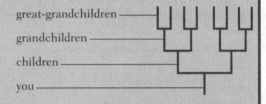

Now, rotate the image upside down and combine it with the first image. You are still the trunk and your parents become the first two sets of roots, with your grandparents filling in as the next set of roots.

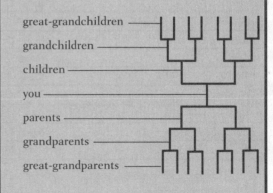

ANCESTORS™

FAMILY GROUP
RECORD

Husband's name: Joseph Patrick KENNEDY

Born: 6 Sep 1888	Place: East Boston, Suffolk Co, MA
Mar. 7 Oct 1914	Place: Boston, Suffolk Co, MA
Died: 18 Nov 1969	Place: Hyannis Port, Barnstable Co, MA
Father: Patrick Joseph KENNEDY	Mother: Mary Augusta HICKEY

Wife's name: Rose Elizabeth FITZGERALD

Born: 22 Jul 1890	Place: Boston, Suffolk Co, MA
Mar.	Place
Died: 22 Jan 1995	Place: Hyannis Port, Barnstable Co, MA
Father: John Francis "Honey Fitz" FITZGERALD	Mother: Mary Josephine HANNON

Children (In order of birth)

1	Sex: M	Name: Joseph Patrick KENNEDY, Jr.	Spouse
Born: 25 Jul 1915		Place: Hull, Plymouth Co, MA	
Mar.		Place	
Died: 12 Aug 1944		Place: an airplane, Suffolk, England	

2	Sex: M	Name: John Fitzgerald KENNEDY	Spouse: Jacqueline Lee BOUVIER
Born: 29 May 1917		Place: Brookline, Norfolk Co, MA	
Mar. 12 Sep 1953		Place: Newport, Newport Co, RI	
Died: 22 Nov 1963		Place: Dallas, Dallas Co, TX	

3	Sex: F	Name: Rosemary "Rose Marie" KENNEDY	Spouse
Born: 20 Feb 1920		Place: Brookline, Norfolk Co, MA	
Mar.		Place	
Died		Place	

4	Sex: F	Name: Kathleen "Kick" KENNEDY	Spouse: William John Robert CAVENDISH
Born: 20 Feb 1920		Place: Brookline, Norfolk Co, MA	
Mar. 6 May 1944		Place: London, England	
Died: 13 May 1948		Place: Ste-Bauzille, Ardeche, France	

Additional Children (In order of birth)

5	Sex: F	Name: Eunice Mary KENNEDY		Spouse: Robert Sargent SHRIVER, Jr.
Born: 10 July 1921		Place: Brookline, Norfolk Co, MA		
Mar. 23 May 1953		Place: New York City, NY		
Died		Place		

6	Sex: F	Name: Patricia KENNEDY		Spouse: Peter LAWFORD
Born: 6 May 1924		Place: Brookline, Norfolk Co, MA		
Mar. 24 Apr 1954		Place: New York City, NY		
Died		Place		

7	Sex: M	Name: Robert Francis KENNEDY		Spouse: Ethel SKAKEL
Born: 20 Nov 1925		Place: Brookline, Norfolk Co, MA		
Mar. 17 Jun 1950		Place: Greenwich, Fairfield Co, CT		
Died: 6 Jun 1968		Place: Los Angeles, Los Angeles Co, CA		

8	Sex: F	Name: Jean Ann KENNEDY		Spouse: Stephen Edward SMITH
Born: 20 Feb 1928		Place: Boston, Suffolk Co, MA		
Mar. 19 May 1956		Place: New York City, NY		
Died		Place		

9	Sex M	Name: Edward Moore KENNEDY		Spouse: Virginia Joan BENNETT
Born: 22 Feb 1932		Place: Boston, Suffolk Co, MA		
Mar. 30 Nov 1958		Place: Bronxville, Westchester Co, NY		
Died		Place		

OTHER MARRIAGES: Edward Moore KENNEDY divorced Virginia Joan BENNETT in 1984.

Edward Moore KENNEDY married Victoria Ann Reggie 3 Jul 1992 in McLean, Fairfax Co, Va.

SOURCES:

Doris Kearns Goodwin, *The Fitzgeralds and the Kennedys: An American Saga.* New York: Simon and Schuster, 1988.

Harvey Rachin, *The Kennedys: A Chronological History.* New York.: Ballantine Books, 1986.

Senator Kennedy's Senate Staff, Public Relations, 1996.

Barbara Gibson, *Rose Kennedy and Her Family: The Best and Worst of Their Lives and Times.* Secaucus, NJ: Carol Publishing Group, 1995.

Ronald Kessler, *The Sins of The Father: Joseph P. Kennedy and the Dynasty He Created.* New York: Warner Books, 1996.

Palladium Interactive, Kennedy sample in *Family Gathering,* 1996.

When you begin to share the information you've found with others, they'll want to know who supplied you with your details and what records you've searched. If you've noted your sources on your research log, you'll be able to supply answers to these questions.

Your ancestors are more than the sum total of names and dates that you will record on your pedigree chart and family group records. From the begininng you should be reading a variety of source material and social history to help you get a better picture of your ancestors.

This resource for your work cannot be underestimated. In your search for ancestors, you'll experience the thrill of the chase. One source will lead you to another and another. Often, during this chase, it is difficult to stop yourself and make detailed notes on your research log. But think of the research log like your checkbook register: you hate to use it, but you know that if you ignore it altogether, the results can lead to disaster. If your great-aunt Sue has a different recollection of the maiden name of your great-great-grandmother than your uncle Charlie, write this discrepancy down in your research log. Any source that you use should be accounted for. If you're careful to keep your log current, when you find conflicting information, it will be easier to decide which is the most accurate. When you begin to share the information you've found with others, they'll want to know who supplied details and what records you've searched. If you've noted your sources, you'll be able to supply answers to these questions. Remember, there is going to be conflict in information that you gather from different sources, and the only way to sort the wheat from the chaff is with strong documentation and sources. This research log has been filled out with sources used to find the information about JFK's birth, death, and marriage. (See page 13.)

Successful family historians and genealogists use the pedigree chart, family group record, and research log as guides for what they know and what they want to learn about their family history. Used carefully, these tools will save you time and effort in finding the information you need. From the start, establish a system for using these records that works for you. Some genealogists use a good three-ring binder, others use a filing cabinet and files. If you have moved quickly into the information age and you want to use computers to help you organize, store, and share your family history, see chapter 9 for more details.

Your ancestors are more than the sum total of names and dates that you will record on your pedigree chart and family group records. From the begining you should be reading a variety of source material that will help you get a better picture of your ancestors. Imagine if the only information you had about your ancestors was the pedigree chart and family group record. Yes, these records tell you who your ancestors were, but they are silent about the actual lives of your ancestors. The tragedies and triumphs, sorrows and joys of your heritage

ANCESTORS

RESEARCH LOG

Ancestor's name

    John Fitzgerald KENNEDY

Objective(s)		Locality
Birth, Marriage, Death		Local library

Date of search	Location/ call number	Description of source (Author, title, year, pages)	Comments (Purpose of search, results, years, and names searched)	Doc. number
Sept. 1996		Doris Kearns Goodwin, *The Fitzgeralds and the Kennedys: An American Saga.* NY.: Simon and Schuster, 1988.	Birth, marriage, death dates for JFK and extended family	
Sept. 1996		Harvey Rachin, *The Kennedys: A Chronological History.* NY.: Ballantine Books, 1986.	Birth, marriage, death dates for JFK and extended family	
Sept. 1996		Palladium Interactive, Kennedy sample in *Family Gathering*, 1996.	Birth, marriage, death dates for JFK and extended family	

☞ Begin with yourself and what you know.

☞ Work from the known back to the unknown, starting with yourself.

☞ Enter what you know on a pedigree chart.

☞ Enter what you know on family group records.

☞ Use your research log from the start to keep track of the sources you are using to build your family history and genealogy.

☞ Be as complete as possible, and use standard formats consistently.

are not found on a pedigree chart or a family group record. The pedigree charts and family group records of the Kennedy family reveal only part of the story. Just as with the Kennedys, you'll want to know more about your family. Your ancestors had friends and neighbors; they probably belonged to religious, political, and social groups. They were a part of historical events. Reading social and local history will help you understand more about your ancestors by placing them in the times and places in which they lived. You'll want to learn about the communities where your ancestors lived and how they played a part in it.

Is genealogy and family history for you? If you are curious about who your ancestors were, if you want to know the great saga of your family, then yes. It is easy to begin, and anyone can do it. Start with yourself and move backward one generation at a time. If you hit roadblocks on a particular family line, work on another. Look for educational opportunities to sharpen your skills, and go back to that problem line when you know more. Join a genealogical society in your community. These societies are filled with people who are there to share resources, tips, and information with you. As you become more involved in family history, you will soon understand why it is one of the fastest- growing hobbies in America. The information you find will have a profound effect on you and your family.

You can start your family history and genealogy now. Begin by building your pedigree chart. It is as easy as beginning with what you already know. Enter as much information as you can, and then build as many family group records as you can. You will have gaps of information in both the pedigree chart and family group record. These gaps will help you decide what information you will need to look for next. Take the pedigree chart, family group record, and research log provided at the back of this book and write down what you know on them. The standard working size for these forms (8½" × 11") is larger than the size of this book so you may want to xerox them up to a larger size or create your own using the layouts provided here. The next step will be looking around your home for clues to missing information.

CHAPTER TWO

Looking At Home

AFTER YOU HAVE

filled in your pedigree chart
with what you know, you will
need to begin searching for
the missing information in order to continue your journey
back in time. The best place
to start your search for more
information about your ancestors is at home. Your home
will provide some of the most
valuable information in your
search for family history.

$\mathcal{S}$HANNON APPLEGATE found most of her family history at home. She took the time to organize and search through her home for clues to her family history and pieced together a compelling history of her pioneer ancestors.

Shannon had been raised, as many of us have, moving frequently and with little sense of permanence. " I had the life of a wanderer as a child and woman. I didn't have any sense of home." It was with a move to Yoncalla, Oregon, in 1971, to live in the old family home, that Shannon began to uncover the legacy of permanence that had been left for her.

"We lived at the old place with the spirit of past, there were layers of living and layers of life in this house. The air was heavy with other people's lives and the things they loved and touched." She found bits and pieces of her family history everywhere. " We found things from five or six generations, a cabinet that my grandfather had built, exquisite antiques. But there were also humble things—baskets with chinese coins and beads on the top that held handfuls of marbles, boxes with different keys, chipped teapots, books and photographs, just the debris of living."

"As I continued my family history research, I got to know the women of this family through their writings and their art, through the things that they toiled at and crafted; I came to appreciate their spirit and independence, even though the times prescribed them to be docile." The women kept the time with slips of paper, "Great-Aunt Irene's notes for the book she was going to write, Sue Applegate Byrd's wedding dress," Great-Grandmammy's alpaca shawl. "When I come into this house, I do have a feeling that time has been kept, quite conciously. I don't know what the motivation was for great-great-grandmother to write so much down, she was a humble, unassuming woman. But somehow there was a sense of life lived being important."

Like Shannon, you will look at your home in a new way when you begin this treasure hunt. Things that have held little or no meaning will suddenly emerge as important pieces in your family history. Many things around your home can hold valuable clues to your family history.

When you begin to look for clues at home, it is important to understand that you are looking for documents that were created around events in your ancestors' lives. Long after the events, such as birth, marriage, or death, the documents that were created at the time are stored away in boxes, drawers, closets, and trunks. Just think of the paper trail that you yourself may have created: a birth certificate, photographs, school records, marriage certificates, military records, deeds and wills, insurance papers, employment records. When pieced together, documents create a personal portrait and provide wonderful sources of biographical information for the family historian.

Two documents that are key to any family history are birth certificates and death certificates. If you have trouble locating these documents at home, refer to the appendix in this book for information on how to send away for them. Both the birth and death certificate are essential for your search, and death certificates can even provide life-saving medical information, as described in chapter 8.

The best way to start at home is to go on a genealogical treasure hunt. Begin by looking for certificates of different events like birth, death, and marriage. Look for letters, photos, cards, and other articles that may have important genealogical significance. This is one of the most important first steps in beginning your research. The materials you find will help document what you already know and can provide new information. If you have found materials already, look at them again. You might see information you missed before or find information that corrects what you have. Family members and old family friends may have relevant genealogical materials in their homes and may be willing to share information with you. So, whenever possible, ask others to help you search for family history documents and information.

Identify yourself to your family as the record keeper and family historian. Begin sharing your interest and you will be amazed at what comes out of the woodwork. Let everyone know that you are doing family history research, and ask for copies of records and photographs. Family reunions are always a good time to share genealogical information and to ask for help in locating documents. Remind family members to keep genealogical materials safe. Let them know the value of looking carefully through all paperwork before discarding it.

Family members and old family friends may have relevant genealogical materials in their homes and may be willing to share information with you. So, whenever possible, ask others to help you search for family history documents and information.

If another family member is also doing genealogical research, find out what area he or she is researching. Share information that is relevant to each other's research. This is very important so that you are not duplicating research but adding to the larger effort. One family member may be interested only in pedigree charts and family group records, while another is interested in the photographs and larger family history of stories and events. These research efforts will clearly complement one another.

When families move or a family member dies, important historical documents are the most vulnerable. During these times of stress, take care to prevent precious family history materials from being lost, thrown out, or destroyed. If a family has lived in a home for more than one generation, younger family members are often unaware of the existence or significance of certain historical documents. So remember to ask all family members to keep an eye out for important documents.

Birth and death certificates, baptism, bar/bat mitzvah, marriage and divorce records, social security cards, Bibles, newspaper articles, passports, immigration and naturalization papers, diplomas, old photos, obituaries, funeral records, letters and diaries, military papers, deeds to property, yearbooks, invitations, and birth or marriage announcements are some of the records you might find in your search.

Regional and ethnic differences play a part in what you will find. Before the turn of the century, when local and state governments began to keep vital records, family Bibles were the source of information about births, marriages and deaths. Unfortunately, family Bibles were not easily duplicated so were passed on to only one family member. Ask relatives if they know of a family Bible and where it might be.

The information that might be in it is well worth the extra effort of finding it.

Other sources of genealogical information that can be found in your home are family keepsakes, such as jewelry, quilts, and photos. These and other objects such as furniture and clothing have their own significance and should be handled as carefully as you would handle paper records. It is a good habit to photograph these items and share them with relatives. In showing the photos around, stories about the items will often emerge that have great significance to your family. It is also a good idea to photograph items that other members of the family share with you because they too could be important clues. We know of one family who has a mirror that has the names of ancestors carefully inscribed on the back. Another family recorded the births of children and grandchildren on the wooden headboard of a large bed. The most important thing to remember is that even the most innocent-looking article could have significance to your family history.

Photographs are extremely valuable in your research, not just for the images of your ancestors, but for many of the details within the photos. These details can tell you about the life of a person. If necessary, find an expert to examine the details in the photos you have. The time period can be determined by the clothing or other objects in the photo. Photos can be dated by the process used in developing. The photographer's name, address, or studio name and address are sometimes found on the photo or on the frame. Be sure to look on the back as well as the front for names, dates, places, or any other information that will be useful to your research. Finding photos of individuals you cannot identify can be very frustrating. Ask older family members to help identify the individuals in your old photos. As with all genealogical materials, copy and preserve your originals. See chapter 10 for more information on preserving and sharing photographic images. When you have your own photos developed, remember to write names and dates on them for future family genealogists.

If you find a quilt in your search, be sure not to overlook its genealogical importance. Quilts are sometimes narrative, telling stories about a family's life, with dates and names embedded in the quilt. They are sometimes dated and signed by the maker. Find an expert or a book about quilts and uncover

ALL KINDS OF objects around your home can have genealogical importance. One family had a copper pot that sat on a fireplace. The family legend was that the paternal great-grandmother had gone to California between 1851 and 1857 in a "prairie schooner" and that she had brought the pot with her. The pot is stamped 1851, along with the manufacturer's name. The grandmother was born in California in 1857, so the date on the copper pot and the grandmother's birth date were valuable in determining when the great-grandmother had arrived in California.

In your rush to get to the past, don't overlook what is right in front of you. Be careful and take your time to look around and find information, and remember that often the most valuable source of information is living relatives.

the story of your quilt. If it is an old quilt, ask older family members what they know about it.

Original records are valuable sources of genealogical information created at the time of an event. These primary sources of family history information are often in our homes because they were created and obtained at the time of an important life event. These documents are often hidden or tucked away in files, drawers, or boxes, long forgotten and overlooked in the wake of daily events. Deeds, wills, certificates, licenses, and insurance documents can all unlock information that is important to your family history.

These original records help determine not only dates and places needed to begin your research but can also reveal family relationships, interesting details about an individual's life, and the times in which he or she lived.

All genealogical records are only as accurate as the information given at the time a document is created. Alternative records are necessary to verify information. Using several documents to support the same information is useful in detecting errors, inconsistencies, or misinformation. There are many stories about family members who have lied about their age at some point in their lives, maybe to get a job or enlist in the military. If you make the mistake of recording this as fact, your genealogical search could get confused. A combination of genealogical records will be useful in establishing what is truly factual or merely hearsay. An example of this is the information found in a family Bible and a birth certificate that are in agreement about names and dates.

Family members may be able to provide you with important clues for your research. Often there are family members who have lived in the same place for many years. Check with these relatives. Because they have not moved, their homes will be museums of the period. They will likely be willing to share information and experiences with you that will help you on your way. In your rush to get to the past, don't overlook what is right in front of you. Be careful and take your time to look around and find information, and remember that often the most valuable source of information is living relatives.

Genealogical treasures are likely to turn up anywhere, so leave no drawer, closet, letter, book, or box unopened. Don't assume that information that appears unrelated to family history will have no value. For one family, a modest brochure for the sale of a home at the turn of the century turned out to refer to the long-lost family home that everyone had forgotten about. The brochure gave many interesting details about the home and was a key to unlocking the memories of some older members of the family. It would have been easy to overlook and throw out, since no one in the current generation knew anything about the home. Create a filing system by type of document or by names on the document—whatever works for you. But be prepared, because once you start, your collection of documents will grow quickly. The most important thing to remember is to not place these documents back in an old box. They must be preserved and cared for. Chapter 10 has more information about the storage and care of old documents and photographs. Once you have located documents around your home, carefully record all the details in these materials and cite the sources of the information in your research log.

When you begin your search at home, you will want to keep the task simple. Use the checklists on pages 22 and 23 to look around your house. Share these checklists with family members and ask them to do the same search in their homes. Often, when family members share the information they have, research is easier and less time consuming. It is also important for other family historians not to duplicate your efforts, or you theirs. Coordination is important. Send a newsletter to your family members announcing your plans to begin compiling your family history. Help them understand that you are interested in what they have to share, in their stories and information.

Searching at home for clues to your family history is an important and exciting step in your research. Use the lists on the next two pages when searching at home:

WHERE TO LOOK

- Attics. Look in old boxes and trunks. Even old furniture can reveal clues. One family inscribed birth dates on the headboard of a bed.

- Bedrooms. Look in drawers and old books for clues. Jewelry is often inscribed with dates and initials.

- Kitchen. Old recipe boxes and cookbooks can hold family history information. China, silver, and crystal will probably have special significance, and silver is often inscribed.

- Living Room. Old photographs often have writing on the back. Some frames hold numerous photos stacked on top of one another. Heirlooms can be inscribed with dates and names. One family kept champagne bottles from weddings and turned them into lamps. On each lamp the marriage was recorded on the label of the bottle.

- Family Room. Trophies often have dates and initials inscribed on them. Don't forget yearbooks and other school memorabilia. Check the backs of old paintings.

- Basement. Much information can be found hidden in boxes that are long forgotten. Old documents, including wills and insurance papers, can reveal clues to your past. Old clothing, such as military or sports uniforms or wedding dresses, can also have special significance.

WHAT TO LOOK FOR

- Certificates (Birth, death, baptism, marriage, school, military, clubs and organizations)
- Naturalization or citizenship records
- Photo albums
- Scrapbooks
- Family Bibles (Often contain dates of marriages, births, and deaths)
- Letters (Can contain valuable information and insight into daily life)
- Baby books (Biographical information and dates)
- Diaries (A rich source of biographical information)
- Family recipe boxes or books (Recipes that have been handed down for generations can be shared today)
- Deeds and wills
- Insurance papers
- Newspaper clippings
- Trophies
- Yearbooks
- Announcements
- Invitations
- Heirlooms
- Furniture (Check for inscriptions or dates)
- Jewelry (Check for initials and dates)
- Health and medical records
- Employment records

BEGINNER'S Checklist

Searching at home for clues to your family history is an important and exciting step in your research. Use the following list when searching at home:

☞ Use your pedigree chart, family group records, and research log to help select the information you need to look for at home.

☞ Be creative when you search at home; look for many different types of records and clues.

☞ Enlist the help of extended family to look in their homes for documents, photographs, and other clues. Provide them with a list of what you are looking for.

☞ Enter the information you find on your pedigree chart and family group record.

☞ Make entries in your research log to keep track of where and when you found information about your ancestors.

CHAPTER THREE
Gathering Family Stories
ORAL HISTORY AND GENEALOGY

ORAL HISTORY IS a cornerstone of everyone's family history and genealogy. It can also be one of the most rewarding and enriching parts of your research.

The initial steps of entering the information you have gathered in your pedigree chart, family group records, and research log will be an important part of the interview process. The information you know will help you determine whom you need to interview and what questions you will need to ask of them. Your search at home will have provided documents and photographs that will help you conduct successful interviews.

The stories we hear from our families are usually one of the reasons we start our family history research. Many of us have treasured memories of stories told by grandparents. Unfortunately, if we have heard the stories more than once, we have a tendency to glaze over when they are repeated. It is often because of this complacency that we let these treasured stories pass with the storyteller when he or she dies. Of all of the elements in genealogy research, oral histories are the most important to capture. Too often parents and grandparents take vast amounts of information quietly with them when they die.

Alex Haley, author of the 1970s phenomenon *Roots,* was clear about the value of the oral tradition. In a 1989 interview by the *Ancestors* team, Haley shared his impressions about the value of oral history:

Whether the stories told by older people are sad or funny, they bring both the children and the people being interviewed closer together than they were before the interviewing process began.

"Every family is as unique as a fingerprint. Seek out the elders in your family—they can tell you things that you can't find in records. What motivated me was my grandmother and her sisters. We used to sit on the front porch in the summer evenings. I was six years old when this first happened. It was the year after my grandfather died, and my grandmother, in her grief, had invited all of her sisters to join her. About early dark, the sisters would trickle out to the front porch. The porch was covered with thick honeysuckle vines and there were hundreds of thousands of fireflies. My grandmother and her sisters would spend a few minutes getting their rocking chairs synchronized, and then they would get out their snuff. They would talk. They would talk about family history. They would talk about Chicken George, and Miss Kizzy and Massa Wallar, and Miss Kizzy's mother. It was talked about night after night."

An interview, even with family memebers, is a process that requires preparation and time for both parties involved. Bill Zimmerman, who has written a book on taping family interviews, shared with us his experience about the the best way to tape interviews with family members:

Some years ago, after a period of estrangement from my mother, I sat down with her to ask her about her life. On the surface, I was trying to test material for a book I had just written, *How to Tape Instant Oral Biographies.*

As a journalist, my goal, in writing my book, was to teach youngsters and grownups how to become family journalists. My premise was that by using a tape recorder or camcorder, families can preserve what is most precious in their lives — the voices and stories of their relatives and the people they love. My hope was that families could establish electronic libraries of spoken and video memories, which they can hand down from one generation to another.

Deep down, though, in writing the book and in interviewing my mother, I was searching for a way to reunite my family. I was trying to make peace between us and repair some of the rupture that had resulted from my marriage to my wife, Teodorina, who is of a different ethnic, racial, and religious background from my family's. Up to that point, my mother had had difficulty in looking beyond the brown skin of my Puerto Rican wife and seeing her as another human being. She had not made her feel welcome into our family.

I had other motivations, too. Coming from a divorced home, I wanted to learn more about my father, who had died when I was only a boy, and to understand better why my parents had such difficulties in living together. I thought, too, that capturing my family's stories and memories on tape would be a wonderful way to preserve some of my family history for my own daughter, Carlota, then six. Carlota needed to know more about the backgrounds of her grandparents, and she accompanied me when I interviewed my mother, chiming in with her own questions, which, ultimately, helped bring her close to her grandmother.

Doing an oral biography of my mother proved to be a wonderful experience. While they did not entirely console my pain, the many hours spent questioning and listening to my mother and piecing together her oral history did bring us closer together—and even helped my wife understand my mother better.

I learned some wonderful stories about my family, and I play the tapes from time to time, gaining something different each time, for as I mature I bring to the listening of the tapes

the wider perspective that comes with time and understanding.

I learned, for example, how my great-grandmother, a peddler of elastic and sundries on New York's East Side, would have her grandchildren stretch the elastic in order to wring out a few more cents of profit on the goods. I learned how, at the beginning of their marriage, after coming to this country from Europe early in this century, my maternal grandparents would perform song-and-dance skits for the family on Saturday evenings to cheer their children and themselves when times were hard — a home vaudeville act. I learned, too, from my mother about the dream of my father, a furrier, to become a gentleman farmer someday. I learned how my parents met in a subway and fell in love.

I listened quietly as my mother told me she was sorry for the harsh way she had treated my wife after our marriage. She was happy, my mother said, that Teodorina and I had made a good life together and had given her a granddaughter.

Later, my wife, our daughter, and I sat down with my mother-in-law, Pastora, to record her life history, too.

She told us how many years earlier she had come to New York by ship from Puerto Rico to join her sister and make a new life on the mainland. Lovingly, she described the farm where she was born and raised and how she would ride a horse and hide from her mother in the orange groves. And so, slowly, tape after tape, my daughter learned about the richness of her background — the Russian, Polish, Jewish side of her father's family and the Hispanic, African, and Indian side of her mother's.

Since that time, I have taught many people how to interview their family members. One of my most rewarding experiences has been to set up "Grandparent Day" programs in local schools, in which youngsters invite older relatives, or neighbors if they don't have nearby relatives, to school to tape reminiscences about their lives.

In many of these instances the children share each other's relatives and older friends when their own can't come to schools. What better way for youngsters to learn about history, social studies, about the richness of different cultural backgrounds, and improve their listening and communications skills?

Whether the stories told by older people are sad or funny,

they bring both the children and the people being interviewed closer together than they were before the interviewing process began. This is because both are listening and talking to each other, and the act of interviewing itself implies there is value in what another person has to say. Oral histories help children see that human experience, no matter what your background, is universal. It's comforting for each of us to learn we are not the only ones who have ever gone through problems in life, and that others have done so and survived. The audio and videotaped memories that accrue from this coming together truly bear witness to the wonderful African saying that when an older person passes away, an entire library, made up of memories and experiences, passes away, too.

In offering you a few pointers about interviewing, I would emphasize first that the best interviewers are those who listen well to what the other person is saying. Be truly interested in the person you plan to interview.

Before the interview, jot down some questions you want to ask and practice them a few times. When calling relatives for an appointment for the interview, ask them to prepare by gathering old family pictures and documents, such as passports, citizenship papers, marriage certificates, family heirlooms, and maps that you can examine together. These materials serve as cues to evoke memories.

On the morning of the day an interview is scheduled, test your equipment; take along extra batteries and cassettes in case something goes wrong. Always carry a notepad and extra pens with you to jot down any notes, further questions, or definitions. And of course, make sure your recorder is turned on or plugged in when you begin the interview.

Conduct the interview in a quiet place that is comfortable to the other person, like the kitchen or a favorite room.

Help people recall stories by giving them cues, such as, "Remember when we did such and such?" or by sharing with them your own recollections of certain events and then asking for theirs.

Don't worry if you don't get all the answers to the questions at one sitting. There's always tomorrow to do another interview. In many respects, it's better to do a series of short interviews over a period of time rather than one very long one that can tire you both out. Remember, part of the reason you

IN ADDITION to using a tape recorder to record these memories and traditions, you can also use a camcorder to capture the person and his or her environment. It will be wonderful for you to have a video that you can watch later that will show you the person's expressive eyes or hands or the smile on her face.

are doing the interviews in the first place is to help you draw closer to another human being.

Try to be as organized as possible when making tapes by marking on the outside of the tapes the date, who was interviewed, your own name, and your relationship to that person. Prepare an introduction for each tape, such as: "This is Bill Zimmerman interviewing my mother, Ruth Strauss, on June 15, 1996, her eightieth birthday."

Round out the interview by talking to others and asking for their stories about the person you're interviewing. Who knows, you might be lucky enough to hear another version of a story that was told to you earlier and that fills in some of the holes.

Now, the most important part of the interview: choosing the questions to ask. Remember that all reporters, in the course of an interview, ask two basic types of questions. The first type is factual questions and these usually elicit short answers. They will also serve to corroborate the information on your pedigree charts and family group records.

Some examples:

- What is your full name?

- What is the date of your birth?

- What is your nationality?

- What were the names of your parents?

- What were the dates of their births and marriage?

- When did our family come to this country and where did they come from?

But the best kind of questions, in my opinion, are the kind that encourage people to open up and offer longer, more interesting answers and stories. Some examples:

- Does our family name have a special meaning?

- What does your name mean, and who were you named after?

- Do you remember any of the stories your grandparents told you about where they came from, why they settled here, or what life was like for them when they were younger?

- What is the happiest memory in your life? What was the saddest time?

- What are your deepest values?

- What is the most important thing you have learned so far in your life?

- Can you tell me what life was like when you were very young and growing up?

- Who was your best friend and what kind of games did you play?

- What are some of your earliest memories?

- What were you like as a child? Serious? Always getting into trouble? Quiet? Sad? Happy? Can you think of any stories to show me the way you were?

- What was your greatest adventure? What do you think is the most important thing that ever happened in your life?

- What special things do you know that you are proud of?

- What is the key lesson you have learned from life that you would want others to know?

- What are the hopes and dreams you still have for your life and for your family?

You might also want to ask those relatives you interview to tell you favorite family stories, sayings, or songs. Are there family superstitions or rituals that you want to recall? What is your favorite food recipe? What is your favorite or most meaningful prayer? Can you speak it in another language, and will you translate for me? What home remedy has been passed along in your family from generation to generation?

After you conduct interviews, always remember to thank the people you interviewed for their time and generosity in sharing their lives with you. In sitting with you and recalling memories and their lives, they have given you a special gift, which you may want to share with others in your family by making copies of the tapes.

Now is the right time to start collecting family history from your living relatives. The stories will help bring life to the documents that you find, and genealogy becomes more than just a collection of dates and names. These treasured tapes or transcriptions can be shared with future generations born too late to meet your grandparents or parents.

One of the first things you need to do is help your family members understand that their lives are important. Many people resist an interview because they feel that they have nothing of interest to tell and share. Each life is unique and brings a rich tapestry of understanding to our own life when shared and understood.

Remember some basic strategies for conducting interviews with members of your family:

BEGINNER'S Checklist

☞ Use your pedigree chart and family group records to identify what you want to learn from your interview.

☞ Be prepared. Give yourself time to get organized for the interview with prepared questions.

☞ Check your equipment to make sure that you have enough tape, batteries, and other accessories for the interview.

☞ Give the person that you are interviewing enough time to prepare. Ask her a week in advance to start gathering photos, letters, documents, or any items that will help her to share her memories with you.

☞ Bring someone else with you to handle the camera or tape recorder. Your attention needs to be focused on the interview.

☞ Ask direct questions to find dates, names, and other genealogical information. Ask more general questions to learn more about your family history.

☞ Take the time to enter what you learn on your pedigree chart, family group records, and research logs.

Chapter Four
The Paper Trail

FAMILY HISTORIANS AND genealogists love paper. Documents hold the clues we need to trace our ancestors. Birth certificates, school and church records, death records, military records, even wills and real estate records carry information that family historians and genealogists need. You will find documents at home and in libraries and archives. Before you do any additional research, it is important to understand the paper trail you will be looking at. There are all kinds of reference tools, such as guides and manuals for genealogical research, catalogs of special collections, alphabetical name indexes, and more.

Records may be original or compiled. Original records are created at the time of an event, usually by an eyewitness. These include, for example, birth, marriage and death records, baptismal and burial records, ships' passenger lists, military service and naturalization records, and the records of private firms, such as funeral homes and insurance companies. Original records are called *primary sources.* They are, for the most part, handwritten, dusty, musty, faded, and fun.

Each original record brings new insight and opportunity for the family historian to unlock clues to the past. Rafael Guber knows the value of original records in family history and genealogy research. Rafael's paternal grandfather, aunts, uncles, and father came through the doors of Ellis Island in 1913 seeking a better life than the one they had left behind in Russia. Rafael's maternal ancestors had come through Ellis Island as well. Rafael knew little of his family history, but always felt pulled to learn more. "When people came to America, some of them wanted to get lost here. Europe meant all kinds of bonds and class systems. They wanted to come here and make it on their own merit." Rafael's family succeeded in America, so much so that assimilation meant giving up their collective past to become Americans. Rafael, a third generation American, wanted to know what others had chosen to forget. "I didn't know much about my family at all. I would

Records may be original or compiled. Original records, or *primary sources,* are created at the time of an event, usually by an eyewitness. Compiled records, or *secondary sources,* are put together by other genealogists or historians and contain records specific to an area or topic.

ask my parents where we were from and they would say, 'Somewhere in Russia.' My parents were so busy being Americans and they felt that there was something un-American about remembering all that came before. I once asked an aunt to tell me about Europe and she said, 'What do you want to know for?' "

After experiencing illness and financial setbacks in the late 1980s, Rafael found himself looking inward and asking questions about his life. "I will admit that my sense of self-esteem was tied to my accomplishments and my bank account, and it was just the perfect time for me to start wondering about who I was. I decided to start as far back as I could. I wanted to understand more about where I came from." One day he went to Ellis Island on what he called a quest. "I remember riding on the ferry with a boatload full of tourists. I had taken a day off from work, and I made a point of going alone. I had this idea that somehow riding on the ferry and passing the great lady in the harbor, the Statue of Liberty, I would be seeing the things that my grandparents saw,

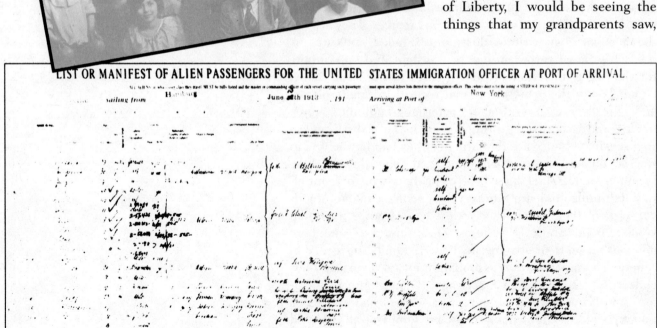

and maybe I would imagine myself being in their place. I got to Ellis Island and it was beautiful, almost too beautiful. It was like Ellis Island under glass. It wasn't enough by itself; it was a disappointment. I wanted more. Walking around I got the sense that the information about who my family was and how they came here was available."

Rafael's trip to Ellis Island fueled his need to know more about his immigrant ancestors. He asked where he could find more information about his ancestors and was told to make a visit to the New York branch of the National Archives. With help from the staff and the information that he already knew, he found the passenger manifest that listed his grandparents' arrival in America. There was more information than he had ever imagined. Passenger manifests are unique original documents and a great example of how much information can be mined from original records. From this one passenger list with thirty different columns of information about his family, Rafael learned the names, ages, occupations, nationality, last permanent residence in Russia, and the city or town in Europe where each member of the family was born. These passenger lists are very detailed because they were created when passengers boarded in Europe as part of a screening process. They are exciting because they are often the first glimpse of family in the old country that many Americans get. Rafael used the information on the passenger list of his paternal family to help jog the memories of older relatives who revealed even more information than he had. Rafael was also successful in finding the passenger list, or manifest, for his maternal immigrants to America. "First, I found out that the family who first came to America on my mother's side was much larger than I had anticipated. The only family history information that I had from my mother was the name of one grandfather. I found his passenger list and there was a name that I didn't recognize. My

To learn more about immigration records and how to find them, read the section about immigration records in *The Source: A Guidebook of American Genealogy*. This is an excellent source for information on finding many different types of original documents.

grandfather had been picked up, the passenger list said, by David Eisenblatt. I called my mother and asked who he was. 'Oh, that was your great-grandfather. I forgot to tell you. He died when I was six.'" With the information from this one original document, Rafael was able to get back to 1835. "My mother could not remember her grandmother's name and it was bothering her terribly. Her grandmother used to bake cookies for her and take care of her. She remembered her as small and full of joy and warmth. I found her name the day before Yom Kippur, which is the holiest day on the Jewish calendar. I felt the spirit of my great-grandmother with me because I was able to give her back her name." The original documents for Rafael Guber were a critical find. The manifests were a bridge between the vague memories of the living and the events that transformed his family's destiny.

Passenger lists are just one example of the many different kinds of original documents that are available to family historians and genealogists. To learn more about immigration records and how to find them, read the section about immigration records in *The Source: A Guidebook of American Genealogy* or consult *They Came in Ships: A Guide to Finding Your Immigrant Ancestor's Arrival Record*. These are excellent sources for information on finding immigration records.

Original records are important, but family historians and genealogists also turn to compiled records for answers to many of their questions. Compiled records, or secondary sources, are as varied as the original records in content. They are put together by other genealogists or historians and contain records specific to an area or topic. Marriages can be found in compiled records, as well as military records and local histories. One of the first places a genealogist should look is in compiled records for a family history that has been published on a particular surname. The Family History Library, in Salt Lake City, Utah, for example, has more than 80,000 compiled family histories available to researchers.

Such books might contain an entire family history, or the history of a state, county, or town, or a compilation of biographical sketches or genealogies. They might contain records transcribed in their entirety, such as the monument inscriptions of a particular cemetery, or they might contain records abstracted down to the bare facts—probate files, for instance, or obituaries from newspapers, or naturalizations.

COMPILED RECORDS are called *secondary sources,* since the primary sources, or original records, were read and interpreted and transcribed by some compiler or indexer. Here are two examples of compiled records:

Passenger Arrivals at the Port of Charleston, 1820–1829, compiled by Brent H. Holcomb from National Archives passenger arrival records, indicates that a large family named Biggart from Belfast, Ireland, arrived on the ship *Caledonia* in December 1824. Alexander was forty, his wife Mary was thirty-eight, and their six sons—James Joseph, John, Archy, Alexander, and W.W.—and two daughters—Betty and Peggy—ranged in age from twenty to three years old. Imagine the trials this hearty family of eight endured forsaking their native village, bobbing for eight weeks on the turbulent Atlantic, and then beginning life anew in a strange land.

Marriages and Deaths from Mississippi Newspapers, Vol. 4: 1850–1861, compiled by Betty Couch Wiltshire, contains this entry from a Vicksburg newspaper of August 18, 1858: "Married at the residence of Major R.H. Crump, the bride's uncle, by the Rev. W.W. Lord, Mr. James W. Gray of Yazoo City, to Miss Ellen Louisa Hart, daughter of R.W. Hart, Esq., of Fredericksburg, Va." Not only does this notice hint at quite an elegant affair, it also points to Fredericksburg as a likely place of origin for the Hart family.

Social history may suggest how your ancestors thought, what their attitudes were, what customs and traditions they observed, and generally why they behaved as they did. Read as much history about the times and the places in which your ancestors lived. The knowledge can help you solve clues along the way, creating a more complete history of your family.

Alphabetical name indexes to particular sets of records, such as ships' passenger lists or colonial land patents, might also be called compiled records.

Today more and more records are being compiled and published electronically. The International Genealogical Index, for instance, is a computer database by the Family History Library of the Church of Jesus Christ of Latter-Day Saints. It contains millions of names extracted from old records, with citations to the sources in which each name was found. There is a rush to make as much genealogical information available in electronic formats. See chapter 9 for more information on electronic databases and genealogical information on the Internet.

To find and follow the paper trail of your ancestors, begin with what you can find at home. When you have gathered everything that is available in original and compiled sources at home, then it is time to head to the libraries and archives in search of more. When you go to the library for the first time, begin with compiled records. They are clean, convenient, and because they are printed, easy to read and use. Their contents form the foundation for all of your future research. However, they are liable to contain errors, and they are very limited in scope. Most old records have not been published. Compiled records constitute only a thin slice of the whole pie of the past. Original records still represent the major source of genealogical information.

Original records can be found at the National Archives and its thirteen regional archives, in state archives, county courthouses, and city and town halls. (See the Resource Directory on page 125). Some original records may still be in the custody of the private firm or government agency that created them, such as a railroad company or the Social Security Administration. Personal papers, including business ledgers, plantation books, and family letters and albums, may be found in manuscript collections in libraries. Millions of original records have been microfilmed, too, making them accessible in libraries all over the country. There are also companies that specialize in providing genealogical microfilm that can be purchased or rented through the mail. A leader in this type of service is AGLL, the American Genealogical Lending Library in Salt Lake City, Utah. It is listed on page 204.

Besides providing additional information about your family, original records will serve to correct the data you found in secondary sources. However, it is wise to bear in mind that primary sources, too, often contain errors. How reliable any record is depends entirely on who created it, and for what purpose. This shortcoming notwithstanding, primary sources are extremely valuable, as they contain all of the information that has come down to us — the whole delicious pie of the past.

Once you have obtained data on your family from compiled and original records, you will want to know more about your ancestors as living, thinking, feeling individuals. By reading social history—books about the everyday life of everyday people, such as Alice Morse Earle's *Home Life in Colonial Days* or Harvey Green's *The Uncertainty of Everyday Life, 1915–1945*—you will learn where your forebears fit into the larger world in which they lived. Social history may suggest how your ancestors thought, what their attitudes were, what customs and traditions they observed, and generally why they behaved as they did. It puts flesh on the bare bones of names and dates. Read as much history about the times and the places in which your ancestors lived. The knowledge can help you solve clues along the way, creating a more complete history of your family.

Rafael Guber found that his knowledge of his family history and genealogy was enhanced by learning everything he could about the history of the villages in Europe that his ancestors came from. He had a revelation based on this research: "In my mind, my family survived the Holocaust because my grandparents came

Rafael Guber and his children with their ancestors' passenger lists.

☞ Records are created by important events that shaped your ancestors' lives.

☞ There are two types of records —original or primary records, and compiled or secondary records.

☞ Original records are created at the time of the event by eye-witnesses.

☞ Compiled records are created and compiled after the events by others.

☞ Together, compiled and original records create a firm foundation for research about your ancestors.

here, but as I did my research I realized that scores of my cousins were killed in the Holocaust. They died in the concentration camps. I was amazed to find records in Eastern Europe, but when the German army was moving east and they made their way into Poland and then into Russia, they were burning synagogues and annihilating the Jews, but they had a particular fondness for records. So very often they would remove the records from a synagogue, store them in a local town hall and then burn the synagogue. It is there that my search continues." Without searching through the history of the period, it would have been difficult for Rafael Guber to put all the different pieces together.

CHAPTER FIVE
Libraries and Archives
WHERE TO FIND WHAT YOU NEED

WHEN YOU RESEARCH your family history and genealogy, you will soon find yourself searching in libraries and archives for information about your ancestors. This research can be exhilarating and sometimes frustrating, but never boring.

Before you go to a library or an archive it is important to be prepared. After you have started at home by gathering as much information as you can, interviewing family relatives, and then entering the information on your pedigree charts and family group sheets, you will be ready to go to a library or an archive to get more information. Remember that answering as many questions as you can about your ancestors before you head to a library or an archive will save you time and energy. The more you have learned, the more you are likely to find.

There are more than 30,000 libraries and archives in the United States. Sorting out where to go can be less difficult if you are first very clear about what you are looking for.

Make your search as specific as possible. Choose an individual or family that you want to learn more about. Select a specific task for learning more about your ancestor. For example, search for a birth date, a marriage date, or a death date. Focusing your search objective in this way will also help you determine what kind of record you need to search.

Libraries and archives in the United States are organized on city, county, state, and national levels. When you think about libraries and archives in relation to family history and genealogy, you might think of the National Archives, the Library of Congress and the Family History Library in Salt Lake City, Utah. These collections are large, impressive, and of great use to the genealogist, but you should first be aware of resources in your own community. Local resources are best for beginning your initiation into libraries and archives as a family historian.

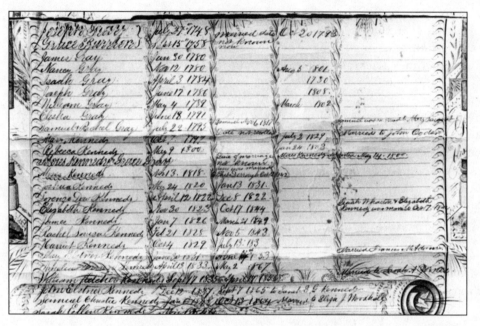

Starting with local community resources will save you time and energy. Many records that are held at the national level in government and private collections are often found in your community on microfilm, microfiche, or computer applications. There are several resources to look for in your community:

Local genealogical and historical societies are often the best place to begin. These societies are staffed by seasoned enthusiasts who can help you with questions. Societies commonly have libraries that are open to members. The members of your local society will be able to introduce you to community resources that are available for research. Networking is one of the best ways for a genealogist to find information. You never know who might be working on a similar line of family history, and genealogical societies are the best place to begin networking. Genealogical and historical societies often have CIGs, or computer interest groups, that can help you take advantage of what computers and the Internet have to offer the genealogist. (See chapter 9 for more information about computers and genealogy.) Check to see if there are local societies that reflect your ancestors' ethnic or national backgrounds; these societies can be of help in tracing your ancestry. The appendix in the back of this book lists local genealogical and historical societies by state.

A discussion about genealogical societies would not be complete without mentioning the Federation of Genealogical Societies, the National Genealogical Society, the New England Historic and Genealogical Society, and the Daughters of the American Revolution. These national organizations are well known for their resources and expertise in genealogy.

THE NATIONAL GENEALOGICAL SOCIETY

4527 17th Street North
Arlington, VA 22207
(703) 525-0050
www.genealogy.org/~ngs

The National Genealogical Society (NGS) was founded in 1903. It is headquartered in the historic Glebe House in Arlington, Virginia. NGS is a national organization with more than 15,000 members, including individual members and member societies. NGS provides many services for its members, including a library and library loan program, a quarterly journal, bimonthly newsletter, home-study course, annual conference, a computer interest group, and more. NGS has an excellent site on the Internet with information for the beginner as well as the seasoned hobbyist.

THE NEW ENGLAND HISTORIC AND GENEALOGICAL SOCIETY

101 Newbury Street
Boston, MA 02116
(617) 536-5740
www.nehgs.org

The New England Historic and Genealogical Society was founded in 1845 and is in Boston, Massachusetts. The society has a library with holdings of more than 150,000 volumes and a 20,000-volume circulating collection that is available to members. There are education programs and a number of seminars held throughout the United States. NEHGS also sponsors annual research and family heritage trips to England, Canada, Washington, D.C., and the Family History Library in Salt Lake City. NEHGS is on the World Wide Web

Starting with local community resources will save you time and energy. Many records that are held at the national level in government and private collections are often found in your community on microfilm, microfiche, or computer applications.

A good reference for finding libraries is the *American Library Directory*. A new edition of the directory is printed annually.

An excellent guide for the genealogist and family historian concerning information on city, county and state resources is *Ancestry's Red Book: American State, County and Town Sources,* edited by Alice Eichholz. This is the definitive guide to local resources for genealogists.

with more information about their services and membership information.

The Federation of Genealogical Societies

P.O. Box 3385
Salt Lake City, UT   84110-3385

The Federation of Genealogical Societies (FGS) was founded in 1976. It is a society of organizations including genealogical societies, historical societies, family associations, libraries, archives, and other organizations involved in genealogy and family history. FGS publishes *The Forum* and is involved in the Civil War Soldiers and Sailors System (CWSS). FGS has marshaled the resources of volunteers nationwide to help the National Park Service create a database, which is available to visitors at some of the park service's Civil War sites. Visitors often wonder if their ancestors fought and died in Civil War; this system gives visitors access to very basic information about soldiers who fought on both sides. Individual memberships are available to FGS.

The Daughters of the American Revolution

1776 D Street, N. W.
Washington, D.C.   20006
(202) 628-1776
www.ultranet.com/~revolt
e-mail: revolt@dar.com

The Daughters of the American Revolution (DAR) is a membership society. This society has an excellent library, open to the public for a small fee. There is original material as well as a large collection of family histories and cemetery records that have been gathered by local chapters around the country. The collection covers local history, including town, state, county, and church materials. Genealogies, biographies, and vital records are also available here.

Other valuable resources in your community include your local public libraries and your county or state library system. Some local libraries have genealogy reading rooms, and most libraries have at least general references on genealogy and family history. A good reference for finding libraries is the *American Library Directory*. A new edition of the directory is printed annually. Other valuable assets in local library collections are local histories and biographies. And one of the most helpful resources in any local library is the librarian. Don't hesitate to ask your librarian about the holdings in your library and about other resources in your community. Understand that the librarian is there to help you find the resources you need, but will not actually do your research for you. Be aware that each city, county, and state is organized in a different manner and has different holdings. An excellent guide for the genealogist and family historian concerning information on city, county, and state resources is *Ancestry's Red Book: American State, County and Town Sources,* edited by Alice Eichholz. This is the definitive guide to local resources for genealogists. It achieves its goal in providing "an expansive guide to the most useful resources in each of the fifty United States and the District of Columbia." *Red Book* also contributes a brief historical background discussion on each of the fifty states. The more familiar you become with the local history of places where your ancestors lived, the easier and more interesting your search will be. *Red Book* will guide you to local information as diverse as land, tax, court, probate, cemetery, church, and military records, and more.

After you have exhausted the resources of your community and state, you may need to use one of the following national resources for your research:

THE FAMILY HISTORY LIBRARY
35 North West Temple
Salt Lake City, UT   84150
(801) 240-2584

The largest international collection of genealogical material is in the Family History Library of the Church of Jesus Christ of Latter-day Saints in Salt Lake City, Utah. The Family History Library (FHL) is open to the public for research. The library has more than 300,000 volumes and two million rolls of microfilm in its collection. The library continues to film original and compiled records from around the world. The 1,800 Family History Centers nationwide provide a non-denominational public service sponsored by the Church of Jesus Christ of Latter-day Saints. To find the center nearest you, call 1-800-346-6044. The Family History Centers also

For more information on the holdings and services of the Family History Library, turn to *The Library: A Guide to the LDS Family History Library,* edited by Johni Cerny and Wendy Elliott.

have access to the International Genealogical Index (IGI), which has more than 200 million names available to search. The resources of the Family History Library and the local Family History Centers are well known and used by seasoned hobbyists in the genealogical community. The centers are staffed by trained volunteers who can help you with research on your family. If the center does not have the film that you need, it can be ordered from the Family History Library in Salt Lake City for a small fee. For more information, turn to *The Library: A Guide to the LDS Family History Library*, edited by Johni Cerny and Wendy Elliott. This is the definitive guide to the holdings and services of the Family History Library.

THE NATIONAL ARCHIVES

Pennsylvania Avenue at 8th Street, N.W.

Washington, D.C. 20408

(202) 501-5400

www.nara.gov

Another nationally recognized resource for genealogists is the National Archives and Records Administration (NARA). NARA is known to most Americans as the building in Washington, D.C., that safeguards and displays the cornerstones of our government: the Declaration of Independence, the Constitution of the United States, and the Bill of Rights. But the National Archives is more than that. It is an independent federal agency that is charged with the responsibility of preserving our nation's history by maintaining and managing all federal records. The National Archives is more than its building in Washington; it is a system that includes thirteen regional branches of the National Archives and twelve presidential libraries. Genealogists compose a majority of the public that uses the National Archives, and as a result NARA makes special efforts to address the needs of genealogists. The Archives offers special publications, or General Information Leaflets (GILs), concerning records for genealogical research. NARA also distributes a free publication called *Aids for Genealogical Research*. This guide describes NARA and works on genealogy and contains information that's important to know before you go to any of the National Archives for research. GILs and *Aids for Genealogical Research* are available by contacting the Publications Distribution (NECD) of the National Archives, Room G9, Seventh and Pennsylvania Avenue, NW, Washington, D.C., 20408. You can call for these publications at (202) 501-7190 or (800) 788-6282; or fax at (301) 763-6025. Request GIL numbers 3, 5, 7, and 30. The National Archives also offers genealogy workshops and courses each year. For more information about the programs, contact the regional archive where you plan to do your research. Before you plan a research trip to the National Archives, it is a good idea to become familiar with *The Archives: A Guide to the National Archives Field Branches* by Loretto Dennis Szucs and Sandra Hargreaves Luebking. Reading this book will give you a better sense of how to use this mammoth archive, what will be available to you, and what you can expect when you get there. Many resources are also available online at the web-

General Information Leaflets and the free publication *Aids for Genealogical Research* are available by contacting the Publications Distribution (NECD) of the National Archives, Room G9, Seventh and Pennsylvania Avenue, NW, Washington, D.C., 20408. You can call for these publications at (202) 501-7190 or (800) 788-6282; or fax at (301) 763-6025. Request General Information Leaflet numbers 3, 5, 7, and 30.

site listed above. As with any resource on the scale of the National Archives, preparation is the key to successful research and will help to keep frustration to a minimum.

The Library of Congress is the largest library in the world. It holds more than 100 million items—books, manuscripts, photographs, maps, and more.

THE LIBRARY OF CONGRESS
1st–2nd Streets, NW
Washington, D.C. 20006
www.loc.gov

The Library of Congress is another national resource that has extensive holdings for avid genealogists. The Library of Congress is an enormous institution housed in three buildings in Washington, D.C. The building most familiar to the public is the Jefferson Building, which sits across from the Capitol.

The size and scope of the holdings at the Library of Congress make it the largest library in the world. In 1992, the library had acquired 100 million items. This collection includes more than fifteen million books, thirty-nine million manuscripts, thirteen million photographs, four million maps, three-and-a-half million pieces of music, and more than half a million motion pictures. This vast collection is a treasure-trove for the genealogist.

The heart of the Library of Congress genealogical collection is found in the Local History and Genealogy Reading Room on the ground floor of the Thomas Jefferson Building, Room LJ G20. The Local History and Genealogy Reading Room has roots that go back to Thomas Jefferson. In 1815, Jefferson sold his personal library to Congress to help rebuild the Library of Congress collection that had been burned by the British in the War of 1812. Jefferson's collection doubled the original holdings and included such titles as Edward Kimber's *Peerage of England, Peerage of Scotland,* and *Peerage of Ireland;* John Winthrop's *Journal of the Transactions and Occurances in the Settlement of Massachusetts and Other New-England Colonies, from the Year 1630–1644.*

The Local History and Genealogy Reading Room is a popular destination for genealogists. Several books can acquaint you with what the Library of Congress has available for genealogical research. One excellent guide is *The Library of Congress: A Guide to Genealogical and Historical Research,* by

James C. Neagles (Ancestry, 1990). The Library of Congress as well as the National Archives has a very strong site on the Internet that provides a variety of information. The Library of Congress catalog can be searched online with LOCIS (Library of Congress Information System).

You should be familiar with a few more nationally recognized libraries that have strong holdings in genealogy and family history and access to archival information:

NEWBERRY LIBRARY
60 W. Walton Street
Chicago, IL 60610
(312) 943-9090
192.231.205.235/isc275

ALLEN COUNTY PUBLIC LIBRARY
900 Webster Street
Fort Wayne, IN 46802
(219) 424-7241
www.acpl.lib.in.us

NEW YORK CITY PUBLIC LIBRARY
Local History and Genealogy Division
Fifth Avenue and 42nd Street
New York, NY 10018
(212) 930-0828
www.nypl.org/research/chss/lhg/genea.html

The research process for genealogists and family historians is a four-step process that is repeated during the course of your research. Especially important to use when you are in a library or an archive, it will streamline your research efforts.

1. IDENTIFY WHAT YOU KNOW.

It is easy to skip this step since it seems so obvious, but you need to be clear about the information you are using as the foundation for your research. The information you have recorded on your pedigree charts and family group records will provide a firm foundation for your work.

2. DECIDE WHAT YOU WANT TO LEARN.

Be as specific as you can. It is best to begin with someone for whom you have at least a full name and when and where he or she lived. Choose a specific event to focus on—a birth, death, or a marriage. Always ask for help when you are unsure; an experienced librarian can help you decide what task will be most productive.

3. CHOOSE A RECORD TO SEARCH.

Choosing the right record to search will have a great impact on your success. Different records give different clues. The list on page 51 will help you decide what types of records or materials to search.

4. LOCATE THE RECORD AND RECORD YOUR FINDINGS.

After you have selected the record you should search, find the record, search it for information, and then enter your findings on your research log, pedigree chart, and family group record. You will then be ready for your next search, and the research process will repeat itself.

When researching family history and genealogy, you may find libraries and archives intimidating at first. If you go to libraries and archives well prepared and follow the research process, your initiation will be easier and less frustrating.

IF YOU NEED:	LOOK FIRST IN:	THEN SEARCH:
Age	Census, vital records, cemeteries	Military records, taxation
Birth date	Vital records, church records, Bible records	Cemeteries, obituaries, census
Birthplace	Vital records, church records, census	Newspapers, obituaries
Death	Vital records, cemeteries, probate records, church records, obituaries	Newspapers, Bible records, military records
Divorce	Court records, vital records	Newspapers
Maiden name	Vital records, church records, newspapers, Bible records	Cemeteries, military records, probate records, obituaries
Living relatives (and adoptions)	Genealogies, directories, court records, obituaries	Census, biography, societies, church records, probate records
Marriage	Vital records, church records, census, newspapers, Bible records	Cemeteries, military records, probate records, naturalization and citizenship, land and property
Parents, children, and other family members	Vital records, church records, census, probate records, obituaries	Bible records, newspapers, emigration and immigration
Immigration date	Emigration and immigration, naturalization, citizenship, genealogies	Census, newspapers, biography
Place-finding aids	Gazetteers, maps	History, periodicals
Places family has lived	Census, land and property records, history	History, biography
Religion	Church records, history, biography	Bible records, cemeteries, genealogy
Occupations	Census, directories, emigration and immigration	Newspapers, court records
Country of foreign birth	Emigration and immigration, census, naturalization and citizenship, church records	Military records, vital records, newspapers, obituaries

BEGINNER'S Checklist

☞ Be prepared. Use libraries and archives *after* you have taken the first steps of learning as much as you can by searching at home and interviewing living relatives.

☞ Start locally. Become familiar with what is available to you in your community. Genealogical and historical societies, Family History Centers, and your local public libraries are good places to start your family history research outside of your home.

☞ Use national resources after you have exhausted what is available to you locally. This approach will save you time and money.

☞ Use the four-step research process when you are in the library. Identify what you know. Decide what you want to learn. Choose a record to search. Find the record, search it for information, and record what you find on your research log, pedigree chart, and family group record.

CHAPTER SIX
Military and Census Records

TWO POPULAR RECORDS used by genealogists
and family historians are military and census records. The
federal census records are some of the first records researched by many beginners. They are a favorite because of
the amount of information they contain about families and
individuals. Military records also provide valuable information for the family historian, but they go a step further. Military records place our ancestors in the wars that we have read
about in history books. Suddenly, history has new meaning,
and the sacrifices that were made for us by our ancestors
strike a chord deep within us.

$\mathcal{G}$ARRY BRYANT was in the Air Force during the Vietnam War. But his service was a source of embarrassment and shame to him. He felt little patriotism or honor serving in a war that he did not support. He had been involved in antiwar activity before his service.

"One evening in the barracks, there were six of us in the room talking and the conversation turned to family history. Someone talked about how he was descended from Puritans, another guy talked about his family history and it finally came around to me. I said I didn't care about America, my family came after the Revolutionary War, so I don't care about the Declaration of Independence, American flag, the Constitution or the Bill of Rights." Garry's conduct during the war was one of begrudging service. He would often avoid saluting the flag and was bitter and sullen about his role as a soldier.

Garry's stepfather, a World War II veteran, found it hard to understand Garry's behavior, and it was a source of great tension at home.

After his service in the Vietnam War, Garry returned home. He became depressed and felt survivor's guilt over the deaths of so many soldiers his age in the war. "Of all the servicemen who had died in Vietnam, probably most of them would like to be alive. I didn't want to be alive." He struggled with his depression. His battle with depression led him to search for his roots. "I needed to know why I was here, what was my purpose." Garry had always been curious about his ancestors. "I remember as a child of about eight sitting on the lap of my great-grandmother, Bertha Hixson, and asking her to tell me about her parents and her great-grandparents. In later years I could recall her stories with great clarity, and I started writing them down. I moved to interviewing elderly members of the family. During the five years that I did family history research, I had an awakening that would change my life and attitude forever. What I found was that most of my ancestors came to America before the Revolution, not after, as I had thought, and that twenty-five had served in American wars." In the Revolutionary War alone, Garry found that ten of his ancestors served and two had died. Garry was taken with an ancestor named John Straughn, who fought in Morgan's Riflemen in 1776 at the tender age of fifteen or sixteen. "He probably had peach fuzz on his face, and yet there he was thrust into some of the bloodiest battles of the Revolution. He was a member of Morgan's Riflemen. They were the eyes and ears of General Washington. The Riflemen served as spies, snipers, and saboteurs. At one point, Morgan's Riflemen marched the length of New Jersey, half of them without shoes, to warn General Washington of impending British forces. It is said that you could follow their trail in the snow because of their bloody feet." Garry was able to find payroll records for John Straughn that showed a payment of five dollars for service in the month of July 1779 and six dollars and some change in June of 1779. Although Garry was only able to find three documents attesting to John's service, the compiled histories about Morgan's Riflemen gave him a good understanding of what his ancestor went through. "Their greatest moment was probably at the Battle of Saratoga in New York. After the Battle, General Burgoyne walked up to Colonel Morgan and said, 'Sir, you command the finest regiment in the world.' And John Straughn, a lowly private, was one of the men standing at that surrender." Garry's knowledge of the

John W. Straughn's re-enlistment record shows that he was twenty-three years of age at enlistment, five feet eleven inches tall with gray eyes and dark hair. He was born in Putnam County, Indiana; he was a farmer; and he re-enlisted in Little Rock, Arkansas, on February 1, 1864, for a duration of three years' service.

Muster rolls give information about such activities as rank change and hospitalizations, and other related service events. This roll shows John Straughn enrolled and mustered in on February 1, 1862, for three years, as a private in Company H of the 43rd Regiment of the Indiana Infantry.

This muster roll shows John Straughn mustered out as a 4th Sergeant in Company H of the 43rd Regiment and then mustered back in as 2nd Lieutenant in the 155th Regiment of the Indiana Volunteers.

"Sir—I would respectfully ask through you that John W Straughn, a Corporal of Company 'H' 43 Infantry be reduced to rank for absence with out leave."

service that preceded him in his family left him humbled. "Once I learned what a legacy my family had in military service, I felt very ashamed for not having been a model soldier. I was ashamed for my attitude and my lack of patriotism. I felt like a very unworthy son; had I known the family history of military service I would have conducted myself differently because there is a legacy to live up to."

John Straughn's grandson, John W. Straughn, fought in Civil War campaigns up and down the Mississippi River. Garry learned a great deal about this Civil War ancestor by researching military records. He noted, "I had often wondered where my rebellious streak comes from and in part I think I have found an answer in the records of John W. Straughn. I find a young man who was busted a few times for insubordination, for being AWOL and for disobeying direct orders." Garry found a letter in John W. Straughn's personnel file that showed a request to bust Corporal Straughn to Private Straughn for being absent without leave, or AWOL.

Another valuable source of information on John W. Straughn was found in his pension records. Pension records are a great source of information for the family historian. Because the government requires background information on the pensioner, pension records often include affidavits from a spouse, marriage certificates proving marriage, and affidavits from comrades who served with the pensioner attesting to his service.

It is the information from original service records and later compiled records that brings Garry's military ancestors to life. Through unit histories of the corps that Straughn served with, Garry was able to follow his ancestor through the course of the war. "On July 4, 1863, Straughn fought in the battle of Helena in Arkansas. The 43rd fought back a Confederate force two to three times larger than themselves. In the end, the 43rd captured the Confederate forces. Later, while guarding a wagon train of supplies, the 43rd was surprised by a cavalry of 6,000. When the smoke cleared, only 38 of the original 400 were alive. John Straughn was one of the survivors."

Garry had been unaware of his rich military legacy until he started researching his family history. This legacy changed his life. It was by combing through the information from the original and compiled military records available to him that Garry was able to put together a compelling history of his family's service to their country and to make peace with his own experience as a soldier in the Vietnam War.

John W. Straughn's first filing for pension in 1888. This record includes John's age and a physical description and shows his occupation after the war as a carpenter. Because of a bout of measles contracted during his service in the war, and a case of piles, he claims that he is unable to work.

An affidavit from John's brother-in-law, Samuel Kennedy. This affidavit claims that John left his unit with the measles and returned home to be cared for until he was fit to return to duty. This affidavit provided valuable information for a search of Samuel Kennedy, placing him in Boone County, Indiana.

Garry's understanding of his family history has become a legacy that he can pass on to his children and future generations.

The types of service records available vary from war to war. Many service records have been indexed or abstracted in book form with copies of the originals available in a microtext format. They can be found in the National Archives and its regional branches. These records are also available on the local level in many state and historical societies and in major genealogical libraries across the country.

(See the Resource Directory

on page 125.)

INFORMATION about your ancestors is available in many different types of military records. There are records for every type of soldier that served. Your ancestor need not have been a medal of honor candidate or a famous general for you to find information about his or her service. Here are the basic types of records that you should search for:

SERVICE RECORDS. A service record is any document that chronicles an individual's military service. Examples of different types of service records include:
   Company musters
   Rolls
   Rosters
   Enlistments
   Discharge records
   Discharge lists
   Prisoner of war records
   Records of burials
   Oaths of allegiance

PENSION RECORDS. Pension records are another type of military record that provides excellent information for the family historian. In order to process a pension claim, the government requires that the veteran document his service and the part of his service that qualified him for a pension. Pension files are usually filled with testimony from fellow comrades or commanders who served with the veteran. Often there is additional testimony or affidavits submitted by family members or doctors during the period after the veteran was discharged from service. Pension files are, therefore, a rich source of biographical information for the veteran. Don't overlook pension files for veterans who died during service. Pensions could be claimed by widows or other survivors. As with service records, there are indexes and abstracts to the various military pension groups with microtext copies of the original records available.

PUBLISHED MILITARY HISTORIES. Both historical and contemporary published military histories have much to offer the genealogist. Military histories provide the background and color to the original documents about military ancestors. Knowing that your ancestor was part of a regiment is the first step; reading about what that regiment did will give you a greater sense of the role that your ancestor played in history. Regimental histories can detail the duties of particular groups of men within the unit as well as the hardships endured and the triumphs enjoyed by the entire unit. Many contain rather complete listings of all the skirmishes, battles, and other engagements in which the unit participated.

The towns and counties in which military soldiers lived and retired have libraries that contain many of the histories of units composed of individuals from the area. Town and county histories often contain significant sections about the veterans who were part of their communities. This emphasizes the importance of investigating local and regional libraries in veterans' home communities. Special or limited-edition publications may make it to state library and state historical society collections, but they will assuredly be in the nearly countless smaller libraries around the country. Special libraries, such as the Daughters of the American Revolution Library in Washington, D.C., and the Newberry Library in Chicago, also have significant collections of military histories.

DIARIES AND LETTERS. Diaries and letters, another significant type of record, closely resemble military histories in some respects. Soldiers' diaries may rival published histories in the amount of detail provided about given military engagements and the people involved. Indeed, for units that have no published histories, soldiers' diaries are a great substitute. Some soldiers go into significant detail in naming the individuals with whom they marched, encamped, engaged the enemy, and commiserated. Sometimes lists of individuals captured, encountered, and reprimanded can be found. Soldiers' letters to and from loved ones may also contain names of other individuals in a particular unit, and most certainly contain many heartfelt stories of the trials of war.

A number of these diaries and collections of letters may be found in local city and county archives as well as a soldier's home state archive. Some have been reprinted, indexed, and published and can be found on the shelves of local public li-

With the continued interest in America's past wars and the activities of patriotic organizations in the United States, expect to find increasing numbers of unit and regimental histories being published. State libraries and state historical societies are great places to look for these histories.

LETTER FOUND BY
Garry Bryant was carefully transcribed. In a camp near Fredericksburg, Virginia, on January 16, 1863, William Day wrote to his wife, Rebecca,

Dear Wife:

I one more time raise my pen to lets you know that I am not right well though I think I am some better. I recieved a letter from you on the 15th of the present month which was wrote the 6th of January which almost broke my heart to hear of the death of little Martha. You can not tell how bad it is to hear such things about my family and be not allowed to go see them. But we all have to die sooner or later. If it is God's will to call the young as well as the old. It is no doubt for the better. It grieves my heart to know that I can not see her agin in this world, But I feel confident that she is better than us.

Dear wife my heart is tender at this time that I hardly know what to write for your benefit. I would give the whole world if I just could get out of this war and come home to my family, but I see no chance for us poor soldiers to get the chance to come to our poor disconcolated families. I hope the great giver of Good will provide for us.

William Day died of typhoid on his way to Gettysburg and never saw his family again. Young Martha was his daughter.

braries as well as state libraries and other major research facilities. *American Diaries: An Annotated Bibliography of Published American Diaries and Journals, 1492–1980* is a helpful publication to use in research.

The publications of the various military and patriotic organizations are another good source of information. *The Confederate Veteran,* the *Daughters of the American Revolution Magazine,* and *Southern Magazine,* published by the United Daughters of the Confederacy, are just a few of the many periodical publications available. The periodical publications of military order societies and patriotic organizations provide the researcher with such resources as copies of actual records, indexes of major collections of military data, lists of recently published regimental histories, and names of individuals to contact for special assistance. These same organizations also publish many books on their particular military focus and may maintain substantial research libraries for their members to use.

Other examples of military records are those one can find in rural libraries, on memorial plaques in courthouse squares, and in those records that seem to grow up around the official military records. Military pension records, discussed previously in this section, are a favorite breeding ground for some of these miscellaneous records. For example, many southern states offered some form of pension to some of their Confederate soldiers, since these were not available from the federal government. In some cases, lengthy questionnaires were sent to the former soldiers as a first step in establishing these pensions.

The Tennessee Civil War Questionnaire was sent to living Confederate veterans around the turn of the century and had a total of forty-four questions. This record as a whole is valuable, but question forty-four of the Tennessee Civil War Questionnaire is a genealogist's dream come true. It states, "Remarks on ancestry. Give here any and all facts possible in reference to your parents, grandparents, great-grandparents, etc., not included in the foregoing, as where they lived, office held, Revolutionary or other war service; what country the family came from to America; where first settled, county and state; always giving full names (if possible) and never referring to an ancestor simply as such without giving the name. It is desirable to include every fact possible and to that end the

Periodical publications of military order societies and patriotic organizations provide such resources as copies of actual records, indexes of major collections of military data, lists of recently published regimental histories, and names of individuals to contact for special assistance.

Because communities had so much pride in their "boys who went off to war," you can find much information about soldiers in local newspapers as well as other town and area publications.

full and exact record from old Bibles should be appended on separate sheets of this size, thus preserving the facts from loss." And, while perhaps surprising, quite a number of veterans did fill out this form in rather great detail, providing several generations of family data and much military information. Arkansas also had such a questionnaire. These are true treasure-troves of genealogical information.

The perennial challenge for genealogists is to be as complete and thorough as possible in uncovering and using records and documents when establishing a family history. In the military arena, such thoroughness can pay significant dividends and lead to some wonderfully amazing discoveries. The importance of local sources of military information simply cannot be overstated. So much significant genealogical data regarding an ancestor's military activities can be gleaned from local sources. Because communities had so much pride in their "boys who went off to war," you can find much information about soldiers in local newspapers as well as other town and area publications. If you know the community from which an ancestor entered service, returned after service, or died, the local history materials available will be crucial in finding as much of the available military data as possible.

Tombstone inscriptions and cemetery markers can provide the unit in which the deceased served. The tombstone art and monuments for military veterans are impressive, particularly in some eastern and New England states. In some instances, veterans returning home were required to record their discharge papers with the county recorder. Special funds were sometimes established in particular jurisdictions to provide for soldiers' widows and dependents. Most state archives have military records for their citizens who served—and for all wars since the creation of the state. In many cases, the same holds true for county and local archives.

There are a number of significant publications that provide more specific details on conducting historical military research and locating military records.
• The Family History Library in Salt Lake City published an extremely useful and affordable research outline entitled *U.S. Military Records* (1993). It describes the various types of military records, lists the resources available to the researcher at the library in Salt Lake City or through the Family History Centers throughout the country, and provides numerous ref-

erences throughout the text to useful book titles and periodical articles. It also gives the researcher a healthy number of suggestions on how to more effectively use military records and how to explore local records to find valuable leads about an ancestor's military service. Less than fifty pages, it is easy to use and can comfortably become part of one's traveling research collection.

• Another outstanding publication is a book entitled *U.S. Military Records: A Guide to Federal and State Sources, Colonial America to the Present* by James C. Neagles. This book begins with a very useful description of the various types of military records and continues with information about post-service records, the records of the National Archives and its regional branches and repositories, and military record resources in Washington, D.C., as well as those in major research centers around the country. In the state resources chapter, each state is treated in an alphabetical listing. A time line showing the military engagements that affected a particular state and its residents is followed by the address and telephone number of the state's archives and/or major historical society. A general listing of state-specific military resources is followed by a chronological list dividing the more detailed materials by war. For a number of states, significant titles and microform collections are listed for wars from the Revolutionary War through the Vietnam War. These lists are a real boon for the researcher who wants to find the most significant titles for a particular state.

Equally important for the genealogist is the final chapter, which lists published sources that pertain to more than one state. In addition to the sheer number of references cited, a benefit is the manner in which the references are arranged. For each military engagement, a list of guides and bibliographies is followed by publications with lists of names. For some engagements, such as the Civil War, the list is further divided—in this case by Union and Confederate publications as well as foreign combatants. This work is a true companion for the genealogist interested in finding and using military records.

With so much valuable data potentially available in military records for genealogical researchers, how do you begin to explore these sources?

First, identify which war or wars your ancestors might have been a part of. Placing them in the right period of time, whether during war or peace, will help you identify which records you should search.

John W. Straughn

King William's War 1689–1697
Queen Anne's War 1702–1713
King George's War 1744–1748
French and Indian War 1754–1763
Revolutionary War 1775–1783
Indian Wars late 18th and 19th centuries
War of 1812 1812–1815
Mexican-American War 1846–1848
Civil War 1861–1865
Spanish-American War 1898
Philippine Insurrection 1899–1902
World War I/European War 1917–1918
World War II 1941–1945
Korean War 1950–1953
Vietnam War 1961–1975

(These dates reflect the United States' declared involvement.)

A meaningful second step would be to construct a checklist of the different types of military records available. Such a list might look like the following:

• Service records
• Pension records (bounty land warrants for earlier wars)
• Claims records
• General military histories
• Unit/regimental histories
• Letters and diaries
• Government documents and special publications
• Other miscellaneous records

A final useful activity to prepare for maximizing chances of locating important genealogical data in military records would be to construct a cheat-sheet of sorts, identifying the various general locations of military records.

- Local libraries and local historical societies
- State libraries and state historical societies
- County courthouses and state archives
- Major public libraries
- Special libraries
- The National Archives and the regional branches
- The Library of Congress

With the use of the first two checklists, the genealogical search is set in the proper historical context, and you are reminded of the different military records available for consultation. It is important to research and explore a few of the details about the particular war and time period.

For example, if you have ancestors that lived during the Revolutionary War, you would discover that pension and service records are widely available, that state militias played an extremely vital role in the war efforts, that there are two major national organizations with state and local chapters for descendants of ancestors who fought in that war, and that many military histories for the Revolutionary War have been published and indexed.

If, on the other hand, you suspect that you have potential Civil War ancestors, you could discover that the Civil War involved more people per capita than any other war in our nation's history; that unit and regimental histories abound; that there was a tremendous amount of pride in towns and communities on both sides of the Mason-Dixon Line, resulting in much locally published data; and that the government published massive compilations of official records for both the Confederate and Union armies and navies.

To make sure you explore all the record possibilities, use the second and third lists to remind yourself of the various types of records and then of the locations, repositories, and institutions that might hold the actual documents and publications.

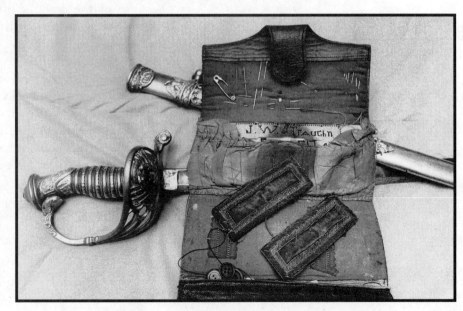

Federal censuses can be divided into three major groups based on the amount of information a researcher can find listed on them. The groupings are 1920–1880, 1870–1850, and 1840–1790.

CENSUS RECORDS

Census records can be some of the most exciting and useful records for genealogists, especially beginning researchers. There are three major types of census records, typically organized by jurisdiction: federal, state, and local. Federal census schedules are the records that come to mind most often when one hears the term census. And while these records are important for genealogists, state and local censuses are too important to ignore.

Federal censuses for genealogists are available from 1790 to 1920. Because of a 72-year privacy cap, the 1920 census is the most recent census available for research. These census records, frequently referred to as population schedules, attempt to be a complete listing of all citizens in the United States. An increasing number of federal censuses have indexes, which makes identifying and locating ancestors that much easier. For the purposes of discussion, federal censuses can be divided into three major groups, based on the amount of information a researcher can find in them. The groupings are 1920–1880, 1870–1850, and 1840–1790.

1920–1880 FEDERAL CENSUSES

The 1920–1880 census records are a favorite of genealogists because of the amount of information that is available on them. One of the major distinguishing factors of this group is that everyone living in the household is listed and there is a column to record the place of birth for each person, as well as each person's father and mother. The 1920 census actually goes a bit further and asks for the mother tongue as well as birthplaces of each person's parents. This grouping of census records also typically includes information about each person's education, ability to read and write, and occupational data along with other personal, identifying information. There are a good number of census guides available as separate publications or as chapters in larger reference works that supply the exact column headings for each census year.

*T*HERE ARE A COUPLE OF important items to note about the 1920–1880 census group. First, the 1890 census was almost completely destroyed by a fire in the District of Columbia in the 1920s. The fragments that did survive are available on five rolls of microfilm and include a few pages for each of the following: Alabama, District of Columbia, Georgia, Illinois, Minnesota, New Jersey, New York, North Carolina, Ohio, South Dakota, and Texas. There is an alphabetical index to these fragments on two rolls of microfilm.

Second, the 1880 soundex only indexes heads of households with children ten years and younger, although everyone is listed on the census itself.

And third, the 1910 census for some states is indexed by soundex while other states are indexed by miracode (a slightly different form of soundex) or not at all. Only twenty-one states were soundexed or miracoded for 1910. They are

Alabama				
Arkansas	Illinois	Michigan	Ohio	Tennessee
California	Kansas	Mississippi	Oklahoma	Texas
Florida	Kentucky	Missouri	Pennsylvania	Virginia
Georgia	Louisiana	North Carolina	South Carolina	West Virginia

A second major distinguishing factor of this group of census records is the manner in which they are indexed. Most of us have grown up using standard alphabetical indexes. While there are some alphabetical print indexes available, with the 1920–1880 censuses, you will encounter a unique indexing system called soundex. The soundex indexing system attempts to arrange names by the way they sound as opposed to a strict arrangement by spelling. At first, this manner of indexing may look a bit odd and even confusing. It is, however, a fairly reliable way of grouping names together by sound rather than by actual spelling. The advantage of this system is that it enables you to do a search that encompasses variant spellings of a surname.

The soundex indexing system for the 1920–1880 censuses attempts to arrange names by the way they sound as opposed to a strict arrangement by spelling.

As soundex is an extremely important indexing tool not just for census records but for passenger and immigration records as well as some contemporary database searching, it is important for you to understand how it works. There are a few basic guidelines to follow in converting a surname into a soundex code:

- The first letter of the surname is used as the first part of the soundex code.

- After the first letter, vowels (a, e, i, o, and u) and the consonants h, w, and y are ignored.

- Soundex codes always contain one initial letter followed by three numbers—no more and no less.

- The numerical values given to the letters have been established in such a manner so that letters that sound alike have the same numerical value.

- After the initial letter of the surname, the next three significant letters of a surname (other than the letters mentioned above) are coded according to the chart below.

- Whenever two letters with the same code appear side by side in a surname, only the first letter is coded. The second is ignored.

1 b,f,p,v
2 c,g,j,k,q,s,x,z
3 d,t
4 l
5 m,n
6 r

A couple of encoding examples are included to demonstrate how this system works.

If a name contains more letters than are needed to have a soundex code of three digits, the remaining letters are simply ignored.

Movopovitch = M-111 (ignore the vowels, t & c)

VanDuessen = V-532 (ignore the vowels, the second s & n)

If there are not enough consonants in the name to form the code, add zeros until there are three digits.

Haas = H-200 (ignore the vowels, code the s and add zeros until three numerals are part of the code)

Lee = L-000 (ignore the vowels and add zeros until three numerals are part of the code)

The surname Smith could have a number of spelling possibilities.

Some of the possibilities would include Smith, Smyth, Smithe, and Smythe. Using the soundex system, all of these names would have the same code, making it easier for the researcher to find more of the possible variant spellings.

Smith = S530 (ignore the vowels & h), Smithe = S530 (ignore the vowels & h), Smyth = S530 (ignore the vowels, y & h), and Smythe = S530 (ignore the vowels, y & h)

Once a particular surname has been coded according to the soundex protocol, the researcher is ready to use the actual soundex microfilm. The soundex films are arranged by state within each census year from 1920 to 1880. Within each state, the films are arranged by soundex code number and then by given name of the head of the household. And though a great deal of data from the census sheets is extracted on the soundex film, using the population schedules is always advisable.

The soundex coding system can be particularly useful when researching a name that has changed spellings or been misspelled over time, such as Weutcher, Weutscher, Wuetcher, Wuetscher, and finally Witcher. For each of these spellings, the soundex code is W-326.

Libraries and archives that have indexes that use the soundex system should have instructions such as these available—no need to memorize the system!

Here is an example of the 1870 census. Notice that this document lists Garry Bryant's ancestor, John Straughn. At the time that this document was created, John was twenty-eight and married to Sarah, a twenty-six-year-old home-maker. Also listed are the names and birth dates of their children as well as the place of birth of each member of the family.

Page No. 75

Inquiries numbered 7, 16, and 17 are not to be asked in respect to infants. Inquiries numbered 11, 12, 15, 16, 17, 19, and 20 are to be answered (if at all) merely by an affirmative mark, as /.

SCHEDULE 1.—Inhabitants in 3rd Ward City of Green Castle, in the County of Putnam, State of Indiana, enumerated by me on the 21st day of June, 1870. 128

Post Office: Greencastle Indiana   Charles G. Bowman, Ass't Marshal.

		The name of every person whose place of abode on the first day of June, 1870, was in this family.	Age	Sex	Color	Profession, Occupation, or Trade of each person, male or female.	Value of Real Estate	Value of Personal Estate	Place of Birth, naming State or Territory of U. S.; or the Country, if of foreign birth.											
1	2	3	4	5	6	7	8	9	10	11	12	13	14	15	16	17	18	19	20	
1		McBeth Ann	83	F	W				Pennsylvania										/	1
2	572 552	Straughn John W.	28	M	W	Carpenter			Indiana											2
3		— Sarah E.	26	F	W	Keeping house			Ohio											3
4		— Carrie L.	3	F	W				Indiana											4
5		— Addie L.	2	F	W				Indiana											5
6		Infant daughter	1/12	F	W				Indiana		May							/	6
7	553	Ramado Samuel	75	M	W	Shoemaker			Virginia	1								/	7
8		— Mary	71	F	W	Keeping house	3000		Maryland										8
9		Adams Mary E.	38	F	W				Ohio										9
10		— Augustin F.	16	M	W				Ohio										10
11	573 554	Puett Austin W.	66	M	W	Farmer			North Carolina									/	11
12		— Avery	46	F	W	Keeping house			Indiana										12
13		— Joseph	13	M	W				Indiana				/						13
14		— Cookie	11	F	W				Indiana				/						14
15		— Lizzie	7	F	W				Indiana				/						15
16		Bruce Mary	20	F	W	At home			Indiana										16
17		Shay Mary	14	F	W	Domestic Servant			Indiana	1	1								17
18	574 554	Hathaway John P.	65	M	W	Teamster			Virginia									/	18
19		— Nancy	62	F	W	Keeping house			Kentucky										19
20		— Mary	19	F	W	At home			Kentucky										20
21	575 555	Puter Reuben	29	M	W	Carpenter	1600		Ohio									/	21
22		— Irene	29	F	W	Keeping house			Indiana										22
23		— Maggie	4	F	W				Indiana										23
24		— Franklin	1	M	W				Indiana										24
25		Webster Harry	26	M	W	Teamster			Kentucky									/	25
26	576 556	Wilson Thomas	29	M	W	Foundry man			Indiana									/	26
27		— Jessie	26	F	W	Keeping house			Scotland	1	1								27
28		— Ada	4	F	W				Indiana		1								28
29		— Nettie	3	F	W				Indiana		1								29
30		— William	1	M	W				Indiana		1								30
31		Fitzgibbons Hanora	11	F	W				Indiana		1		/						31
32	577 557	Emison Daniel	48	M	W	Heater	9200		Pennsylvania									/	32
33		— Elizabeth A.	41	F	W	Keeping house			Hessen	1	1								33
34		— Mary E.	21	F	W	At home			Pennsylvania		1								34
35		— Daniel W.	12	M	W				Pennsylvania		1		/						35
36		— William E.	7	M	W				Pennsylvania		1								36
37		— Harrie	5	M	W				Pennsylvania		1								37
38	578 558	McHie Thomas B.	28	M	W	Engineer			Pennsylvania									/	38
39		— Mary	24	F	W	Keeping house			Pennsylvania										39
40		— Clara	3	F	W				Ohio										40

No. of dwellings 7 No. of white females 24 No. of males, foreign born 4
No. of families 8 No. of colored males No. of females 21 No. of insane 9

1870–1850 FEDERAL CENSUSES

This group of census records is a very good source of information. The census in this period still counts every person in the household. Listed as well are the birthplace of each person, age, occupation, and property value.

Most states have printed alphabetical indexes that are widely available. There are a few remaining states that do not have indexes for the 1870 census, but most are being compiled presently. The indexes are in alphabetical order by surname of the head of household. Persons with surnames different from those of the heads of households are typically listed in the index as well. Following the name, one will usually find the county abbreviation (or parish in the case of Louisiana), the page number on the actual census microfilm where the person or family is listed, and a township or district abbreviation.

Be aware that besides statewide census indexes in book form, many areas of the country have county- or town-specific census indexes for the federal population schedules. There is also a set of microfiche entitled *Accelerated Indexing Systems (A.I.S.) Census Searches*. This source indexes some censuses from 1790 to roughly 1870 (though it claims to go to 1907) and some miscellaneous tax lists for large portions of the United States by nine-year and regional/area groupings. For cities or localities that are not indexed, you can use *A Handy Guide to Record-Searching in the Larger Cities of the United States* by E. Kay Kirkham to determine how to narrow your search.

1840–1790 FEDERAL CENSUSES

The 1840–1790 censuses are characterized by the fact that only heads of households are mentioned by name. Other household members are enumerated strictly by age and sex categories. The head of household was usually the oldest male or main male property holder, but it could also be the primary female (again, the oldest or main property holder), often a widow. The further back in time one researches, the less specific the age categories become. In 1840, there are more than a dozen age categories for each sex, while in 1790 there are a total of six categories for both sexes, free and slave.

Most states have printed alphabetical indexes that are widely available. There are a few remaining states that do not have indexes for the 1870 census, but most are being compiled at present.

The 1840–1790 censuses are characterized by the fact that only heads of households are mentioned by name. Other household members are enumerated strictly by age and sex categories.

While this census group may be somewhat of a disappointment compared to the other groups of census records one encounters earlier in his or her research, they should not be undervalued. Used in conjunction with other town and county records, these earliest of federal censuses can still provide a good look at an ancestor's family. Remember that families are grouped together by district, township, and county or parish. And the census taker typically recorded families and households in the order in which he encountered them—keeping ethnic and migratory groups intact. This can be important as people of the same family and from the same homeland tended to settle together in the same area. A final benefit of this census group is the fact that literally all of the federal censuses taken during these years are indexed, sometimes by several different groups or companies.

A publication that can really provide an up-close-and-personal look at the questions asked and instructions given to census enumerators is entitled *Twenty Censuses, Population and Housing Questions 1790–1980.* Knowing the column headings for each year, the specific instructions by census year for filling in the data, and the actual census year for each enumeration is vital for getting the most complete and accurate picture of what the census has to offer the careful researcher. For example, the 12th Census of the U.S., Indian Division, 1880, gave the following instructions: "The Census year begins October 1, 1879, and ends September 31, 1880. All persons will be included in the enumeration who were living on the 1st day of October, 1880. No others will. Children born since October 1, 1880, will be omitted. Members of families who have died since October 1, 1880, will be included." Knowing this part of the instructions for who should be listed on the 1880 Indian schedules could explain why one may be having difficulty locating a particular ancestor.

SPECIAL FEDERAL CENSUS SCHEDULES

There are several special enumerations or census schedules that were taken in conjunction with the federal population census schedules for particular years. They include the slave schedules, the mortality schedules, the agricultural and man-

ufacturing schedules, and the Special Census of Union Civil War Veterans and Their Widows.

SLAVE SCHEDULES list slaves in the southern states for the census years 1850 and 1860. Like the population schedules, they are arranged in order by state and county, with some states having published indexes to facilitate searching for data about a particular owner. While called slave schedules, the owner is the principal party named. And typically very little information is supplied beyond the owners' names and sexes and ages of the slaves, although occasionally a few slaves were named.

MORTALITY SCHEDULES list those residents of a particular region who died during the twelve months prior to the taking of the census. These schedules are often confused with actual death records. One should be careful to maintain the distinction. The mortality schedules tend to mirror the population schedules of the corresponding years. The additional information one would find on them would have to do with the circumstances of the various individuals' deaths. For example, if the census was taken on 1 June 1850, the enumerator would ask who in the household had died between 1 June 1849 and 31 May 1850 and would gather information on name, age, sex, birthplace, occupation, and cause of death. With few exceptions, mortality schedules survive for the census years of 1850, 1860, 1870, and 1880. Some are indexed in book form while others are in a microtext format.

AGRICULTURE AND MANUFACTURING SCHEDULES can provide you with extra information about an ancestor or an ancestor's family. With agricultural schedules, you can document land holdings, glean information about how the land was used by a particular family, and possibly gather some migration data. Many people find it fascinating to see what crops their ancestors grew and what animals were on their farms. On manufacturing schedules, depending on the year, one can find out how many employees were used at a particular shop, the type of items manufactured, the annual income, and other general pieces of information.

THE 1890 SPECIAL CENSUS of Union Civil War Veterans and Their Widows was intended to list only Union

With agricultural schedules, you can document land holdings, glean information about how the land was used by a particular family, and possibly gather some migration data. Many people find it fascinating to see what crops their ancestors grew and what animals were on their farms.

veterans and widows, but occasionally Confederate veterans were included. This census is available for states from the second alphabetical half of Kentucky to the end of the alphabet. Schedules for Alabama through the first half of Kentucky were destroyed and are not available. Some of these surviving schedules are indexed either in book form or on microfiche.

OTHER CENSUS RECORDS: STATE AND LOCAL

While federal census records are the most commonly used population schedules, some states also took their own separate censuses in what are sometimes called the off-years or nonfederal census years. State censuses were usually taken in the middle of the decade. State census records tend to mirror their closest federal counterparts, that is, an 1855 state census will resemble an 1850 or 1860 federal census.

State census records can be an added asset for genealogical researchers. Not only do they shorten the ten-year gap between federal census records, many have more data than what is found on their federal counterparts. For example, the place of birth for most individuals on federal census schedules is typically no more specific than a state or foreign country. On the 1895 Iowa State Census, though, if the person listed was born in Iowa, the county is listed as well. In addition to that is something that no federal census has ever had as a category—religious belief. Just these two little extras make this a uniquely valuable census record for anyone researching in Iowa in the 1890s. The importance of this particular state census is increased by the fact that the 1890 federal census was destroyed by fire.

When conducting research in any given geographic area, it is always wise to watch for local censuses. Many local jurisdictions had taxing issues as well as other rules and codes that required a special census. In old local records there is evidence of families with school-aged children, of persons living in areas under consideration for railroad or canal construction, and of special groups of citizens based on ethnicity or on age. The census and censuslike records that you can find digging through local government documents, ordinances, and annual reports are impressive.

A source used in attempting to locate more of the local and regional enumerations is the *Periodical Source Index*. Numerous genealogical and historical societies publish indexes, transcriptions, or abstracts of federal, state, and local census schedules in their newsletters and quarterlies. This index provides subject access to these periodicals, including their census-related materials.

FINDING AND USING DATA
FROM CENSUS RECORDS

Because of the popularity and utility of federal census records, they are widely available for research. The National Archives and its regional branches have complete sets of all the federal census materials currently available for research. Many large public libraries and most state libraries have at least the federal census records pertaining to their particular geographic areas if not all of the contiguous areas. Libraries with large genealogical collections try to have the complete set of federal censuses as well as many of the indexes.

Along with the information that they provide, copies of census pages from the turn of this century are useful when interviewing older family members about their parents, neighbors, and early life. Often families lived near one another, and it is not unusual to find more information when the census is examined by the individual listed there. Aunts, uncles, even grandparents could be listed on the census in adjacent homes.

*T*HERE ARE A NUMBER OF challenges in using census records of all types. First, though valiant attempts were made to be as inclusive as possible, for some years and geographic regions, significant numbers of people were simply missed by the census takers. In the same manner, some indexes are a little more thorough than others. Regrettably, some of the most popular indexes have some of the highest error rates. And just because the index does not list a person does not necessarily mean the person is not on the census. That is why it's important to look for and use all available indexes. And if there is enough other evidence to suggest that a person should have lived in a particular county and year but is not listed in an index, a good researcher must be prepared to scan the entire county.

Handwriting can be another challenge when using census records. Some enumerators had either such sloppy handwriting or such artistic-looking penmanship that reading names and deciphering exact spellings can be difficult at best. Check all possible spellings when looking for an ancestor in older records.

Census and military records provide some of the most interesting and compelling insights into our ancestors' lives. These records prove time and time again to be among the most popular and extensively used records in genealogy because of the valuable information they provide. If you make sure to include these records as part of your research when you are working on your family history, you are sure to meet with success.

Checklist
BEGINNER'S

☞ Each war in American history has generated military records that are valuable in genealogy research.

☞ Each war has generated different types of service and pension records to examine.

☞ Regardless of the rank, from private to general, all servicemen have records.

☞ Census records are a favorite record among family historians for finding information about families and individuals.

☞ The federal census records that are available for research span the years 1790–1920.

☞ There are also local and state and special census records that are valuable to search.

CHAPTER SEVEN
African-American Research
STRATEGIES FOR THE BEGINNER

EACH OF US HAS an ethnic heritage that we look to for a sense of identity in our lives. Often, much of our cultural and religious heritage is derived from our ethnic roots. It is wise in the beginning of your research to contact a genealogical or historical society that focuses on the specific ethnic group that you are researching. There are a number of national and local genealogical societies that are listed by ethnic classification in the Resource Directory on page 125. While each ethnic group faces different research challenges within United States records, most use the same basic resources to conduct research. There are, however, unique challenges for the African-American who begins family history and genealogy. Because of the special nature of African-American experience in the United States, research takes a different turn very quickly from other ethnic groups researching family history in the United States.

African-American genealogy does *begin* with the same principles as any other genealogy research: begin with yourself and work back in time; start at home and find documents, letters, and other information that will help you to define your search; and remember to interview all living relatives for information about your ancestors. But there are five distinct periods of the African-American experience that are important to consider when approaching your research and that make African-American genealogical research different from other ethnic research:

CIVIL RIGHTS MOVEMENT	1954–1970
SEGREGATION	1896–1954
RECONSTRUCTION	1865–1877
CIVIL WAR	1861–1865
SLAVERY	1526–1865

ORAL HISTORY has a strong tradition in African-American culture. Alex Haley's journey into his family history began because of oral history. It was during his research that he learned how vital the African tradition of oral history could be. When Haley's grandmother and aunts would tell the stories of the family history, the stories always began with "the African" who was kidnapped by slavers and brought to America. In the narrative that the grandmother and aunts told, remnants of "the African" Kinte's language were used in telling the story. With the help of an African linguist and with documents that he found during his research, Haley was able to make his way back to Africa to trace the steps of his ancestor. Once in Gambia, Africa, he found a caste of singers called *griots* who could recite and act out centuries-old histories of villages, clans, families, and heroes. After more research, Haley returned to Gambia with a group that included four translators. They went to the village of Jaffure, where an old *griot* specialized in the history of the Kinte clan. The old man, named Kebbe Kanji Fofana, began chanting the history of the Kinte clan for Alex Haley. The chant was epic in its breadth, and two hours into the chant, the old man spoke of Kunte who went from his village one day to chop wood and was never seen again. Kunte, the son of a king, Haley realized, was "the African" of the narratives that his grandmother and aunts had told on the porch in Tennessee. What a treasure he had found in this African *griot* who could recite centuries of history related to his family and village.

It was not uncommon for slaves to carry this tradition of the *griot* forward in the form of storytellers. Haley's grandmother and aunts were storytellers who had committed to memory stories that were rich in family history and tradition. Although this oral history may reveal only fragments of history, they nevertheless provide valuable clues that can lead to important research.

Learning about history is important for any family historian. History provides a frame of reference for research and helps to identify search strategies that will be valuable to follow. Without a clear understanding of history, research will be difficult and frustrating for any family historian. That's why it is important to consider African-American genealogy in the context of American and African history.

THE CIVIL RIGHTS MOVEMENT
1954–1970

The Civil Rights movement was a time of great change within the African-American community, and it is important for you to learn what this movement meant to your family. Interview living relatives who lived through this movement, and document this period of African-American history for your family. Remember that at first, many people think they don't have a story to tell, or that their lives don't matter because they are not famous. Help them understand the value of what they have contributed by interviewing them and learning about the challenges and sacrifices they have endured (see chapter 3).

SEGREGATION 1896–1954

Beginning with *Plessy* v. *Ferguson* in 1896, and ending with *Brown* v. *Board of Education, Topeka, Kansas,* in 1954, segregation was a legal convention that marked the lives of all African-Americans. It is because of segregation that African-American research takes a different tack from conventional genealogy. African-Americans use the same records that other genealogists use; vital, military, census, and city directories. There is, however, a clear difference in using these records to find what you will need. As African-Americans were segregated in every aspect of their lives, so were their records. Birth, death, and marriage records were often segregated in city, county, and state repositories. Listings in city directories, a precursor to the telephone book, were segregated by white and colored listing, often placing African-Americans in the back of the book, as if riding the back of the bus. Cemeteries, as well as cemetery records, were segregated. An African-American might find an ancestor buried in a segregated cemetery or in the colored section of a white cemetery. When researching in communities where records are segregated, it is important to search both, as nonwhites often appear in white records. Clerks might not be aware of the separate records that were created, so always be persistent when searching for records created during the period of segregation. When you write to request original records from city or county courthouses, be sure to specifically ask for black

It is because of segregation that African-American research takes a different tack from conventional genealogy. African-Americans use the same records that other genealogists use; vital, military, census, and city directories. But, as African-Americans were segregated in every aspect of their lives, so were their records.

records as well as white. Many birth certificates, death certificates, and marriage records are segregated by race. This varies from state to state, county to county, and even by time period within the same county. The only way to know for sure is to research "inventories," or indexes, of vital records in the states and counties you are researching. The Works Progress Administration (WPA) conducted an inventory of county records in the 1930s. The inventories are part of their Historical Records Survey. These inventories indicate which vital records existed in each county at the time the inventory was taken. Many of these inventories were published and are available in genealogical and academic libraries across the country. Ask your librarian if they have county inventories from the WPA Historical Records Surveys. Otherwise, check with the county clerks in the offices where you are applying for vital records, and determine if the records are segregated for the location and time period you are researching. The reality is that you don't know where the records might be, so check both white and black records for the period of segregation. Also check for ancestors who may have been passing as whites or might have been counted as white because of their light tone of skin. Seventy-five percent of American blacks have at least one white ancestor and fifteen percent have a predominantly white ancestry.[1]

Compiled records are often used by genealogists and family historians as a first step in locating original records. But African-American records were routinely omitted from these compiled records, often created by local genealogists. Recent compiled records, published from the mid 1960s forward, may have corrected this omission, but

*T*HERE IS A TYPE of death record that is available for African-American research that is, unfortunately, important to note here. Tony Burroughs, a leader in African-American genealogy, has written, " It is a very painful source, but we cannot overlook it. That is a record of a lynching. Lynchings were very common in the South during the period of segregation. In fact, sometimes when we run into road blocks during our oral interviews, it's because one of our ancestors may have been lynched and family members are reluctant to talk about it. Researchers have studied lynchings and kept records on them. Tuskegee Institute kept a clipping file on lynchings, and Ralph Ginsburg edited a book *100 Years of Lynchings,* which contains 5,000 lynchings in America. The dead are listed alphabetically, by state. So even if a researcher did not know their ancestor was lynched, they can look up the names of their ancestors alphabetically to see if one is mentioned. Many have newspaper articles referenced to the names."

be mindful of the possibility of omission. If you don't find what you are looking for in a compiled record, persist in looking for the original record. It is a common mistake for a beginner in African-American research to assume that if an ancestor is not listed in a compiled record, original records do not exist. Marriage indexes and birth and death records from many cities, counties, and states omitted African-Americans. Also, be careful with CD-ROM compiled records because these records often contain the original omissions from the earlier works. The best reference for African-American research during segregation is original documents.

RECONSTRUCTION 1865-1877

Reconstruction was a time dedicated to repairing the damage done to this country during the Civil War, and a time for assisting former slaves in making the transition from slavery to freedom. Reconstruction was a very important period in this nation's history, and very important for African-American genealogists. The federal government created volumes of records then that are now valuable for genealogy research.

During Reconstruction, a banking system for former slaves and veterans of the Civil War was established. The Freedman's Savings and Trust Company's records are rich resources of genealogical material. These records can be found at the National Archives.

The Bureau of Refugees, Freedmen, and Abandoned Lands was established in March 1865. It became known as the Freedmen's Bureau. The bureau corresponded with those seeking assistance, established schools to teach former slaves to read and write, passed out food and medical supplies to refugees of the Civil War, managed property abandoned and confiscated from former Confederates, established hospitals, conducted trials for acts of violence, supervised labor contracts between former slaves and former slave owners, monitored apprenticeship contracts, and legalized marriages of former slaves who were prohibited from legal marriages during slavery. Each one of these policies created records that were preserved by the federal government and are available for research at the National Archives or one of its branches.

During the same time, but not as a part of the Freedmen's Bureau, a banking system was established for former slaves and veterans of the Civil War. It became known as the Freedman's Savings and Trust Company. There were thirty-seven branches, primarily in the South. These bank records are rich in genealogical data, listing places of residence and birth, other family members' names, and sometimes names of former slave owners and Civil War regiments. An example of one of the records available from the Freedman's Savings and Trust Company is signature cards. These cards, or registers, contain basic information about the depositor, such as name and address, but they also include birthplace, place of residence as a child, age, complexion, occupation, name of husband or wife, and names of other family members, including children. Also included are the names of the former master and mistress. This information is critical in beginning the research back into the slavery period as most records relating to slaves were kept by the master or mistress of the plantation. The records of the Freedman's Savings and Trust can be found at the National Archives.

CIVIL WAR 1861–1865

There were approximately 180,000 African-Americans who fought for the Union in the Civil War. There were another 10,000 to 20,000 who served in the Civil War Navy, and others who were not soldiers but assisted in the war effort. There were countless other slaves who went to war with their masters on the side of the Confederacy. The National Archives, and many states, have records for these African-American participants in the Civil War. You can search the Index to Compiled Records of Volunteer Union Soldiers Who Served with the United States Colored Troops, M594 (98 rolls), at the National Archives to locate an ancestor who served in the Union Army. These troops also were granted pensions. Pension files and service records are a wonderful source of information for the family historian and an important find for African-Americans (see chapter 6). As in other genealogical research, it is best to begin by reading, studying, and understanding this important part in American history. African-Americans played an important role during the Civil War, but because of racism and segregation, that role revolved around a different set of circumstances than the role other Americans played.

SLAVERY 1526–1865

By the time you reach as far back in your research as 1865, you should have determined whether your ancestors were slaves or not. Don't assume that they were slaves and skip directly to slave research. You must work back in time, step by step, to achieve your goal. It is a false assumption that all African-Americans are descended from slaves.

Attempting to trace a slave ancestor can be challenging, but it's not impossible. This research is complicated and demanding, requiring patience and attention to details. It is not for beginners. Much of the documentation relating to slave records has not been compiled or extracted and is not located in a central repository. Research into the slavery period usually requires examination of records in local

*A*N EXCITING SOURCE for information on African-American ancestors during the slave period is related to the Underground Railroad. From 1786 to 1865, fugitive slaves escaped to northern states and Canada, some 50,000 slaves in all. If your ancestors settled in a northern city, Canada, or a city in the Midwest before the end of the Civil War, chances are that they traveled on the Underground Railroad. There are records available that list stationkeepers and agents of the Underground Railroad. You can also check to see if journals and account books were kept. Fugitive journals are also available, and they contain genealogical information.

and state public libraries where the records were created. The researcher usually needs to contact each library in question to determine what records are available relating to black research. The Resource Directory on page 125 provides listings by state of African-American libraries, archives, and genealogical societies. Don't hesitate to ask for help from African-American genealogical societies; they can save you time and effort in your search for your slave ancestor.

In searching for proof of a slave ancestor, the first task is to determine the name of his or her last owner. If possible, use family resources to determine this. If family resources don't help, you will need to search plantation records carefully. There is no compiled source or index to plantation records, nor is there any indication of how many of these records still exist. Many may still be in the possession of the original family and not available for research. The first place to search for plantation records is in local archives and libraries in the slave state.

After determining who the slave owner was, you must determine what the owner did with his property, because slaves were property. Researchers must turn to records such as probate records, deeds, and tax transactions. Bills of sale were commonly filed at the local level in county courthouses, with probate records or land records, or often in a miscellaneous file. Bills of sale frequently include the name and value of the slave as well as the name of the buyer. Sometimes the slaves were purchased out of slavery by family members. Once the slave owner's identity is established, the slave schedules created by the federal census in 1850 and 1860 can be a valuable source for tracing slave ancestors. Comparing the age, sex, and color of each slave tallied on these census records against data in deed books containing bills of sale, probate, and other owners' records can help confirm what happened to a particular slave. The information from these slave schedules can also be compared against later records from the Freedmen's Bureau and the Freedman's Savings and Trust.

Other records that can be helpful in slave research include manumission records and slave advertisements. Before the Emancipation Proclamation, many slaves were granted their freedom. This freedom was documented by a manumission record, which was often recorded at the county courthouses. Some manumission records can be located in state libraries

According the the U.S. Census, there were 4,441,830 Negroes in the United States in 1860. Most of these antebellum Negroes were slaves (3,953,760). However, there were free blacks in both the North and the South. In fact, while 200,112 free blacks lived in the North in 1860, there were more (278,958) free blacks living in the South at the time.[2]

When searching for slave ancestors, check slave narratives. It is estimated that there are over 8,300 slave narratives.

and archives. Slave advertisements are difficult to research but can be valuable. They have not been indexed. You will have to determine what newspapers were printed in the area that your ancestors lived in and then search page by page for advertisements. These advertisements often announced a sale or runaway slave, which can lead you to other records.

Slave narratives are another resource to check when searching for slave ancestors. It is estimated that there are over 8,300 slave narratives. Many of these narratives are preserved on microfilm or have been published. The largest collection is the Works Projects Administration (WPA) Slave Narratives. The collection was published in 1972 and has been made available to researchers. One part of the WPA Slave Narratives collection has been published as *The American Slave: A Composite Autobiography* by George P. Rawick. This work is composed of nineteen volumes that span 2,194 interviews. Two supplements published in 1977 and 1979 bring the total interviews to 3,600. *Index to the American Slave* lists all of the interviews conducted.

Although research in the slavery period is difficult, many African-Americans have met with success when they follow standard research principles and apply what they learn about African-American history and records to their search. The more you learn about available records and successful searches, the more successful your own search will be.

CENSUS RECORDS

One record that you will use over and over again in your research for African-American ancestors is the census record. Research in federal census records (see chapter 6) is the same for African-Americans except for a few differences that you need to be aware of:

- Federal census records from 1790–1840 contain information on only the head of the household. The 1790–1810 census listed free nonwhites and "all other [free] persons." It did not *specifically* mention free African-Americans. It is important to understand that in the federal census between 1790 and 1840 the categories "other free" and "free

persons of color" did not distinguish between African-Americans and Native Americans.

- 1850 was a watershed year for the federal census. The census listed the names of each free member of the household, white and nonwhite. Other categories on the 1850 census include age, race (white, black, or mulatto), sex, and profession or occupation of men over the age of fifteen.

- The 1860 census is important for African-Americans because it was the last census tallied before the Civil War. This census can help to determine whether African-American ancestors were free or slave prior to the Civil War. There were many free blacks prior to the Civil War. "By 1860, one out of every eight blacks was already free. As early as 1830, some 3,765 free blacks owned slaves themselves. Men often purchased their wives and children born in slavery and then set them free." [3]

- The 1870 census began to list the names of all nonwhites, and the information contained therein was similar to that of 1850. It is important to understand that the census did not submit information regarding the relationships in the households. Do not assume any relationship without establishing it with other documentation.

- The 1880 census did give more information on family relationships. It is the first census to establish relationships to the head of household, marital status, health, and birthplace of each member of the family and of the parents of each.

☞ Begin your search at home, and interview living relatives.

☞ Enter the information you have gathered on a pedigree chart, family group record, and research log.

☞ Join an African-American genealogical society.

☞ Learn about African-American history and the records that are available to you.

Research in African-American genealogy continues to advance. With more activity in this area, new and exciting opportunities are forthcoming. Today there are more and more groups dedicated to compiling and conducting original research on African-American ancestry, and many universities are involved in this area of research. The Internet is a great place to share information about African-American genealogy. There are sites that specialize in African-American genealogy and that provide great links to other resources on the Internet. Beyond cyberspace, your best bet in beginning African-American genealogical research is to find a local genealogical society that has members who work in this area of research. See the Resource Directory on page 125 for listings of African-American genealogical resources nationally and by state.

THE FOLLOWING BOOKS, available from Gale Research, provide information on ethnic groups that have research challenges:

• *African American Genelogical Sourcebook*

• *Asian American Genealogical Sourcebook*

• *Hispanic American Genealogical Sourcebook*

• *Native American Genealogical Sourcebook*

See Chapter Notes for more specific information.

CHAPTER EIGHT

Your Medical Heritage

BEGINNING YOUR MEDICAL PEDIGREE

HOW IMPORTANT IS a medical pedigree to your family? A family medical pedigree can be lifesaving. A medical pedigree of your family gives you the ability to provide any health-care provider with essential information that is often necessary when diagnosing and treating family members. With the advent of health maintenance organizations and the complex environment of health care, keeping track of family medical records can be a challenge. A family with a medical pedigree is one step ahead in the world of medical records and information.

Family history and genealogy is a natural link to creating a medical pedigree. In the course of researching your ancestors, you will run across the records that can be used to build a medical pedigree. More and more family historians are using the information they find to create a family medical history. Examples of records that family historians use to build medical pedigrees include:

DEATH CERTIFICATES. A death certificate is an original document that is created at the time of someone's death. This record is valuable in building a medical pedigree because it usually includes the primary and secondary causes of death, the date of onset of the illness, and surgeries that were performed as a part of treatment. A death certificate is usually completed by an attending physician, which renders its information accurate and valuable to other physicians in diagnosing possible conditions in your family. What your family remembers as the cause of death and what is on the death certificate can be very different. Don't rely on the memories of others as your only source of information; get a copy of the death certificate to verify the information. Death certificates are kept in the state where the deceased passed away, not where they were buried. To send for copies of death certifi-

Family history and genealogy is a natural link to creating a medical pedigree. In the course of researching your ancestors, you will run across the records that can be used to build a medical pedigree.

Service records and pension records can often reveal medical information that is important to the genealogist uncovering a family medical history. For more information about these records,

see chapter 6.

cates, use the Where to Write for Vital Records section on page 187. Vital statistics, death certificates, and birth certificates have been kept by states since the early 1900s. The cost of copies and years available vary from state to state.

MORTALITY SCHEDULES. Mortality schedules were kept by the federal government between the years of 1850 and 1885. These schedules list deaths of the twelve months prior to the census. For example, the mortality schedule of 1859 would record deaths from 1 June through 31 May 1849.

These schedules provide a state-by-state register of deaths. Mortality schedules predate the registration of vital statistics at the turn of the century. The deaths that are recorded represent only about 13 percent of all deaths, but it is still an important source in lieu of vital statistics. The schedules include the name, age, sex, color, marital status, free or slave status, place of birth, occupation, disease or cause of death, and number of days of illness. These schedules can be found in state archives, the Daughters of the American Revolution Library, the National Archives, and in the Family History Library in Salt Lake and its Family History Centers.

INSURANCE RECORDS. Insurance records often contain medical information. If you find information on an insurance company document in the course of your research, follow up on it and see if you can find more. Life insurance, in particular, can be a great source of information. As early as 1865, medical information was included on life insurance applications. Important information about the general health, lifestyle, and condition of your ancestor could be found here. Each insurance company is different. Try to deal with corporate headquarters and tell them that you are interested in the information in order to complete a medical file on your family. Be prepared to show proof of descent. This research is difficult but can be done. *The Source: A Guidebook of American Genealogy* has a list of insurance companies from the 1800s forward. Your best bet for determining what insurance companies your ancestors used is home sources, such as boxes of old papers, and relatives.

CEMETERY AND FUNERAL RECORDS. Cemetery records often contain information about the cause of death. Check the sexton's office in the cemetery where your

ancestor was buried to see what information is available. Some tombstones or markers identify the cause of death or illness. Churches often keep funeral records, and mortuary records can also be valuable.

OBITUARIES. Modern obituaries do not usually identify the disease or illness that contributed to the cause of death, but older newspaper accounts usually do. An important clue in modern obituaries is often the charity that the family requests donations for, such as the American Cancer Society or the American Heart Association.

All of these records are important when you are beginning to build a medical pedigree for your family. But you will need to gather all available information about family relationships and health history. Since this information is emotionally charged, it is natural that your family may want to avoid the issue. Be sensitive to family members who are unwilling to be involved or discuss medical history, but help them recognize that the information they provide can be lifesaving to you or to future generations of your family.

There are genetic traits that are visible to everyone: a hitchhiker's thumb, eye color, a widow's peak, or a curved pinkie finger. Your genetic makeup also harbors information that is not apparent on the surface but is important to know about. "Each of us carries roughly 5 to 20 mutant (altered or abnormal) genes which have the potential to cause diseases or abnormalities. This is a potential only; some of these genes require the interaction of environmental factors to cause disease while others are rendered inactive by stronger, dominant healthy genes. As of [1995], more than 5,000 genetic conditions have been identified, ranging from rare and obscure diseases to fairly common ones."[1] The identification of genetic conditions has provided physicians with the ability, in some cases, to recommend early screening or treatment that can alleviate pain and suffering.

Because of the sensitive nature of the information that you will be looking for, it is important to be concerned with the issue of privacy. Information in the wrong hands can have devastating consequences. The information that you compile should be shared only with your health-care provider and blood relatives. Assure your extended family that your research will remain confidential and will be treated with dis-

Hospital and medical records are often difficult to access. If you suspect that you need access to these records, enlist the help of your physician.

It is important to gather genetic information about your horizontal (brothers and sisters, aunts, uncles, and cousins) as well as your vertical (mother and father, grandparents, and great-grandparents) ancestors. So that your genetic information can be helpful to you and your doctors, it is important to trace your genetic history back four generations.

cretion. Discrimination can occur in the workplace and with health and life insurance if information about genetic conditions is treated casually.

Blood relationship determines the shared gene percentage between family members. A basic understanding of this relationship can help you understand the importance of gathering information for your medical pedigree. The closer the blood relationship, the greater percentage of common genes.

RELATIONSHIP	PROPORTION OF GENES IN COMMON
FIRST-DEGREE RELATIVES	
Parent, sibling (brother or sister), child	**1/2**
SECOND-DEGREE RELATIVES	
Grandparent, uncle, aunt, nephew, niece, half sibling, grandchild	**1/4**
THIRD-DEGREE RELATIVES	
First cousins	**1/8**

THE PORTION OF COMMON GENES FOUND IN BLOOD RELATIVES

Understanding how genetic traits are shared by blood relationship underscores the importance of gathering information on horizontal (brothers and sisters, aunts, uncles, and cousins) as well as vertical (mother and father, grandparents, and great-grandparents) ancestors. It is generally agreed that gathering four generations of medical information is usually enough to be helpful for your medical diagnostic purposes.

A medical pedigree chart is the final graphic product of a medical genetic history. This graphic format allows for identification of family relationships, which is the easiest place to start. Use your medical pedigree as a foundation for gathering more information. Share it with your family and have them fill in the information they know. Whenever possible, obtain a copy of each death certificate to verify the information. Identify your children, their children, and so on; move to your brothers and sisters, their children, your parents, your aunts and uncles, and soon you will have a page full of circles, squares, and lines. In addition to those individuals who are alive, it is often important in medical history to document miscarriages and stillbirths. Often, it is easiest to number the

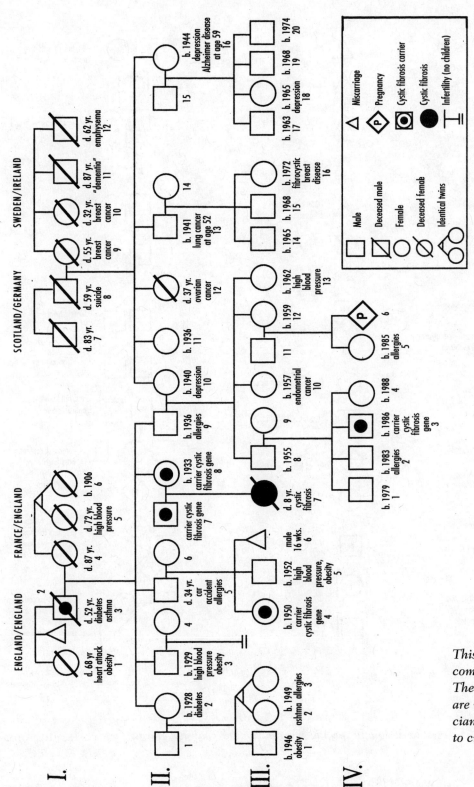

This is an example of a complete medical pedigree. The key shows symbols that are used universally by physicians and genetic counselors to create a medical pedigree.

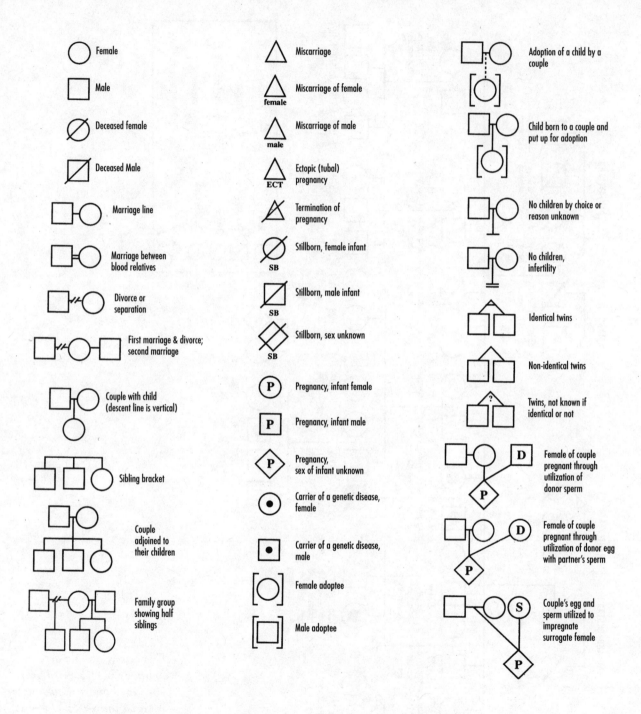

○ Female	△ Miscarriage	Adoption of a child by a couple
□ Male	△ female Miscarriage of female	Child born to a couple and put up for adoption
⊘ Deceased female	△ male Miscarriage of male	
⧄ Deceased Male	△ ECT Ectopic (tubal) pregnancy	No children by choice or reason unknown
□—○ Marriage line	△ Termination of pregnancy	No children, infertility
□═○ Marriage between blood relatives	⊘ SB Stillborn, female infant	Identical twins
□⫽○ Divorce or separation	⧄ SB Stillborn, male infant	Non-identical twins
□⫽○—□ First marriage & divorce; second marriage	◇ SB Stillborn, sex unknown	Twins, not known if identical or not
Couple with child (descent line is vertical)	Ⓟ Pregnancy, infant female	Female of couple pregnant through utilization of donor sperm
Sibling bracket	🅿 Pregnancy, infant male	Female of couple pregnant through utilization of donor egg with partner's sperm
Couple adjoined to their children	◇P Pregnancy, sex of infant unknown	Couple's egg and sperm utilized to impregnate surrogate female
Family group showing half siblings	⊙ Carrier of a genetic disease, female	
	▪ Carrier of a genetic disease, male	
	[○] Female adoptee	
	[□] Male adoptee	

These are the standard symbols used to designate specific information on pedigree charts.

MEDICAL FAMILY TREE SKELETON

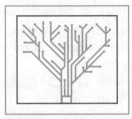

ANCESTORS™

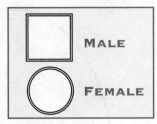

MALE

FEMALE

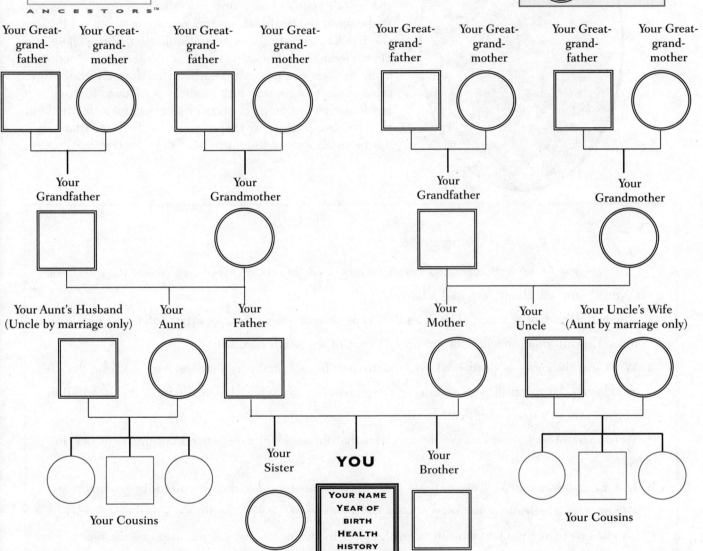

Your Great-grand-father

Your Great-grand-mother

Your Great-grand-father

Your Great-grand-mother

Your Great-grand-father

Your Great-grand-mother

Your Great-grand-father

Your Great-grand-mother

Your Grandfather

Your Grandmother

Your Grandfather

Your Grandmother

Your Aunt's Husband (Uncle by marriage only)

Your Aunt

Your Father

Your Mother

Your Uncle

Your Uncle's Wife (Aunt by marriage only)

Your Cousins

Your Sister

YOU

YOUR NAME YEAR OF BIRTH HEALTH HISTORY

Your Brother

Your Cousins

This is a classic block for a medical pedigree. Women are circles and men are squares. Include as much information as you can about date of death, cause of death, and age of onset. Begin your own medical pedigree by writing down what you know and drawing a diagram to show family relationships.

symbols and write information about the people on additional sheets of paper. You can reduce the confusion by developing a key or legend which identifies the consistent information that is relevant to interpreting the pedigree.

Once the family relationships have been identified, the next step in developing a medical family history is to identify the health status of as many individuals as possible. As you think about the health status of a person, ask yourself if he or she has had any surgeries or hospitalizations (especially as a child), long-term illness, or need for medications. Document as many events as possible: death, birth dates, dates of hospitalization, or beginning of a medical condition. If there is a particular condition of concern, it is essential to learn about that condition to see if there are subtle findings that might not be so obvious as to require medical attention.

THE QUESTIONS that you ask family members are important. Here are some of the questions that you should ask about deceased relatives:

1. What was the date of death? The exact date is preferred, but get an approximation if it is not available. This information will help you order a copy of the death certificate.

2. What was the cause of death? Ask your relatives to be as specific as possible. Ask how long the illness lasted. Try to get the age of onset of the cause of death, if possible. Again, seek documentation of the event in a death certificate.

3. Were there other known illnesses or surgeries that my ancestor experienced during his or her lifetime?

4. Did my ancestor smoke? If so, indicate how much he or she smoked daily and for how many years.

5. Did my ancestor drink or use drugs? Be aware of patterns of substance abuse. Substance abuse can also be an environmental factor in many diseases, including diseases of the liver and the heart.

6. Were there any miscarriages or stillbirths? This information can help in treating pregnancies and can flag possible problem pregnancies.

Be as inclusive as possible when gathering information about your family. Sometimes, something as simple as family pictures can help identify particular physical characteristics that may not have been clinically important but may be subtle signs of a more serious condition. Vickie Venne, a genetic counselor, remembers:

"One family several years ago came for genetic counseling because they had a newborn son who was deaf. While collecting information about the family, I noticed that the mom had one blue eye and one brown eye. I asked them to bring in family pictures. You could see in the colored picture that her father also had different eye colors and a bit of white in his bangs and although the picture of her grandparents was in black and white, her grandfather had a very clear streak of white in the middle of his hair. It turns out that the family had a condition called Waardenburg Syndrome, in which the mildest forms show up as individuals who have eye colors that are different and a white forelock of hair. The more serious version of this syndrome causes deafness. And the family just thought it was a funky family characteristic that you could mask with hair coloring, as the mother had done."

Since some genetic diseases are more prevalent among different ethnic groups, it is important to know your ethnic heritage as you compile a medical pedigree.

TAY-SACHS DISEASE is a fatal genetic disorder found in children that leads to the progressive destruction of the central nervous system. This genetic disease appears more often in people of eastern European Jewish (Ashkenazi) descent. Eighty-five percent of the children affected are of eastern European Jewish descent.

MALIGNANT HYPOTHERMIA is a hereditary condition that results in high temperature and muscle rigidity when exposed to certain anesthetics. This disease is found most commonly in people of French-Canadian, European, Italian, Norwegian, and Welsh descent. It is rarely found in African-Americans or Japanese.

THASSELEMIA is a group of anemias that vary in severity. It is usually found in people of Mediterranean, Southeast Asian, Middle Eastern, or African descent.

There are many books that go into substantial detail about creating a medical history for your family. *Genetic Connections: A Guide to Documenting Your Individual and Family History* is a comprehensive guide that can help you build a medical pedigree.

SICKLE CELL ANEMIA is a form of anemia found primarily in African-Americans. It is estimated that sickle cell anemia is present in 1 in 625 live births among African-Americans. It is also found in people of Mediterranean descent and has been found among Caucasians.

CYSTIC FIBROSIS is characterized by the thick mucus that the body produces, causing damage to the pancreas and the lungs. It is most common in families of European descent. It is present in African-American families, but rare in Asian families.

CONGENITAL NEPHROSIS is a kidney disease that is hereditary and found most often in people of Finnish or Scandinavian descent. It is noted in newborns before three months of age.

As research continues, more information will become available about the different types of diseases that are transmitted by the genetic code we carry.

If you have any concerns about what you discover in collecting your family's medical history, make an appointment with your physician or a genetic counselor. A professional review of the research you have gathered will help identify what additional information may be needed and will help determine what, if any, medical treatment you should seek.

Genetic counselors can help you understand your family medical history. They are members of medical teams who provide information and support to individuals and families who are dealing with a birth defect or genetic condition. Genetic counselors work with people during various time of their lives: pregnant couples concerned that their child might have a problem, parents of a newborn who has a birth defect, or teens and adults diagnosed with a condition that runs in the family.

Genetic counseling is a new area of practice in medicine. The process of genetic counseling was defined by the American Society of Human Genetics in 1975 as a communication process dealing with the problems associated with the occurrence or risk of occurrence of a genetic disorder in a family. This process includes understanding the medical facts and the way in which heredity contributes to the disorder in specified relatives. To do this, genetic counselors obtain the complete individual and family social, reproductive, and health history. Genetic counselors then help determine the risk assessment and provide information about available clinical and testing options. Communication is crucial: the more information given to a genetic counselor, the easier it is to define diagnosis and genetic implications.

We are entering an exciting century, in which the possibilities of treating genetically transmitted diseases will increase as a result of the work being done today. The last quarter of this century has seen unprecedented advances in the field of human genetics. Today, there are tests available to help diagnose and treat some genetic illnesses. In clinical research programs, tests are helpful for early diagnosis of cancerous and precancerous cells. Carrier testing is also done to help couples learn if they will risk passing such diseases as cystic fibrosis, sickle cell anemia or Tay-Sachs disease to their children. The most common form of testing today is newborn screening, which is done to find missing or abnormal genes in newborn infants.

*I*F YOUR PHYSICIAN doesn't already work with a genetic counselor, he or she may be able to locate one at a local university or medical center. The National Society of Genetic Counselors is a professional membership organization of genetic counselors. Although the executive office does not maintain or disseminate information about specific genetic disorders, it will provide referrals to local genetic counselors:

National Society of Genetic Counselors
233 Canterbury Drive
Wallingford, PA 19086-6617

Although there are many exciting and disturbing issues that revolve around this type of scientific knowledge, the more information you have about your family medical heritage, the more capable you will be of making informed decisions for you and your family.

ACH OF US enters this world with a genetic legacy. The Krause sisters learned that the silent legacy they carried with them was a deadly bequest. Because of their diligence and interest, they were able to save their own lives and to help extended family members be aware of the dangers they faced.

When Carol Krause was forty, she was diagnosed with colon cancer. Because Carol had learned about her family's medical history, she had a better chance than most to survive her battle with cancer. After their mother's death at the age of fifty-two from ovarian cancer, Carol and her sisters began to piece together a medical pedigree. They found a pattern of cancer in their mother's family, but not enough to alarm them. When Carol's father became ill with cancer at age seventy-two, the women still weren't concerned about their own health. Their father was diagnosed with prostate cancer, which was not unusual for a man his age, but during more testing, the doctors found a rare cancer in their father's ureter; the sisters wanted to know more about their family medical history. They questioned their father gently and learned an ominous truth. Cancer had been a constant companion on both the paternal and maternal lines of their family. "There were too many different kinds of cancer, from both sides of the family. And I assumed that very few cancers were thought to be genetic. I knew that breast cancer tended to run in families. But that was one of the few organ cancers we didn't have anywhere on our family tree. . . . So I decided simply not to worry about it."[2] What Carol didn't realize was that even the limited information the sisters had gathered could prove to be lifesaving.

Carol's father eventually died of his cancer, and at the funeral, Susan, age thirty-eight, mentioned that she had been experiencing a mild pain in her side. Because she was trying to get pregnant, Susan was anxious to clear up any problems. She was examined, and it was determined that she had an ovarian cyst. Susan shared her mother's medical history with her doctor, who said she was too young, and she didn't have to worry about cancer. The cyst became worse, and when finally removed, it revealed a cancerous tumor. More tests showed the cancer had spread to the uterus and a lymph node. Alarmed by this discovery, the sisters continued to do more research. They started to consult experts in the field of oncology and genetics. The opinions that came back were startling. "It appeared our family had been hit by a syndrome of cancers. . . . 'Cancer of the colon, uterus, and ovary can be connected,' we were told by Dr. Leo Lagasse at the Cedars-Sinai Medical Center in Beverly Hills, California. 'You must have your colons checked immediately, and consider having your uteruses and ovaries surgically removed.' "

The women were shocked. They had considered themselves to be quite healthy. Carol, age forty, was trying to have a second baby. Kathy, at age forty-two, was an active jogger and health-food advocate, still wanting to start a family. Peggy was forty-five and was finished having babies, but was uncomfortable with the idea of removing healthy organs. Second and third opinions met with the same urgent tone from the professionals: get the organs out, and get them out fast.

The sisters did as suggested. Each had a colonoscopy and had their uteruses and ovaries removed. At the urging of the doctors, they also had mammograms, because they were told that breast cancer can be linked to uterine cancer. The results of the tests and surgeries that the sisters endured were staggering. Kathy's organs, removed as a precaution, revealed a tiny tumor in her ovaries and an early malignant growth in her uterus. She would fight a later reappearance of ovarian tumors in her pelvis, even though the ovaries had been removed. "We were convinced that she was genetically programmed for this disease and there was nothing she could have done to prevent it. But she now had a fighting chance only because doctors had our medical family tree and convinced her to act quickly." After removal, Peggy's organs were found to be cancer-free. It was with the colonoscopy that Carol was in for a shock. "Doctors found a malignant tumor in my colon. In fact, it sat right in the cecum, the exact resting place of the tumor that killed my paternal grandfather, Ernst, when he was only thirty-three." Carol's colonoscopy proved to be a lifesaver. "My colon tumor might not have shown symptoms for another year or so, and my chances would have been far worse. I did have to experience a difficult surgery, but I was spared chemotherapy. My tumor was discovered early only because we found aggressive, savvy doctors."

The efforts and experiences of the four Krause sisters paid off by saving three of the four sisters' lives. Carol's sister Kathy fought her ovarian cancer for five years and unfortunately, she died in 1995. Carol believes that Kathy had an additional five years that she would not have had because of the family medical history that led to an early diagnosis. Carol's continued diligence paid off when a mammogram at age forty revealed a suspicious spot. A biopsy followed that revealed the beginning of a small malignant tumor. Surgery followed and Carol's prognosis remains good.

BEGINNER'S Checklist

☞ Every family needs a medical pedigree to help physicians treat family members more effectively.

☞ The records you find in researching your family history will help you build a medical pedigree. Death certificates, insurance records, and obituaries contain information that can be important.

☞ Medical information should be gathered on living as well as deceased members of your family. Information from the horizontal line (brothers and sisters, aunts, uncles, and cousins) is as important as information from the vertical line (parents, grandparents, and great-grandparents).

☞ Four generations of information is usually sufficient for professional counseling.

☞ Don't rely on family members' accounts of cause of death or illnesses in the family; document as much information as you can.

☞ Treat the information you gather with discretion.

☞ If you have questions or concerns about the information you find about your family's medical history, consult a physician or a genetic counselor. These professionals will be able to answer questions and suggest possible action.

CHAPTER NINE

High-Tech Help

COMPUTERS AND GENEALOGY

THE PERSONAL COMPUTER has revolutionized the hobby of genealogy. Tasks that were once painstaking and tedious are now made easy with the click of a mouse. Information that could only be used in libraries is now available at home. The genealogist has now been let loose on the Internet. As a result, there is a virtual feeding frenzy of family history taking place in cyberspace.

The computer has made it easier for anyone to become involved in family history and genealogy. Software programs can now take on the responsibility of sorting and listing all of the information that you have gathered about your family. For the beginner, it often makes the process of genealogy research painless. *Almost.*

Many people are under the impression that they can sit down at a computer with a request about family history and be greeted with hundreds of years' worth of ancestry at the stroke of a key. It's not that easy, yet. Right now, you still need to do your research personally. What you *can* do with a computer is store, retrieve, and share information faster and more easily than before.

Storing genealogical information used to mean sorting boxes full of documents and photographs and placing them carefully in three-ring binders that had to be carried to libraries and archives when you did your follow-up research. Family historians used to spend many hours updating information and correcting pedigree charts to reflect their latest discovery from the library. With a good genealogy software program, the genealogist can now enter the information, and the computer will store, make changes to, and organize your material. Some family historians even carry a laptop computer to the libarary and enter the changes as they do their research. Elaborate pedigree charts can be printed out from the information that you have discovered about your family. You

The home page of the Ancestors *web site at* http://www.kbyu.byu.edu/ancestors.html.

can keep track of medical information that you discover, and old photographs and home videos can be digitized and enhanced on your home computer. Family histories can be published with relative ease at home, and many families share family history newsletters that they create on the computer. You can even post everything that you have learned through your research on the Internet to share it with the rest of the world and network with family historians worldwide at any time of the day or night.

If you have determined that you are ready to use this technology, where do you start? Determine what kind of a computer you will need in order to do family history and genealogy. A computer that is state of the art will help you take full advantage of what technology is available to genealogists. Most software programs for genealogists need a fast computer and lots of memory. Much of the published archival information is on CD-ROM. If possible, a computer with at least 16 megabytes of RAM, a four-speed CD-ROM, a Pentium processor, and a 28.8 baud modem will help you start off on the right foot. Since the technology is changing so quickly it is best to talk with members of a CIG (computer interest group) in your local genealogical society. Many community colleges also offer classes in genealogy on computers. These local resources will help you decide what type of computer and programs you will need.

Many of the records that have been available to genealogists in libraries and archives over the years are now being digitized and placed on CD-ROM. Businesses are anxious to provide this information to genealogists and are developing products as fast as they can. One example of the scope of this effort is that 145 years' worth of one quarterly genealogical journal is now available on CD-ROM. In printed form, this journal would take up more than thirty feet of shelf space at home. Thanks to technology, you can have it at home on a CD-ROM for a fraction of the cost. Not only is storage easier, accessing these records on your computer takes a fraction of the time that it would take to search through the volumes on your shelf. Many of the published journals have search engines that find the information you need in a keystroke. Marriage and death certificates, social security indexes, census information, deeds, and more are being put on CD-ROM for the hobbyist. And this trend is growing. Be aware, however,

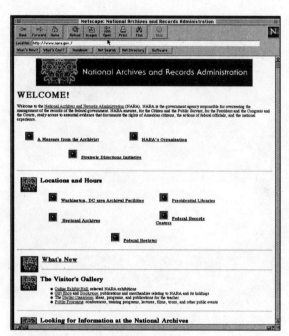

The web site of the National Archives at http://www.nara.gov.

of one problem in using the information found on these CD-ROM records. The CD-ROMs that are available have been created from compiled and original sources that have been scanned. There is an error rate of about 10 percent in most compiled records. Always try to refer to original sources to verify what you find on CD-ROM, or in any compiled source.

Once you have decided to begin using your computer for genealogy and family history, you need to choose a software product to use. There are many different software programs on the shelf today.

• *Family Tree Maker* by Broderbund is the best-selling genealogy program on the market and is the official software of the *Ancestors* television series. This is a program that is easy for beginners to use. The deluxe version, *Deluxe Family Tree Maker,* includes two sample CDs from the *Family Tree Maker* collection, a group of CDs that are accessories to the basic software program. The first sample CD contains volumes one and two of the *World Family Tree,* which includes more than 12,000 actual family trees contributed by customers. Trees date from before 1600 to the present. More than six million individuals are named. The other CD in the deluxe version is the social security death benefits records for the United States from 1937 to 1993. This two-CD set contains 55,000,000 names of deceased social security recipients whose relatives applied for social security benefits. *Family Tree Maker* also has online support and search capabilities through its exciting and comprehensive site on the Internet at http://www.familytreemaker.com. *Family Tree Maker* is available for Windows and Macintosh at most software retail outlets. For more information, contact Broderbund's Banner Blue Division, 500 Redwood Boulevard, Novato, CA 94948-6121. Telephone 415-382-4770.

• *The Master Genealogist* is a heavy-duty genealogy program that is available in both Windows and MS-DOS versions. A Macintosh version is in development. The Master Genealogist has the capability to track each and every piece of information found in genealogy research, including conflicting data obtained from different sources. It also tracks all sources of information and even has a database of libraries, courthouses, and other locations researched. One of *The Master Genealogist*'s features that is not found elsewhere is an extensive research log of tasks already accomplished and

The web site of Family Tree Maker *at* http://www.familytreemaker.com

others planned for the future. For more information about *The Master Genealogist,* contact Wholly Genes, Inc., 6868 Ducketts Lane, Elk Ridge, MD 21227. Telephone 410-796-2447 or send e-mail to 74774.653@compuserve.com or look on the World Wide Web at: http://www.WhollyGenes.com.

• CommSoft's *Roots IV* and *Family Gathering* are two leading genealogy programs that provide power and flexibility not found in the simpler programs. *Roots IV* is an MS-DOS program that tracks all phases of a genealogy project. (*Roots V* will be released in a Windows version.) It records all the facts involved in family research, including conflicting information received from different sources. *Roots IV* also produces some of the finest printed reports, including a complete book of one's ancestors. *Family Gathering,* available for Windows and Macintosh, is a genealogy program that contains approximately 80 percent of the functionality found in *Roots IV.* For more information about either of these products, contact CommSoft, Inc., 7795 Bell Road, Windsor, CA 95492-0310. Telephone 707-838-4300 or send e-mail to 74774.522@compuserve.com or look on the World Wide Web at http://www.sonic.net/~commsoft.

• *Family Origins* is an excellent inexpensive genealogy program available for Windows and for DOS. It has many features normally found in programs that sell for twice its price. *Family Origins* is sold in many retail outlets and by mail order. The price in discount stores is usually about $30. For more information, contact Parsons Technology, One Parsons Drive, Hiawatha, IA 52233. Telephone 319-395-9626 or look on the World Wide Web at http://www.parsonstech.com/software/famorig.html.

• *Reunion* is available in both Windows and Macintosh versions. It has a long list of features similar to those of any high-quality genealogy program. *Reunion* uses your existing word processing program for all text entry. It also produces excellent printed charts, including huge wall charts that are impressive at family get-togethers. For more information, contact Leister Productions, Inc., P.O. Box 289, Mechanicsburg, PA 17055. Telephone 717-697-1378 or send e-mail to 74774.1626@compuserve.com or look on the World Wide Web at http://www.LeisterPro.com.

• *Personal Ancestral File* is a very popular genealogy program produced by the Church of Jesus Christ of Latter-day

The web site of Reunion at http://www.LeisterPro.com.

Saints (Mormons). It is available in two versions: Macintosh and MS-DOS. No Windows version is available yet. *Personal Ancestral File,* or *PAF,* allows the recording of basic genealogy information such as names, dates, and places. It also has the capability to record text notes on each individual. Unlike the other programs listed here, *PAF* does not have any capability to accept scanned images or to produce the fancier reports such as complete genealogy books. While not as powerful as the previously mentioned programs, *Personal Ancestral File* has a simple interface that is very easy to use. It sells for $35, which is lower than many other genealogy programs. For more information, contact Salt Lake Distribution Center, 1999 West 1700 South, Salt Lake City, UT 84104-4233. Telephone 1-800-537-5950.

Once you have chosen your software program, it is time to go online. The Internet is a network of networks that connects computers and their users all over the world. If you are unfamiliar with the Internet, the best thing to do is just jump in and try it out. There are many books available that will guide you through this journey, but the interface has become so user-friendly that getting online and exploring is usually the best thing to do. The commercial Internet providers that are most familiar are America Online, CompuServe, and Prodigy. These are national services that provide usage time on the Internet based on a monthly flat rate and then hourly fees for additional hours. There are also local Internet providers that supply basic packages for Internet access and e-mail accounts.

Once you decide on a service provider and get online, you will have a variety of resources available to you as a genealogist and family historian. This is one of the most exciting environments for finding information and networking.

• CHAT ROOMS AND FORUMS. If you sign on with America Online, Prodigy, or CompuServe, you will find a variety of genealogical references available to you. One of the unique features that these services have to offer is the chat rooms and forums. The chat rooms and forums give you the ability to "chat" in real time with other genealogists from around the world. On the screen before you is dialogue that is happening as you are connected. To join in, type a response to the dialogue on the screen, and it is posted immediately. This is a great way to meet people in the old country that your

The best decision is an informed decision when it comes to choosing an Internet provider. Compare local Internet services against the national providers for the best rate. After you have signed on with a provider, check rates again in six months—this is a competitive field and everyone wants your business. Shopping around can save you money because there can be a great difference in fees. One advantage to America Online, CompuServe, and Prodigy is the genealogical forums and chat rooms that are available. Before you make a decision on an Internet service provider, get in touch with a local genealogical society's computer interest group, or CIG; they will be familiar with what services are available to you locally. You can also check for classes at your local community college. See state resources in the Resource Directory on page 125 for genealogical societies.

ancestors came from. They can often help you understand record sources overseas. You can also network with other genealogists who are interested in sharing what they know. It is exciting to find someone working on one of your lines, or to gather information about local records from someone who lives in the area you are trying to research. You might even meet distant family relations that you don't know about.

• **ELECTRONIC MAIL.** Anyone may exchange e-mail quickly and easily with anyone else who has an Internet-compatible e-mail address. Writing e-mail to other genealogists is faster and easier than sending it through the postal service, or snail mail, as e-mail advocates call it. E-mail is fast becoming a favorite mode of communication for many hobbyists. Families often attach digital photos of family and ancestors to their mail when they send it through cyberspace.

• **THE WORLD WIDE WEB.** The Web, as it is commonly referred to, is the glamour child of the 1990s. It is a means of electronic publishing that is very popular and user-friendly: the Web is for anyone who can read. Browsers are software products that help you navigate the Web. Netscape and Microsoft Explorer are popular browsers. When you publish a page on the Web, you can link to pages on other computers. For instance, you might be looking at a document of George Washington's life as stored in a computer in Virginia. There may be a reference to his ancestry, as stored in a computer in California. By moving the mouse to that reference and clicking, the data from the California computer appears on your screen. In turn, it may have references to other information stored on still other computers in other states or countries. Each of these computers may have more of these links to still other computers. Hence, the word *web* in the name World Wide Web.

• **SEARCH ENGINES.** Search engines help you gather information from the Web. There are many search engines; some of the most popular are Yahoo, Excite, AltaVista, and Infoseek. Type genealogy on any of these search engines and you will find a wide array of listings that you can access. Just click and you are there. Visit the *Ancestors* site at http://www.kbyu.byu.edu/ancestors.html. The *Ancestors* site is a good place to start surfing the Web for information about genealogy and family history.

• **PERSONAL HOME PAGES.** You might wish to

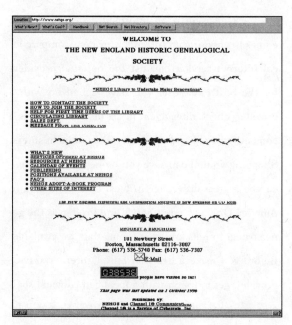

The New England Historical Genealogical Society's web site at http://www.nehgs.org.

publish information about your ancestors on the World Wide Web so that others can find it. You can do this with a personal home page. Personal home pages are available from most Internet service providers, usually bundled in at no extra charge. You must create your home page in a language called HTML (Hyper Text Markup Language). Luckily, new HTML creation tools are available today that shield you from all the computer lingo involved. You can create your home page in a manner similar to using a word processor. It is no longer necessary to write the HTML code as several programs will create that for you automatically. Once it is completed, you transfer the newly created file to the Internet provider. Then your home page is visible to everyone else on the World Wide Web.

• SUBSCRIPTION HOME PAGES. Initially, all the home pages on the World Wide Web were free. That is, anyone could look at them at no charge. However, that limits the information available to advertising or other information that companies or individuals can afford to give away at no charge. More and more companies are now providing information on the World Wide Web for a fee. To access the information, you must be a subscriber of that service. The number of subscription home pages is still small, but it is growing. Real-time stock market quotes and the daily editions of several internationally recognized newspapers are now available via subscription home pages. Genealogy materials that cost money to collect and publish will probably be offered by subscription home pages in the near future. The reality is that this new practice is the only method for a company to recover the expenses of providing high-quality information.

• USENET NEWS GROUPS. These message boards are places where many people congregate to exchange messages. These are public messages; unlike e-mail, you can send a message to a news group, where it can be read by hundreds of people around the world within a few hours. Others may be able to answer your questions by responding with another public message on the news group. There are more than a dozen genealogy-related news groups, including those dedicated to Scandinavian ancestry, French-Canadian ancestry, and Afro-American genealogy. Most providers give access to usenet groups, and you can search for genealogy usenet groups on any of the major search engines.

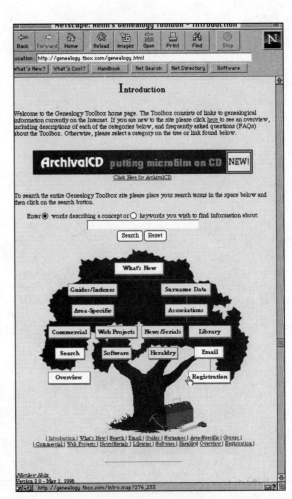

Helm's Genealogical Toolbox at http://www.genealogy.tbox.com/genealogy.html

Unlike the commercial online services, many of the files available on the Internet have not been checked for viruses. You should make sure that your computer has an up-to-date virus-checking program and that you know how to use it properly before you transfer files from the Internet to your computer.

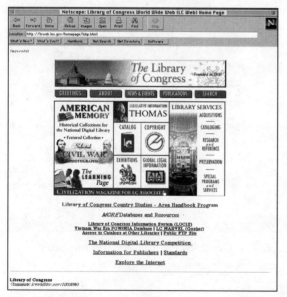

The home page of the Library of Congress at http://lcweb.loc.gov/homepage/lchp.html.

• **FILE TRANSFER PROTOCOL (FTP).** Text information and binary files, such as genealogy programs, may be transferred across the Internet. While there is no central clearinghouse for such files, you can find repositories of how-to guides, lists of ancestors, shareware, and public domain genealogy programs and other items of interest to anyone researching a family tree. These files can be transferred to your computer by a process known as File Transfer Protocol, or FTP. You transfer the file one time across the telephone lines and then store it on your computer's disk drive. You can then use the file time and time again as you wish.

• **ONLINE DATABASES.** While the majority of genealogy-related databases are available only on CD-ROM, a few items of interest are available on the Internet. Online telephone directories may make it possible to find other descendants of an ancestor with an unusual surname. One state, Kentucky, has placed their death records online on the Internet, although the only records available are for the early twentieth century and later. Information about public land sales in Michigan is also available on another Internet database. There are no online databases on the Internet of census records, immigration records, military records, birth or marriage records, etc. The cost of collecting such data and computerizing it is still too high to make it available at no cost.

• **LIBRARY CARD CATALOGS (TELNET).** One of the best-kept secrets of the Internet is the wide access to library card catalogs. You can check out great library catalogs from all over the world. Many major libraries, some with major genealogy collections, keep their card catalogs online and available to the general public. Not only is this useful before a visit to a particular library, but it can help you find books you didn't even know existed. A search of a card catalog by a topic can often produce pleasant surprises. Almost all library card catalogs require Telnet access, a technology by which your computer connects to the card catalog computer as if it were a terminal that is directly connected. Most Internet providers supply Telnet access, but a few do not. If you want to access library card catalogs, make sure that the Internet provider you select gives you that capability.

The online environment is ever changing and is growing at a phenomenal rate. In the short time that it takes to get this book to print, new resources and databases will be available to the genealogist and family historian online. The Internet might seem overwhelming, but getting online today is easy, and once you are there it is hard to walk away from.

There are also databases that are made available through the Church of Jesus Christ of Latter-day Saints. These are the International Genealogical Index (I.G.I.) and Ancestral File. Although not currently available online, these databases are among the most used by genealogists and family historians. You can access them through Family History Centers and some libraries around the United States. For information about the Family History Center or library closest to you that carries the I.G.I. and Ancestral File, call 1-800-346-6044.

• ANCESTRAL FILE. The Ancestral File is a huge database with all data contributed by both Latter-day Saints members and nonmembers. These individuals submitted computerized files of information they have found about their ancestors. Each person in the Ancestral File is linked to parents or children or spouse and often to all three. Complete family trees are frequently available that cover many generations. Quite often you may discover one of your ancestors listed in the Ancestral File along with another five to ten generations of his or her ancestors. The information in the Ancestral File has been collected from many sources and is offered as is. That is, the validity of the information has not been checked. While much of the data in the Ancestral File is correct, there is still a significant error rate. Never accept Ancestral File data directly; always verify each record by comparing it with primary records. However, the Ancestral File can reveal a path that others have taken, often saving you much work.

• INTERNATIONAL GENEALOGICAL INDEX. The International Genealogical Index is a different database produced by the Latter-day Saints church. Again, it is a huge collection of information about individuals. However, this database contains entries about births, christenings or baptisms, and marriages. It may also contain occasional references to census entries or wills. It almost never contains death dates. Unlike in the Ancestral File, the individuals listed in this database are not linked together from one generation to the next. Each entry is about one individual and may connect to a spouse or a child or parents. But each record is

The National Genealogical Society's web site at http:www.genealogy.org/~ngs.

BEGINNER'S Checklist

☞ Computers help genealogists and family historians store, retrieve, and share information faster and more easily than ever before.

☞ Local genealogical societies sponsor CIGs (or computer interest groups) that can help you decide what computer and software program will help you in your family history research. Check the Resource Directory on page 125 for a genealogical society near you.

☞ Check the *Ancestors* home page at http://www.kbyu.byu.edu/ancestors.html for links to great sites in cyberspace for family history information.

limited to only one entry. The International Genealogical Index is available on CD-ROM for almost all countries that use the European alphabet. Similar information is collected for Asian and Arab countries and other places that use different forms of writing, but those records have not yet been computerized because of the difficulty in dealing with those alphabets. Since the International Genealogical Index refers to specific records and events, it is the database that serious genealogists refer to first. However, the same disclaimers about accuracy apply: the data have not been verified, and you should by wary of any information in the I.G.I. until you have verified it against other sources. The I.G.I. does contain references to the sources of the information, so it is easier to validate data in the International Genealogical Index than it is in the Ancestral File.

The computer has indeed revolutionized the way that genealogical information is stored, retrieved, and shared. From CD-ROMs with archival information to software that organizes your information to the online environment that allows networking, the computer and the genealogist are often inseparable. To find out more about how to use your computer for genealogical research, it is important to become aware of resources in your community that can help you begin your ancestral journey into cyberspace. For your first steps online, consult the *Ancestors* home page at http://www.kbyu.byu.edu/ancestors.html.

CHAPTER TEN
Leaving a Legacy

SHARING WHAT YOU HAVE learned about your ancestors is an important part of being a family historian. The gift of legacy can heal and strengthen families. Children with a rich sense of heritage are likely to be graced with strong self-esteem, and adults can be guided by the lessons left behind by ancestors. This chapter is designed to give you some simple guidelines on sharing, creating, and continuing a legacy for your family that will impact generations to come.

There are many different ways to create and share a lasting legacy for your family. Family traditions can be elaborate or simple, but they all have one thing in common: one person must make the time to begin.

The More Family Association shares a rich and treasured legacy. They find strength and direction in a common link to John and Betty More. In 1772, John and Betty More came to New York from Scotland as a young married couple with two small children. They eventually settled in a cabin that John built in the wilderness of the Catskills and raised a family of eight children. By carving a humble homestead out of the wilderness with little more than determination and hard work, the More family waxed strong. When John More died in his ninety-fourth year, his legacy included nine children and eighty-nine grandchildren. One man, Jay Gould, a great-grandson of John and Betty More, felt that the memory of his pioneer ancestors should be remembered by future generations. In 1890, Jay Gould gathered cousins representing the descendants of John and Betty More from fourteen states and held the first More family reunion. It was at this first reunion in 1890 that the family formed the More Family Association, dedicated a monument to John and Betty More, and decided to hold a family reunion every five years.

Members of the More Family Association have taken different responsibilities over the years in sharing their heritage with one another. The family has filmed each reunion since 1915. Grace Van Dyke More published a book in 1930, *John*

JOHN AND BETTY STORIES

Tales of
JOHN MORE AND BETTY TAYLOR MORE
Pioneers in Delaware County, New York
by
GRACE VAN DYKE MORE

Illustrated
by
VIRGINIA MORE ROEDIGER

This children's book, written by a descendant of John and Betty More's, is a collection of ancestral stories.

Descendants of John T. More Reunion, 1890.

and Betty Stories. This book is a collection of stories about John and Betty More's life adventure. The book was written for children and over the years has been a source of bedtime stories for the descendants of John and Betty More. In 1893, David Fellows More wrote a history of the family, which has served as a touchstone for the members of the association. More recently, the association has made the effort to use a computer to keep track of more than 10,000 descendants.

Eric More Marshall, current president of the More Family Association, helps keep track of the 10,000-plus members of the More Family Association that trace their roots back to these two original pioneers. A family journal is published, as well as a directory that can be used to find relatives. At the reunions, members pay respect to John and Betty and to members of the family who have died in the previous five years. The family visits the ruins of the original cabin. Each member of the More Family Association draws something special from the legacy that has been left and is being shared today. The More Family Association motto gives special meaning to the mission that one man, Jay Gould, inspired over 100 years ago and to the immigrant ancestors, John and Betty: *with reverence to the past . . . vision for the future.*

Not all families share a legacy as rich as the More family's. Some of us need to search for the legacy that has been left to us. Many of us are not fortunate enough to be raised in the shadow of family reunions and leagues of ancestors that we can share stories about. The wonderful thing is that a simple gesture can begin a legacy today that will last for years to come.

Nancilu Burdick found a rich legacy in a simple gesture that her grandmother left behind. She had remembered her grandmother Talula as, "a dear, little old-fashioned woman of sweet disposition, who loved everyone, sat in a homemade chair, and serenely pieced quilts all day." Nancilu had married a Yankee and left her southern home in 1940. Her children slept under the quilts that Talula had made, took them away to college, and wore them out. It wasn't until a hot July afternoon in 1978 that Nancilu's perspective about her grandmother changed. "My mother opened a cedar chest in the Alabama home where I grew up and matter of factly lifted out a half-dozen quilts; she revealed a far different world from the one I remembered as a child. It was like being awakened suddenly from a sleep and plunged into awareness. How could it have happened that I *never really knew my grandmother.*" [1] That day was a transformation for Nancilu; she knew that she had discovered a treasure in that chest. She was a teacher at the time and left her job to start working on the old family papers that her mother's sister had left for her. Nancilu began a journey to find out more about her grandmother's life and the quilts she made. Over the course of her life, Talula made more than 200 quilts. She made them for family members to sleep under, to keep warm, and, on occasion, to fight the diseases that took lives too early. Behind each quilt was a story that revealed different layers of her grandmother's life. In looking for clues, Nancilu turned up a memoir that Talula had written in 1940 at the age of eighty-one. A treasure and key to the past, this 200-page memoir, handwritten and hidden in a box beneath a pile of letters, became a cornerstone for Nancilu's research.

Nancilu has gone on to learn the quilting techniques of her grandmother and to piece together the story of her family's history from the rich legacy of quilts that were almost lost to obscurity. The quilts, along with the memoir that Talula wrote, have given Nancilu the ability to share and pass on a legacy rich in heritage and artistry that would have otherwise been lost. It all began with a few stitches.

Hannibal Lakumbe created a musical legacy for his family based on his great-grandfather's life. In the fall of 1995, Hannibal gathered his family at the grave of his slave ancestor in Texas. His great-grandfather was a slave who escaped as a young man and settled in Texas to work and start a new life. He worked hard building the railroad that was leading a new path through the Texas territory for travelers and commerce. Hannibal brought his great-grandfather's descendants together at the grave to hold a ceremony rich in African her-

Hannibal Lakumbe

A journal of your life can be treasured by generations to come. The challenges that you face today will be faced by your descendants; how you handle them can help your children and your grandchildren in the challenges that they will face. A journal can be a simple yet elegant way to share your life with others. A small daily entry is all that is necessary to begin a lasting legacy.

itage. Music and dancing combined with the introduction of the youngest child and the oldest living descendant mark a coming together of the line that was created by the slave ancestor. Hannibal has said, "I think that we should be responsible for those that came before us. The elder's presence lets the children know where they came from and what they are part of." He has written a symphony, *African Portraits,* that has been performed by orchestras across the country. Hannibal also works in classrooms across the country calling young African-Americans to be aware of their rich heritage and to be thankful for the sacrifices and challenges that their progenitors endured for their benefit. Hannibal takes his legacy beyond the walls of his own home to influence the lives of others in his community. Through his awareness of his ancestors he draws on the strength of his great-grandfather's legacy to give him direction in his own life.

The More family, Nancilu Burdick, and Hannibal Lakumbe have all heeded the call to make the past a part of the future. Each has created a different type of legacy to leave behind. Film, books, quilts, and music mark their creative expression. Your family has treasures that are waiting to be discovered and shared. What you will find can influence what you choose to leave behind. The important thing is to do something and to start now.

Talula began with stitching remnants of cloth together and by writing her thoughts down in a book. Her beginnings were humble. Jay Gould gathered some relatives together, and more than 100 years later, 10,000 Mores share a common legacy. Hannibal Lakumbe gathered his family together at his great-grandfather's grave one fall afternoon and his efforts are heard in music around the world. What will be your beginning?

A journal can be a simple beginning. A journal of your life can be treasured by generations to come. Your efforts to find and record your family history can be shared with others. The things in your life that have meaning will not wither with the years. The challenges that you face today will be faced by your descendants; how you handle them can help your children and your grandchildren in the challenges that they will face. A journal can be a simple yet elegant way to share your life with others. The most important hurdle to cross is the belief that your life is important enough to write about. It is.

The age that you live in is an exciting age. Write about your dreams and goals, about your challenges and setbacks, about your values and ideas. Each of us has a unique story and perspective to share with others. You can purchase blank books to make your entries in, or it can be as simple as a notebook that you keep by your bed. A small daily entry is all that is necessary to begin a lasting legacy.

Preserving the photographs and documents of your family history is an important step in sharing a legacy. Beginning with photos, you may wish to share what you find with others and preserve what you have. Photos are subject to deterioration and discoloration over time. The primary enemies of photographs include acid, heat, humidity, fluorescent and incandescent light, and sunlight. It is important to wear linen or cotton gloves when handling photographs. The advances in photo restoration and preservation have come a long way and will help you preserve and share your memories with others.

Preservation is the first consideration when handling old photographs from the nineteenth and twentieth centuries. Learning simple preservation techniques can help you safeguard these memories and share them with others. Many of us have photographs that are stored in the popular magnetic-page albums of the seventies and eighties. The acidic adhesives and plastic covers used in these magnetic albums contribute to the deterioration of photographs stored in them. Some plastic covers are so destructive that the photographic image will stick to the plastic. Remove your photos from these albums and place them in photo albums made of archival-quality materials. The albums should be made of pH-balanced materials and treated with calcium carbonate to retard acid migration. The album pages should be made of acid-free paper or polypropylene or polyester (Mylar) plastic. Be wary of the plastic protector sheets that fit in conventional three-ring binders: many of these plastics are unstable and will cause damage over time by releasing acid. The worst plastic is PVC, which is the primary plastic used in store-bought three-ring binders. It will emit hydrochloric acid over time. Archival-quality binders and fillers for photographic preservation are available at photographic supply stores and sometimes art supply stores. If local stores do not carry the items, you can find them through mail-order suppliers. Your local genealogical society is a good place to ask for information

Preservation is the first consideration when handling old photographs from the nineteenth and twentieth centuries. Simple preservation techniques can help you safeguard these memories and share them with others. Use archival-quality storage products to preserve your photos.

Photographs can be enhanced with digital technology at photo retailers and at home.

about archival-quality binders and fillers in your area. Major distributors of archival-quality storage products include Gaylord Brothers 1-800-448-6160, Conservations Resources 1-800-634-6932, Light Impressions 1-800-828-6216, and University Products 1-800-762-1165. The prices of archival materials vary widely, so shop around.

Once you have taken steps to preserve what you have found, it is a good idea to make copies of the originals for your files as well as to share with other members of your family. The technology that exists today makes this process easier than ever before.

Many photo retailers in your community now have access to the new Kodak Image Magic Digital Enhancement Station 100. This station lets your retailer scan your family photos and restore them for you. You no longer need the negatives to make copies of old photographs. The station can remove creases, tears, spots, and stains. The retailer can print the restored image on a glossy print up to 8 × 10 inches on archival-quality paper. The best part about it is that it is done in the store while you wait, eliminating the possibility of losing a one-of-a-kind print. Many retailers have added the Kodak CopyPrint Station II and the Kodak Image Magic Creation Station. The Creation Station is a self-serve unit that lets you copy photos from a print and then add borders or text. These products let the family historian and genealogist restore old photos and share them with family in a way that has not been possible before.

Other digital options for sharing and storing photographs are the photo CD and the photo picture disk. You can use your negative to create photo CDs and photo picture disks from old photographs. These images can then be imported into the genealogy software that you are using on your computer to create scrapbooks that will not be damaged by the elements that destroy many printed images. Today, most genealogy software gives you the option of creating these digital scrapbooks, which are easy to create and fun to share. When you get your film developed, ask your retailer to also make a photo CD or photodisk of the images; this will help you to preserve your heritage. Families share photos over the Internet, saving time and money. You can also use these images to create a wonderful home page of your family on the World Wide Web. Creating a digital scrapbook for your family will be a legacy that they can take into the twenty-first century.

Photographs are not the only things that you may wish to preserve and share with your family. The old certificates, letters, and other documents that you find should be preserved first in order to be shared. Old documents need to be treated with care and stored well to assure survival. When handling old documents, wear gloves, and get the documents into protective sleeves as soon as possible. Again, the plastic sleeves you use should be made of Mylar or polypropylene plastic. Do not use common PVC plastic sleeves. Many old documents will have been rolled or folded and may have been stapled or clipped together. Documents should be stored flat with all staples, rubber bands, and clips removed, as they can tear or stain the documents. Old newspapers should be photocopied onto acid-free paper because of the high rate of deterioration in newsprint. The original items should be stored carefully. If you are interested in displaying a document, you should frame a copy and store the original. Never laminate documents. The lamination process uses great heat and acidic adhesives, causing a fast rate of deterioration and leaving little recourse for restoration. If you have a computer, you can digitize the documents by scanning them. This requires a scanner, but it is a good way to ensure the survival of the image for a long time. It also helps to enhance the digital scrapbook for your family. Many libraries are digitizing collections as a means of sharing and preserving information. Good resources for understanding more about photographic and document preservation and restoration are *An Ounce of Preservation: A Guide to the Care of Papers and Photographs,* by Craig Tuttle, and *Care and Identification of Nineteenth Century Photographic Prints,* by James M. Reilly. Don't overlook your local genealogical society as a resource. Society members often have areas of expertise such as photo and document restoration and preservation.

Family reunions are a popular way to share family history. Reunions can be elaborate affairs like the More family reunions, or as simple as a backyard barbecue. There are many guides and books that can help you plan a good reunion. The basic steps to a successful reunion are fundamental:

- Plan well in advance. A year or two gives everyone time to get ready and to place the reunion on the calendar.

As you discover documents and photographs in your home, take the time to make a list of the documents, the date you find them, and what genealogical information they contain. Cite the information that you find in a research log. Keeping track of the sources and dates of your research is a very important step for successful and efficient research. It saves time to record information as you go along, rather than trying to reconstruct where you found particular information.

- Create a reunion committee. A good reunion is planned by a good committee. Elect the following:

CHAIR: Must be able to work with everyone and guide the group. Responsible for coordinating the committee and for preventing bloodshed.

TREASURER: Collects and spends the money for the event. Handles logistics such as reservations, bookkeeping, and registration.

SECRETARY: Responsible for member list and newsletter, sending invitations and registration materials.

ACTIVITIES CHAIR: Should be creative and willing to bring the diverse talents and skills of the members together for memorable activities at the reunion. Selects the entertainers and hires the photographer.

FAMILY HISTORIAN: Shares information about family history with the group. Collects family history information before the gathering. Creates family pedigree chart to share with everyone. Can print a family history or build a display for the event. Collects oral history at the reunion.

BEYOND FAMILY REUNIONS, there are simple activities that you can start at home that will have a lasting impression on your family. You can create a family calendar with the birth dates of ancestors from your pedigree chart. This can be a special addition to your family tradition. Celebrating the birthday of an ancestor can be fun and memorable. Special emphasis can be placed on remembering the time in which the ancestor lived and making it a theme for the evening. If your ancestor's birthday was in the 1800s, you might want to turn off the electricity, telephones, and TV for the evening. Candles and period food will bring a special glow to your ancestor's birthday party. Share stories of your ancestor at the birthday party.

The committee will be responsible for the form and function of the family reunion. Issues such as lodging, events, meals, transportation, and communication should be addressed. A great resource for reunion planning, published by *Reunions* magazine, is *Reunions: Workbook and Catalogue*. This publication and the quarterly magazine can be found at newsstands or by contacting *Reunions* magazine at P.O. Box 1127, Milwaukee, WI 53211-0727. Telephone (414) 263-4567. You can also visit their website at http://www.execpc.com/~reunions. The best reunions are those that are planned well in advance and that include the participation of as many family members as possible.

Many family historians use art to share what they have learned about family history. Joan Landis researched her ancestors' lives and created paintings that show important events in their lives. Landis is a painter and commercial artist. Her love of family history is combined with her passion for the primitive style in art to capture moments of her family history that she shares with others. She has used old documents and photographs she has found as inspiration for her paintings. You don't need to be a professional artist to create art from your family history research. Collage, painting, ink drawings, or anything that you enjoy can be adapted to your family history research. If you are a skilled seamstress or a woodworker, you can adapt your hobby to reflect the work that you have done in family history. Samplers and hope chests can be favorite items to pass forward with family history stitched and carved into them.

The more creative you are with your traditions and legacies, the more willingly your family will be involved in passing the traditions of your ancestors forward. Make a special cookbook of family recipes. Gather them from relatives, and when you interview family members, ask what favorite meals were served. Good food is a sure way to anyone's heart, and family recipes are a natural way to bring people together. Some food will even be of the old country and give families the opportunity to learn more about the culture of their ancestors.

The more creative you are with your traditions and legacies, the more willingly your family will be involved in passing the traditions of your ancestors forward.

A painting by Joan Landis illustrates some of her family's history.

☞ Preserve and enhance the family history you have learned about and share it with others.

☞ Be careful to store your old photographs and documents in archival-quality binders, paper, and sleeves.

☞ Your expression of family history can include family reunions, a published family history, photographs, videos, quilts, art, music, journals, recipes, and more. Be creative and have fun.

☞ Whatever you choose to do, begin today. A simple gesture by you can have a lasting impact on generations to come.

Sharing the music that your ancestors enjoyed will bring smiles to many faces. You will have to do a little research to find the popular songs of the earlier periods in American history, but many of the songs have special meaning within the context of the lives that were lived at that time. The strong tradition of religious freedom in the United States leaves a rich legacy of sacred music. Finding music in common with your ancestors can bring an awakening and deep feeling of reverence for their lives. Some family historians write music in praise of their ancestors and share them with family members, as did Hannibal Lakumbe.

From quilts to family medical pedigrees, art and music, food and reunions, family history and genealogy can be celebrated and shared with family members in a number of ways. Elaborate or simple, legacies are rich in meaning and give the gift of continuity and balance to our lives. Whatever you choose to do, do something. Take the time to learn about your family history and to share it with your family.

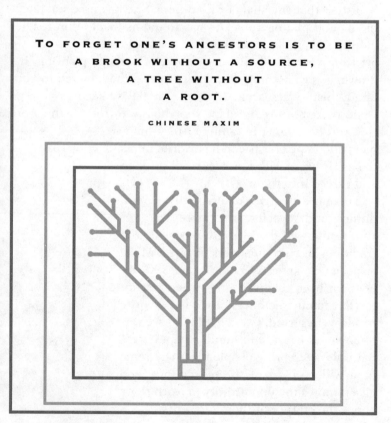

TO FORGET ONE'S ANCESTORS IS TO BE A BROOK WITHOUT A SOURCE, A TREE WITHOUT A ROOT.

CHINESE MAXIM

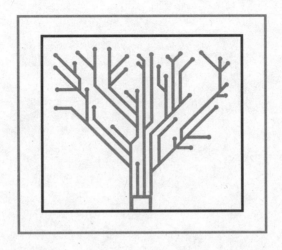

RESOURCE DIRECTORY

WHERE TO WRITE
FOR VITAL RECORDS

CHAPTER NOTES
AND SUGGESTED READING

This directory is not a comprehensive source, but a general listing of resources available to you. Telephone numbers and URLs (web-site addresses) are subject to change as are addresses for genealogical societies. The libraries and archives listed here are state resources. For local libraries and archives, check the American Library Directory (New Providence, NJ. R.R. Bowker Company, 49th edition, volume 1). This directory is published annually and is a comprehensive listing of libraries and archives in the United States with detailed information on holdings. Most libraries carry the American Library Directory. Other state-by-state resources available include: Elizabeth Petty Bentley, *The Genealogists Address Book* (Baltimore: Genealogical Publishing Co., Inc., fourth edition, 1994–95); *The Handy Book for Genealogists* (Logan, Utah: Everton Publisher, eighth edition, 1991); and Alice Eichholz, *Ancestry's Red Book: American State, County and Town Sources* (Salt Lake City, Utah: Ancestry, Inc., 1992).

NATIONAL ARCHIVES AND RECORDS ADMINISTRATION REGIONAL ARCHIVES SYSTEM

The regional archives listed below, except for the Pittsfield Region, receive the permanently valuable, noncurrent records of federal courts and agencies in the areas they serve. All regional archives have extensive holdings of National Archives microfilm publications. For more information on each regional facility see the National Archives home page at www.nara.gov.

National Archives —
New England Region
380 Trapelo Rd.
Waltham, Massachusetts 02154
Phone: (617) 647-8100
Fax: (617) 647-8460
e-mail: Archives@waltham.nara.gov
Connecticut, Maine, Massachusetts, New Hampshire, Rhode Island, and Vermont

National Archives —
Pittsfield Region
100 Dan Fox Dr.
Pittsfield, Massachusetts 01201
Phone: (413) 445-6885
Fax: (413) 445-7599
e-mail: archives@pittsfield.nara.gov

National Archives —
Northeast Region
201 Varick St.
New York, New York 10014
Phone: (212) 337-1300
Fax: (212) 337-1306
e-mail: archives@newyork.nara.gov
New York, New Jersey, Puerto Rico, and the Virgin Islands

National Archives —
Mid Atlantic Region
9th & Market Sts., Rm. 1350
Philadelphia, Pennsylvania 19107
Phone: (215) 597-3000
Fax: (215) 597-2303
e-mail: archives@philarch.nara.gov
Delaware, Maryland, Pennsylvania, Virginia, and West Virginia

National Archives —
Southeast Region
1557 St. Joseph Ave.
East Point, Georgia 30344
Phone: (404) 763-7477
Fax: (404)763-7033
e-mail: archives@atlanta.nara.gov
Alabama, Florida, Georgia, Kentucky, Mississippi, North Carolina, South Carolina, and Tennessee

National Archives —
Great Lakes Region
7358 S. Pulaski Rd.
Chicago, Illinois 60629
Phone: (312) 581-7816
Fax: (312) 353-1294
e-mail: archives@chicago.nara.gov
Illinois, Indiana, Michigan, Minnesota, Ohio, and Wisconsin

National Archives —
Central Plains Region
2312 E. Bannister Rd.
Kansas City, Missouri 64131
Phone: (816) 926-6272
Fax: (816) 926-6272
e-mail:
archives@kansascity.nara.gov
Iowa, Kansas, Missouri, and
Nebraska

National Archives —
Southwest Region
501 West Felix St., P.O. Box 6216
Fort Worth, Texas 76115
Phone: (817) 334-5525
Fax: (817) 334-5621
e-mail: archives@ftworth.nara.gov
Arkansas, Louisiana, New Mexico,
Oklahoma, and Texas

National Archives —
Rocky Mountain Region
Bldg. 48, Denver Federal Center
P.O. Box 25307
Denver, Colorado 80225
Phone: (303) 236-0817
Fax: (303) 236-9354
e-mail: archives@denver.nara.gov
Colorado, Montana, North Dakota,
South Dakota, Utah, and Wyoming

National Archives —
Pacific Southwest Region
24000 Avila Rd.

Laguna Niguel, California 92677-6719
Phone: (714) 360-2641
Fax: (714) 360-2644
e-mail: archives@laguna.nara.gov
Arizona; southern California; and
Clark County, Nevada

National Archives —
Pacific Sierra Region
1000 Commodore Dr.
San Bruno, California 94066
Phone: (415) 876-9009
Fax: (415) 876-9233
e-mail: archives@sanbruno.nara.gov
California except southern California, Hawaii, Nevada except Clark
County, American Samoa, and
Guam

National Archives —
Pacific Northwest Region
6125 Sand Point Way NE
Seattle, Washington 98115
Phone: (206) 526-6507
Fax: (206) 526-4344
e-mail: archives@seattle.nara.gov
Idaho, Oregon, and Washington

National Archives —
Alaska Region
654 W 3rd Ave.
Anchorage, Alaska 99501
Phone: (907) 271-2441
Fax: (907) 271-2442
e-mail: archives@alaska.nara.gov
Alaska

ARCHIVES AND LIBRARIES

Allen County Public Library
Fred J. Reynolds Historical Genealogy Collection
P.O. Box 2270
900 Webster St.

Fort Wayne, IN 46801-2270
Phone: (219) 424-7241
Fax: (219) 422-9688
www.acpl.lib.in.us

Family History Library
35 North West Temple
Salt Lake City, UT 84150
Phone: (801) 240-2331
Fax: (801) 240-5551

National Archives and Records
Administration
8th & Constitution Ave. NW
Washington, DC 20408
Phone: (202) 501-5400
Fax: (202) 501-5005
www.nara.gov

Library of Congress
Genealogy Reading Room
James Madison Memorial Bldg.
Washington, DC 20540
Phone: (202) 707-2726
lcweb.loc.gov/rr/genealogy/

National Genealogical Society
Library
4527 17th St. N.
Arlington, VA 22207-2399
Phone: (703) 525-0050
www.genealogy.org/NGS

New England Historic Genealogical
Society
101 Newbury St.
Boston, MA 02116
Phone: (617) 536-5740
www.nehgs.org

Newberry Library
60 W. Walton St.
Chicago, IL 60610
Phone: (312) 943-9090
192.231.205.235/isc275

New York City Public Library
Local History and Genealogy
Division
Fifth Ave. & 42nd St.
New York, NY 10027
Phone: (212) 930-0828
www.nypl.org/research/chss/lhg/ge-
nea.html

National Society, Daughters of the
American Revolution
1776 D St. NW
Washington, DC 20006-5392
Phone: (202) 879-3229
www.ultranet.com/~revolt
e-mail: revolt@dar.com

GENEALOGICAL SOCIETIES

Afro-American Historical and
Genealogical Society
P.O. Box 73086
Washington, DC 20056-3086

African-American Family History
Association
P.O. Box 115268
Atlanta, GA 30310

American-Canadian Genealogical
Society
P.O. Box 668
Manchester, NH 03105

American Family Records
Association (AFRA)
P.O. Box 15505
Kansas City, MO 64106

American-French Genealogical
Society
P.O. Box 2113
Pawtucket, RI 02861

Association of Jewish Genealogical
Societies
1485 Teaneck Rd.
Teaneck, NJ 07666

Daughters of the American
Revolution,
National Society
1776 D St. NW
Washington, DC 20006-5303
Phone: (202) 879-3229
www.ultranet.com/~revolt

Federation of Genealogical
Societies
P.O. Box 3385
Salt Lake City, UT 84110-3385
Phone: (214) 907-9727
www.connect.net/beau/fgs/

German Genealogical Society of
America
P.O. Box 291818
Los Angeles, CA 90029

Hispanic Genealogical Society
P.O. Box 810561
Houston, TX 77281-0561

International Genealogy Fellowship
of Rotarians
c/o Charles D. Townsend
5721 Antietam Dr.
Sarasota, FL 34231

Irish Genealogical Society
P.O. Box 16585
St. Paul, MN 55116-0585

Jewish Genealogical Society, Inc.
P.O. Box 6398
New York, NY 10128

National Genealogical Society
4527 Seventeenth St. N.

Arlington, VA 22207-2399
Phone: (703) 525-0050
www.genealogy.org/NGS

New England Historic Genealogical
Society
101 Newbury St.
Boston, MA 02116
Phone: (617) 536-5740
Fax: (617) 536-7307
www.nehgs.org

Northwest Territory Canadian and
French Heritage Center
P.O. Box 29397
Brooklyn Center, MN 55429

Orphan Train Heritage Society of
America
4912 Trout Farm Rd.
Springdale, AR 72764

Palatines To America
Capital University, Box 101G4
Columbus, OH 43209-1294

Polish Genealogical Society of
Michigan
Burton Collection
Detroit Public Library
5201 Woodward Ave.
Detroit, MI 48202

Polish Genealogical Society
6640 W. Archer Ave.
Chicago, IL 60638

Scandinavian-American Genealogi-
cal Society
P.O. Box 16069
St. Paul, MN 55116-0069

Vesterheim Genealogical Center
4909 Sherwood Rd.
Madison, WI 53711

ADOPTION

American Adoption Congress
1000 Connecticut Ave. NW, Ste. 9
Washington, DC 20036
Phone: (202) 483-3399

International Soundex Reunion
Registry
P.O. Box 2312
Carson City, NV 89702

National Adoption Clearinghouse
10530 Rosehaven St.
Suite 400
Fairfax, VA 22030
Phone: (703) 246-9095

ALABAMA

ARCHIVES AND LIBRARIES

National Archives —
Southeast Region
1557 St. Joseph Ave.
East Point, GA 30344
Phone: (404) 763-7477
Fax: (404)763-7033
e-mail: archives@atlanta.nara.gov
Alabama, Florida, Georgia, Kentucky, Mississippi, North Carolina, South Carolina, and Tennessee

Alabama Department of Archives
and History
624 Washington Ave.
Montgomery, AL 36130-0100
Phone: (205) 242-4363
Fax: (205) 240-3433

Auburn University
Ralph Brown Draughon Library
Auburn, AL 36849-3501
Phone: (205) 844-4500
Fax: (205) 844-4424
Birmingham Public Library

Tutwiler Collection of Southern
History
2100 Park Place
Birmingham, AL 35203
Phone: (205) 226-3600
Fax: (205) 226-3743

Samford University Library
Institute of Genealogical and Historical Research
800 Lakeshore Dr.
Birmingham, AL 35229
Phone: (205) 870-2642

University of Alabama
Amelia Gayle Gorgas Library
P.O. Box 870266
Tuscaloosa, AL 35487-0266
Phone: (205) 348-7561
Fax: (205) 348-8833

GENEALOGICAL SOCIETIES

Alabama Genealogical Society
AGS Depository and Headquarters
Samford University Library
800 Lakeshore Dr.
Birmingham, AL 35229

Autauga Genealogical Society
Prattville, AL 36067

Montgomery Genealogical
Society, Inc.
P.O. Box 230194
Montgomery, AL 36123-0194

Tennessee Valley Genealogical
Society
P.O. Box 1568
Huntsville, AL 35807

Natchez Trace Genealogical Society
P.O. Box 420
Florence, AL 35631-0420

Tuscaloosa Genealogical Society
1439 49th Ave.
East Tuscaloosa, AL 35404

HISTORICAL SOCIETIES

Alabama Historical Association
P.O. Box 2877
Tuscaloosa, AL 35486

Birmingham Historical Society
1 Sloss Quarter
Birmingham, AL 35203

Historic Chattahoochee
Commission
P.O. Box 33
Eufaula, AL 36027

CHURCH RECORDS

BAPTIST

Harwell Goodwin Davis Library
Samford University
800 Lakeshore Dr.
Birmingham, AL 35229-0001

METHODIST

Huntington College
Houghton Memorial Library
1500 E. Fairview Ave.
Montgomery, AL 36194

Charles Andrew Rush Library
Birmingham-Southern College
800 Eighth Ave. W.
Birmingham, AL 35254

ROMAN CATHOLIC

Diocese of Mobile-Birmingham
400 Government St.
P.O. Box 966
Mobile, AL 36633

ETHNIC RESOURCES

AFRICAN-AMERICAN

Alabama A & M University
J.F. Drake Memorial Learning Resources Center
Box 489
Normal, AL 35762
Phone: (205) 851-5760
Fax: (205) 851-5768

Mobile Public Library
Local History and Genealogy
Division
704 Government St.
Mobile, AL 36602-1499
Phone: (205) 434-7093
Fax: (205) 434-5866

HISPANIC

Bienville Historical Society
Center for Gulf Studies Library
606 Government St.
Mobile, AL 36602
Phone: (205) 457-5242

ALASKA

ARCHIVES AND LIBRARIES

National Archives —
Alaska Region
654 West 3rd Ave.
Anchorage, AK 99501
Phone: (907) 271-2441
Fax: (907) 271-2442
e-mail: archives@alaska.nara.gov

Alaska State Archives & Records
Management Services
141 Willoughby Ave.
Juneau, AK 99811-1720
Phone: (907) 465-2270
Fax: (907) 465-2465
Alaska State Library

Alaska Historical Collections
State Office Bdng.
P.O. Box 110571
Juneau, AK 99811-0571
Phone: (907) 465-2910
Fax: (907) 465-2665

University of Alaska, Fairbanks
Elmer E. Rasmuson Library
310 Tanana Dr.
Fairbanks, AK 99775-1000
Phone: (907) 474-7224
Fax: (907) 474-6841

GENEALOGICAL SOCIETIES

Alaska Genealogical Society
7030 Dickerson Dr.
Anchorage, AK 99504

Anchorage Genealogical Society
c/o Barbara Samuels
P.O. Box 212265
Anchorage, AK 99521

Fairbanks Genealogical Society
P.O. Box 60534
Fairbanks, AK 99706

Genealogical Society of S.E. Alaska
P.O. Box 6313
Ketchikan, AK 99901

Gastineau Genealogical Society
3270 Nowell Ave.
Juneau, AK 99801
Wrangell Genealogical Society
P.O. Box 928
Wrangell, AK

HISTORICAL SOCIETIES

Alaska Historical Library and
Museum
P.O. Box G

Eighth Floor, State Office Building
Juneau, AK 99811
Phone: (907) 465-2925

Alaska Historical Society
524 W. Fourth Ave., Suite 208
Anchorage, AK 99501

CHURCH RECORDS

MORAVIAN

Alaska Moravian Church
P.O. Box 545
Bethel, AK 99559

ROMAN CATHOLIC

Diocese of Juneau
419 Sixth St.
Juneau, AK 99801

Chancery Office
Diocese of Fairbanks
1316 Peger Rd.
Fairbanks, AK 99701

Archdiocese of Anchorage
3925 Reka Dr.
P.O. Box 2239
Anchorage, AK 99510

RUSSIAN ORTHODOX

St. Herman's Theological Seminary
Box 728
Kodiak, AK 99516

ARIZONA

ARCHIVES AND LIBRARIES

National Archives —
Pacific Southwest Region

24000 Avila Rd.
Laguna Niguel, CA 92677-6719
Phone: (714) 360-2641
Fax: (714) 360-2644
e-mail: archives@laguna.nara.gov
Arizona; southern California; and
Clark County, Nevada

Arizona State Archives
Department of Library, Archives &
Public Records
1700 W. Washington St.
Phoenix, AZ 85007
Phone: (602) 542-4159 (Archives)
Phone: (602) 542-4035 (Public
Records)
Fax: (602) 542-4972

University of Arizona Library
Rm. A-349
Tucson, AZ 85721
Phone: (602) 621-2101
Fax: (602) 621-9733

GENEALOGICAL SOCIETIES

Arizona Genealogical Advisory
Board
P.O. Box 5641
Mesa, AZ 85211

Arizona Society of Genealogists
6565 E. Grand Rd.
Tucson, AZ 85715

Arizona State Genealogical Society
Box 42075
Tucson, AZ 85733-2075

Genealogical Society of Yuma,
Arizona
P.O. Box 2905
Yuma, AZ 85366-2905

Genealogical Workshop of Mesa
P.O. Box 6052
Mesa, AZ 85216-6052

Green Valley Genealogical Society
P.O. Box 1009
Green Valley, AZ 85622

Jenson-Peterson-Elkjer Family
Association
c/o Edmund C. Elkjer
605 E. Drowsey Cir.
Payson, AZ 85541

Mesa Family History Center
41 S. Hobson
Mesa, AZ 85204

Northern Arizona Genealogical
Society
P.O. Box 695
Prescott, AZ 86302

The Phoenix Genealogical Society
1 E. St. John Rd.
Phoenix, AZ 85022-1847

Sun Cities Genealogical Society
Library
P.O. Box 1448
Sun City, AZ 85372-1448

W. W. Genealogy Club
c/o Ellen S. Hogue
6222 E. Joshua Tree Ln.
Scottsdale, AZ 85253

HISTORICAL SOCIETIES

Arizona Historical Foundation
Hayden Memorial Library
Arizona State University
Tempe, AZ 85287

Arizona Historical Society
949 E. Second St.
Tucson, AZ 85719

Arizona Historical Society
Century House Museum

240 Madison Ave.
Yuma, AZ 85364
Phone: (602)782-1841

CHURCH RECORDS

ROMAN CATHOLIC

Diocese of Phoenix
400 E. Monroe
Phoenix, AZ 85004

Diocese of Tucson
192 S. Stone Ave.
P.O. Box 31
Tucson, AZ 85702

ETHNIC RESOURCES

AFRICAN-AMERICAN

Afro-American Historical and
Genealogical Society, Tucson
7739 E. Broadway
Suite 195
Tucson, AZ 85710

HISPANIC

Arizona State University
Chicano Research Collection
Department of Archives and
Manuscripts
Hayden Library
Tempe, AZ 85287-1006
Phone: (602) 965-3145
Fax: (602) 965-9169

Northern Arizona University
Library
Special Collections Division
CU Box 6022
Flagstaff, AZ 86001

Tempe Historical Museum
Library

809 E Southern Ave.
Tempe, AZ 85282
Phone: (602) 350-5100

NATIVE AMERICAN

Apache Genealogical Society
P.O. Box 1084
Sierra Vista, AZ 85635-1084

Navajo Nation Library System
Drawer K
Window Rock, AZ 86515
Phone: (602) 871-6376
Fax: (602) 871-7304

ARKANSAS

ARCHIVES AND LIBRARIES

National Archives —
    Southwest Region
501 West Felix St., P.O. Box 6216
Fort Worth, TX 76115
Phone: (817) 334-5525
Fax: (817) 334-5621
e-mail: archives@ftworth.nara.gov
Arkansas, Louisiana, New Mexico,
Oklahoma, and Texas

Arkansas State Library
One Capitol Mall
Little Rock, AR 72201
Phone: (501) 682-1527
Fax: (501) 682-1529

Little Rock Public Library
700 Louisiana St.
Little Rock, AR 72201-4698
Phone: (501) 370-5954
Fax: (501) 375-7451

Southwest Arkansas Regional
Archives
Old Washington Historic State Park
P.O. Box 134
Washington, AR 71862
Phone: (501) 983-2633

University of Arkansas
Special Collections Division
Fayetteville, AR 72701
Phone: (501) 575-6702
Fax: (501) 575-5558

GENEALOGICAL SOCIETIES

Arkansas Genealogical Society
P.O. Box 908
Hot Springs, AR 71902-0908

Arkansas Genealogical Society
4200 A St.
Little Rock, AR 72205

Professional Genealogists of
Arkansas, Inc.
P.O. Box 1807
Conway, AR 72033

HISTORICAL SOCIETIES

Arkansas Historical Association
History Department
Ozark Hall, 12, University of
Arkansas
Fayetteville, AR 72701
Phone: (501)575-5884

Arkansas Historical Society
422 S. Sixth St.
Van Buren, AR 72956

Arkansas History Commission
One Capitol Mall
Little Rock, AR 72201
Phone: (501) 682-6900

CHURCH RECORDS

BAPTIST

Arkansas Baptist State Convention
Collection
Riley Library
Ouachita Baptist University

410 Ouachita
P.O. Box 3742
Arkadelphia, AR 71923

METHODIST

Little Rock Conference Depository
Methodist Headquarters Building
1723 Brdwy.
Little Rock, AR 72004

North Arkansas Conference
Depository
Olin C. Bailey Library
Hendrix College
Washington & Front St.
Conway, AR 72032

ETHNIC RESOURCES

AFRICAN-AMERICAN

Southwest Arkansas Regional
Archives
Box 134
Washington, AR 71862
Phone: (501) 983-2633

CALIFORNIA

ARCHIVES AND LIBRARIES

National Archives —
Pacific Southwest Region
24000 Avila Rd.
Laguna Niguel, CA 92677-6719
Phone: (714) 360-2641
Fax: (714) 360-2644
e-mail: archives@laguna.nara.gov
Arizona; southern California; and
Clark County, Nevada

National Archives —
Pacific Sierra Region
1000 Commodore Drive
San Bruno, CA 94066
Phone: (415) 876-9009
Fax: (415) 876-9233
e-mail: archives@sanbruno.nara.gov
California except southern California, Hawaii, Nevada except Clark County, American Samoa, and Guam

California Genealogical Society —
Library
P.O. Box 77105
San Francisco, CA 94107-0105

California State Archives Library
Room 130
1020 "O" St.
Sacramento, CA 95814
Phone: (916) 653-7715
Fax: (916) 653-7134

California State Genealogical
Alliance
c/o Wendy Elliott
4808 E. Garland St.
Anaheim, CA 92807

California State Library
P.O. Box 942837
914 Capitol Mall
Sacramento, CA 94237-0001
Phone: (916) 654-0183
Fax: (916) 654-0064

California State Library
Sutro Branch
480 Winson Dr.
San Francisco, CA 94132

Carlsbad City Library
Genealogical Division
1250 Carlsbad Village Dr.
Carlsbad, CA 92008-1991

Phone: (619) 434-2870
Fax: (619) 729-2050

Los Angeles Public Library
History and Genealogy Department
630 W. 5th St.
Los Angeles, CA 90071-2097
Phone: (213) 228-7000
Fax: (213) 228-7429

San Francisco Public Library
Larkin and McAllister St.
Genealogical Research Center
Dept. of Special Collections
San Francisco, CA 94102-4796
Phone: (415) 557-4400
Fax: (415) 557-4252

San Francisco State University
J. Paul Leonard Library
1600 Holloway Ave.
San Francisco, CA 94132-1789
Phone: (415) 338-1854
Fax: (415) 338-6199

GENEALOGICAL SOCIETIES

Boyt-Boyette Family
4808 E. Garland St.
Anaheim, CA 92807-1005

California Genealogical Society
P.O. Box 77105
300 Brannan St., Suite 409
San Francisco, CA 94107

Computer Genealogical Society of
San Diego
P.O. Box 370357
San Diego, CA 92137-0357

Conejo Valley Genealogical Society
P.O. Box 1228
Thousand Oaks, CA 91358-1228

Contra Costa County Genealogical
Society
P.O. Box 910
Concord, CA 94522-0910

East Kern Genealogical Society
c/o William and Gale Young
16693 Alexander Ave.
North Edwards, CA 93523

Genealogical Society of Morongo
Basin
P.O. Box 234
Yucca Valley, CA 92284

Genealogical Society of Riverside
P.O. Box 2557
Riverside, CA 92516

Genealogical Society of Santa Cruz
County
P.O. Box 72
Santa Cruz, CA 95063-0072

Genealogical Society of Stanilaus
County
P.O. Box 4735
Modesto, CA 95352-4735

Genealogical and Historical
Council
Sacramento Valley
P.O. Box 214749
Sacramento, CA 95821-0749

Glendora Genealogical Group
P.O. Box 1141
Glendora, CA 91740

Immigrant Genealogical Society
P.O. Box 7369
Burbank, CA 91510-7369

Jurupa Valley Genealogical Society
11519 Jurupa Rd.
Mira Loma, CA 91752

Kern County Genealogical Society
P.O. Box 2214
Bakersfield, CA 93303-2214

Lake County Genealogical Society
P.O. Box 1323
Lakeport, CA 95453

Lake Elsinore Genealogical Society
P.O. Box 807
Lake Elsinore, CA 92531

Livermore-Amador Genealogical
Society
P.O. Box 901
Livermore, CA 94551

Los Angeles Westside Genealogical
Society
P.O. Box 10447
Marina Del Ray, CA 90295

Monterey County Genealogical So-
ciety
P.O. Box 8144
Salinas, CA 93912-8144

Napa Valley Genealogical and
Biographical Society
1701 Menlo Ave.
Napa, CA 94558-4725

North San Diego County
Genealogical Society
Carlsbad, CA

Orange County Genealogical
Society
P.O. Box 1587
Orange, CA 92668

Pasadena Genealogy Society
P.O. Box 94774
Pasadena, CA 91109-4774

Placer County Genealogical Society

P.O. Box 7385
Auburn, CA 95604

Pomona Valley Genealogical Society
P.O. Box 286
Pomona, CA 91769-0286

Questing Heirs Genealogical
Society
P.O. Box 15102
Long Beach, CA 90815

Rose Family Association
1474 Montelegre Dr.
San Jose, CA 95120-4831

San Diego Genealogical Society
1050 Pioneer Way, Suite E
El Cajon, CA 92021-1943

San Fernando Valley Genealogical
Society
20357 Londelius St.
Canoga Park, CA 91306

San Francisco Bay Area-JGS
3916 Louis Rd.
Palo Alto, CA 94303-4541

San Luis Obispo County
Genealogical Society
P.O. Box 4
Atascadero, CA 93423

San Mateo County Genealogical
Society
P.O. Box 5083
San Mateo, CA 94402

Santa Barbara County Historical
and Genealogical Society
P.O. Box 1303
Santa Barbara, CA 93116-1303

Santa Clara County Historical and
Genealogical Society

City Library
2635 Homestead Rd.
Santa Clara, CA 95051-5387

Santa Maria Valley Genealogical
Society and Library
P.O. Box 1215
Santa Maria, CA 93456

Shasta Genealogy Society
c/o Gail Goetz
1200 Palisades Ave.
Redding, CA 96003

Society of California Pioneers
456 McAllister St.
San Francisco, CA 94102

Solano County Genealogical
Society
P.O. Box 2494
Fairfield, CA 94533

South Bay Cities Genealogical
Society
P.O. Box 11069
Torrance, CA 90510-1069

Southern California Genealogical
Society
P.O. Box 4377
Burbank, CA 91503
Vandenberg Genealogical Society
P.O. Box 81
Lompoc, CA 93438-0814

Whittier Area Genealogical Society
P.O. Box 4367
Whittier, CA 90607

California Historical Society
2090 Jackson St.
San Francisco, CA 94109

CHURCH RECORDS

METHODIST

Stuart Library of Western
Americana Church Archives
University of the Pacific
Stockton, CA 95204

PRESBYTERIAN

Library, San Francisco Theological
Seminary
San Anselmo, CA 94960

ROMAN CATHOLIC

Santa Barbara Catholic Mission
Santa Barbara (Old Mission)
Santa Barbara, CA 93105

Diocese of Los Angeles
1531 W. Ninth St.
Los Angeles, CA 90015

Diocese of Sacramento
1119 K St.
P.O. Box 1706
Sacramento, CA 95808

Diocese of San Diego
Alcala Park
San Diego, CA 92111

ETHNIC RESOURCES

AFRICAN-AMERICAN

Oakland Public Library
History/Literature and Oakland
History Room
125 14th St.
Oakland, CA 94612
Phone: (510) 238-3136

Richmond Public Library
Special Collections
325 Civic Center Plaza
Richmond, CA 94804
Phone: (510) 620-6561

University of California,
Los Angeles
Center for Afro-American Studies
Library
44 Haines Hall
405 Hilgard Ave.
Los Angeles, CA 90024-1545
Phone: (310) 825-6060
Fax: (310) 206-3421

Afro-American Genealogical
Society
California Afro-American Museum
600 State Dr.
Exposition Park
Los Angeles, CA 90037

California African American
Genealogical Society
P.O. Box 8442
Los Angeles, CA 90008-0442

BRITISH ISLES

British Isles Family History Society
of L.A.
2531 Sawtelle Blvd. #134
Los Angeles, CA 90064-3163

ASIAN

Oakland Public Library
Asian Branch
449 9th St.
Oakland, CA 94607

University of California,
Los Angeles
Asian American Studies Center

Reading Room
3230 Campbell Hall
Los Angeles, CA 90024-1546

University of California, Berkeley
Asian American Studies Library
3407 Dwinelle Hall
Berkeley, CA 94720
Phone: (510) 642-2218
Fax: (510) 642-6456

Chinese Culture Foundation of
San Francisco
750 Kearny St. 3rd Floor
San Francisco, CA 94108

GERMAN

German Genealogical Society of
America
2125 Wright Ave. C-9
La Verne, CA 91750

German Research Association, Inc.
P.O. Box 711600
San Diego, CA 92171-1600

German Research Association
c/o Irene Palmer, President
11233 Tierra Santa Blvd. #34
San Diego, CA 92124-2886

Sacramento German Genealogy
Society
P.O. Box 4327
Davis, CA 95617-4327

HISPANIC

Genealogical Society of Hispanic
America
South California Branch
P.O. Box 2472
Santa Fe Springs, CA 90670

Charles W. Bowers Memorial
Museum
2002 N. Main St.
Santa Ana, CA 92706

Monterey County Historical Society
Boronda History Center
Research Center and Archive
333 Boronda St.
P.O. Box 3576
Salinas, CA 93912

Stanford University
Chicano Reference Library
590S The Nitery
Stanford, CA 94305

University of California, Berkeley
Chicano Studies Library
3404 Dwinelle Hall
Berkeley, CA 94720
Phone: (510) 642-3859
Fax: (510) 642-6456

University of California,
Los Angeles
Chicano Studies Research Library
58 Haines Hall
405 Hilgard Ave.
Los Angeles, CA 90024-1380
Phone: (213) 206-6052
Fax: (213) 206-1784

University of California,
San Francisco
Gleeson Library
Archives Collection
513 Parnassus Ave.
San Francisco, CA 94143

University of Southern California
Library
Special Collections Department
University Park
Los Angeles, CA 90007

Centro de Studios Chicanos
Research
San Diego State University
San Diego, CA 92182

Cuban Index
P.O. Box 15839
San Luis Obispo, CA 93406
Phone: (805) 546-9015

Hispanic Family History
Researchers
c/o Mimi Lozano-Holtzman
15892 Redlands St.
Westminster, CA 92683

Hispanic History and Ancestry
Research
9511 Rockpoint Dr.
Huntington Beach, CA 92646

Historical Society of Long Beach
Rancho Los Alamitos
6400 Bixby Hill Rd.
Long Beach, CA 90815

La Puente Valley Historical Society
La Puente City Hall
15900 E. Main
La Puente, CA 91744

Los Californianos
P.O. Box 1693
San Leandro, CA 94577-0169

Los Fundadores y Amigos del
Condado Santa Clara
1053 S. White Rd.
San Jose, CA 95127
Phone: (408) 926-1165

Los Pobladores
10686 S. Meads Ave.
Orange, CA 92669

St. John's Seminary
Edward Laurence Doheny
Memorial Library
Estelle Dohney Collection
5012 E Seminary Rd.
Camarillo, CA 93010

JEWISH

Jewish Genealogical Society of Los
Angeles
P.O. Box 55443
Sherman Oaks, CA 91413

San Diego Jewish Genealogical
Society
255 S. Rios Ave.
Solana Beach, CA 92075

San Francisco Bay Area Jewish
Genealogical Society
34 Craig Ave.
Piedmont, CA 94611

NATIVE AMERICAN

Indian Action Council Library
P.O. Box 1287
Eureka, CA 95502-1287

COLORADO

ARCHIVES AND LIBRARIES

National Archives —
Rocky Mountain Region
Building 48, Denver Federal Center
P.O. Box 25307
Denver, CO 80225
Phone: (303) 236-0817
Fax: (303) 236-9354
e-mail: archives@denver.nara.gov
Colorado, Montana, North Dakota,
South Dakota, Utah, and Wyoming

Colorado Division of State Archives and Public Records Library
1313 Sherman St.
Room 1820
Denver, CO 80203-2236
Phone: (303) 866-2055
Fax: (303) 866-2257

Colorado State Library
201 E. Colfax Ave.
Denver, CO 80203-1704
Phone: (303) 866-6900
Fax: (303) 866-6940

Denver Public Library
Genealogy Department
10 W. 14th Ave. Pkwy.
Denver, CO 80204-6123
Phone: (303) 640-6200
Fax: (303) 640-6320

University of Denver
Penrose Library
Special Collections
2150 E. Evans Ave.
Denver, CO 80208-0287
Phone: (303) 871-2007
Fax: (303) 871-2290

GENEALOGICAL SOCIETIES

Aurora Genealogical Society of Colorado
P.O. Box 31732
Aurora, CO 80014-0732

Boulder Genealogical Society
P.O. Box 3246
Boulder, CO 80307-3246

Colorado Chapter/Ohio Genealogical Society
P.O. Box 1106
Longmont, CO 80502-1106

Colorado Council of Genealogical Societies
P.O. Box 24379
Denver, CO 80224-0379

Colorado Genealogical Society
P.O. Box 9218
Denver, CO 80209-0218

Columbine Genealogical and Historical Society
P.O. Box 2074
Littleton, CO 80161

Foothills Genealogical Society of Colorado
P.O. Box 15382
Lakewood, CO 80215-0382

Larimer County Genealogical Society
P.O. Box 9502
Ft. Collins, CO 80525-9502

Longmont Genealogical Society
P.O. Box 6081
Longmont, CO 80501

Penrose Genealogy Library
P.O. Box 2999
Colorado Springs, CO 80901

Pikes Peak Genealogical Society
P.O. Box 1262
Colorado Springs, CO 80901

Weld County Genealogical Society
P.O. Box 278
Greeley, CO 80632-0278

HISTORICAL SOCIETIES

Colorado Historical Society
Stephen H. Hart Library
1300 Brdwy.

Denver, CO 80203
Phone: (303)866-2305

CHURCH RECORDS

BAPTIST

American Baptist Historical Society
1106 S. Goodman St.
Rochester, NY 14620

EPISCOPAL

Diocese of Colorado
1300 Washington
P.O. Box 18 M
Capitol Hill Station
Denver, CO 80203

METHODIST

Rocky Mountain Conference Historical Society
Ira J. Taylor Library
Iliff School of Theology
2201 S. University Blvd.
Denver, CO 80210

PRESBYTERIAN

Presbyterian Historical Society
United Presbyterian Church in the U.S.A.
425 Lombard St.
Philadelphia, PA 19147

ROMAN CATHOLIC

Archives of the Archdiocese of Denver
200 Josephine St.
Denver, CO 80206

Chancery Office
1426 Grand Ave.
Pueblo, CO 81003

ETHNIC RESOURCES

AFRICAN-AMERICAN

Black Genealogical Research Group
4605 E. Kentucky Ave., 5F
Denver, CO 80222

HISPANIC

Genealogical Society of Hispanic
America
P.O. Box 9606
Denver, CO 80209-0606

CONNECTICUT

ARCHIVES AND LIBRARIES

National Archives —
New England Region
380 Trapelo Road
Waltham, MA 02154
Phone: (617) 647-8100
Fax: (617) 647-8460
e-mail: Archives@waltham.nara.gov
Connecticut, Maine, Massachu-
setts, New Hampshire, Rhode Is-
land, and Vermont

Connecticut State Library and
Archives
231 Capital Ave.
Hartford, CT 06106
Phone: (860) 566-5650
Fax: (860) 566-2133

GENEALOGICAL SOCIETIES

Connecticut Professional
Genealogists Council
P.O. Box 4273
Hartford, CT 06147-4273

Connecticut Society of
Genealogists, Inc.
P.O. Box 435
2106 Main St.
Glastonbury, CT 06033-0435
Phone: (203) 569-0002

Stamford Genealogical Society
P.O. Box 249
Stamford, CT 06904

HISTORICAL SOCIETIES

Connecticut Ancestry Society
P.O. Box 249
Stamford, CT 06940

Connecticut Historical Commission
59 S. Prospect St.
Hartford, CT 06106

Connecticut Historical Society
1 Elizabeth St. at Asylum Ave.
Hartford, CT 06105
Phone: (203)236-5621

Connecticut League of Historical
Societies
P.O. Box 906
Darien, CT 06820

CHURCH RECORDS

BAPTIST

American Baptist Historical Society
1106 S. Goodman St.
Rochester, NY 14620

CONGREGATIONAL

Connecticut Historical Society
1 Elizabeth St.
Hartford, CT 06105

EPISCOPAL

Episcopal Diocese of Connecticut
135 Asylum Ave.
Hartford, CT 06105-2295

ROMAN CATHOLIC

The Catholic Center
238 Jewett Ave.
Bridgeport, CT 06606

Diocese of Norwich
201 Brdwy.
P.O. Box 587
Norwich, CT 06360

Diocese of Hartford
134 Farmington Ave.
Hartford, CT 06103

ETHNIC RESOURCES

AFRICAN-AMERICAN

Prudence Crandall Museum
Library
P.O. Box 58
Canterbury, CT 06331
Phone: (203) 546-9916

Connecticut Afro-American
Historical Society
444 Orchard St.
New Haven, CT 06511

DELAWARE

ARCHIVES AND LIBRARIES

National Archives —
Mid Atlantic Region
9th & Market Streets, Room 1350
Philadelphia, PA 19107

Phone: (215) 597-3000
Fax: (215) 597-2303
e-mail: archives@philarch.nara.gov
Delaware, Maryland, Pennsylvania,
Virginia, and West Virginia

Delaware Division of Libraries-State
Library
Department of State
43 S. Dupont Highway
Dover, DE 19901
Phone: (302) 739-4748
Fax: (302) 739-6787
www.kentnet.dtcc.edu

Delaware State Archives
Dover, DE 19901
Phone: (302) 739-5318
Fax: (302) 739-6710

GENEALOGICAL SOCIETIES

Delaware Genealogical Society
505 Market Street Mall
Wilmington, DE 19801

HISTORICAL SOCIETIES

Historical Society of Delaware
Town Hall
505 Market St.
Wilmington, DE 19801
Phone: (302) 655-7161

CHURCH RECORDS

ROMAN CATHOLIC

Diocese of Wilmington Archives
P.O. Box 2247
Greenville, DE 19807

DISTRICT OF COLUMBIA

ARCHIVES AND LIBRARIES

Library of Congress
American Folklife Center
Thomas Jefferson Bldg.
Washington, DC 20540-8100
Phone: (202) 707-6590
Fax: (202) 707-2076

Library of Congress
Local History and Genealogy
Section
Thomas Jefferson Bldg., Rm. G20
Washington, DC 20540-5554
Phone: (202) 707-5537

National Archives
Pennsylvania Ave. at 8th St. NW
Washington, DC 20408
Phone: (202) 501-5415
Fax: (202) 219-1543

National Archives and Records
Administration
8th & Constitution Ave. NW
Washington, DC 20408
Phone: (202) 501-5400
Fax: (202) 501-5005
www.nara.gov

District of Columbia Office of
Public Records
1300 Naylor Court NW
Washington, DC 20001-4255
(202) 727-2054

District of Columbia Public Library
Martin Luther King Memorial
Library
901 G Street NW
Washington, DC 20001
Phone: (202) 727-2255
Fax: (202) 707-1129

National Society of the Daughters
of the American Revolution Library
Memorial Continental Hall
1776 D St. NW
Washington, DC 20006-5392
Phone: (202) 879-3229
Fax: (202) 879-3227

Library of Congress
Genealogy Reading Room
James Madison Memorial Bldg.
Washington, DC 20540
Phone: (202) 707-2726
lcweb.loc.gov/rr/genealogy/

GENEALOGICAL SOCIETIES

District of Columbia Genealogical
Society
P.O. Box 63467
Washington, DC 20029-3467

Genealogical Speakers Guild
3421 M St., Suite 329
Washington, DC 20007

HISTORICAL SOCIETIES

Columbia Historical Society
1307 New Hampshire Ave. NW
Washington, DC 20036

CHURCH RECORDS

EPISCOPAL

The Episcopal Church Historian
Washington Cathedral
Mount Saint Alban
Washington, DC 20016

ROMAN CATHOLIC

Historiographer
Archdiocese of Washington
5001 Eastern Ave.
P.O. Box 29260
Washington, DC 20017

ETHNIC RESOURCES

AFRICAN-AMERICAN

The Afro-American Historical and
Genealogical Society
P.O. Box 73086
Washington, DC 20056
Howard University

Moorland-Spingarn Research
Center
Manuscript Division
500 Howard Pl. NW
Washington, DC 20059
Phone: (202) 806-7480
Fax: (202) 806-6405

Afro-American Historical and
Genealogical Society
National Capitol Area
P.O. Box 34683
Washington, DC 20043

NATIVE AMERICAN

Daughters of the American
Revolution National Society
1776 D. St. NW
Washington, DC 20006-5392
Phone: (202) 879-3229
Fax: (202) 879-3252

FLORIDA

ARCHIVES AND LIBRARIES

National Archives —
Southeast Region
1557 St. Joseph Avenue
East Point, GA 30344
Phone: (404) 763-7477
Fax: (404)763-7033
e-mail: archives@atlanta.nara.gov
Alabama, Florida, Georgia, Kentucky, Mississippi, North Carolina,
South Carolina, and Tennessee

Florida State Archives
R. A. Gray Building
500 S. Bronough St.
Tallahassee, FL 32399-0250
Phone: (904) 487-2073
Fax: (904) 488-4894

State Library of Florida
R.A. Gray Building
500 South Bronough
Tallahassee, FL 32399
Phone: (904) 487-2651
Fax: (904) 922-3678
www.dos.state.fl.us/fglls

St. Augustine Historical Society
Research Library
271 Charlotte St.
St. Augustine, FL 32084-5099
Phone: (904) 824-2872

University of Florida
204 Library Way
P.O. Box 117001
Gainsville, FL 32611
Phone: (904) 392-0342
Fax: (904) 392-7251

University of Miami
Otto G. Richter Library
1300 Memorial Dr.

Coral Gables, FL 33124
Phone: (305) 284-3551
Fax: (305) 665-7352

University of West Florida
John Chandler Pace Library
11000 University Pkwy.
Pensacola, FL 32514-5750
Phone: (904) 474-2492
Fax: (904) 474-3338

GENEALOGICAL SOCIETIES

Alachua County Genealogical
Society
P.O. Box 12078
Gainsville, FL 32604

Amelia Island Genealogical Society
P.O. Box 6005
Fernandina Beach, FL 32035-6005

Central Florida Genealogical
Society
P.O. Box 177
Orlando, FL 32802

Citrus County Genealogical Society
P.O. Box 2211
Inverness, FL 34451-2211

Citrus Springs Genealogical Society
Citrus Springs Memorial Library
1826 W. Country Club Blvd.
Citrus Springs, FL 34434

Florida Genealogical Society
c/o Diane Covert Broderick
303 W. Violet St.
Tampa, FL 33603

Florida Genealogical Society, Inc.
P.O. Box 18624
Tampa, FL 33679-8624

Florida State Genealogical Society
P.O. Box 10249
Tallahassee, FL 32302

Genealogical Society of Broward
County
315 NW 40th Ct.
Fort Lauderdale, FL 33309-5135

Genealogical Society of Collier
County
P.O. Box 7933
Naples, FL 33941

Genealogical Society of Hernando
County
P.O. Box 1793
Brooksville, FL 34605-1793

Genealogical Society of North
Brevard, Inc.
P.O. Box 897
Titusville, FL 32781-0897

Genealogical Society of Sarasota
P.O. Box 1917
Sarasota, FL 34230-1917

Genealogical Society of South
Brevard
P.O. Box 786
Melbourne, FL 32902

Imperial Polk Genealogical Society
P.O. Box 10
Kathleen, FL 33849-0010

Indian River Genealogical Society
P.O. Box 1850
Vero Beach, FL 32961

Jacksonville Genealogical
Society, Inc.
P.O. Box 60756
Jacksonville, FL 32236-0756

Kinseekers Genealogical Society of
Lake County
P.O. Box 492711
Leesburg, FL 34749-2711

Lee County Genealogical Society
P.O. Box 150153
Cape Coral, FL 33915-0153

Manasota Genealogical
Society, Inc.
1405 4th Ave. W.
Bradenton, FL 34205

Palm Beach County Genealogical
Society
P.O. Box 1746
West Palm Beach, FL 33402-1746

Pinellas Genealogical Society
1 Pin Tail Place
Safety Harbor, FL 34695-5028

Putnam County Genealogical
Society
P.O. Box 2354
Palatka, FL 32178-2354

Roots and Branches Genealogical
Society
P.O. Box 612
De Land, FL 32721-0612

Suncoast Genealogical Society, Inc.
P.O. Box 818
Ozona, FL 34660

Treasure Chest Genealogical
Society
P.O. Box 3401
Fort Pierce, FL 34948

HISTORICAL SOCIETIES

Florida Historical Society
P.O. Box 3645, University Station
Gainesville, FL 32601

Florida Historical Society
Special Collections Department
University of South Florida Library
Tampa, FL 33620

Pensacola Historical Society
405 S. Adams St.
Pensacola, FL 32501

St. Augustine Historical Society
c/o St. Johns County Public Library
1960 N. Ponce de Leon Blvd.
St. Augustine, FL 32084

CHURCH RECORDS

BAPTIST

Florida Baptist Historical Society
Stetson University
P.O. Box 8353
De Land, FL 32720

METHODIST

Florida United Methodist History
Collection
E. T. Roux Library
Florida Southern College
Lakeland, FL 33802

ROMAN CATHOLIC

Archdiocese of Miami
9401 Biscayne Blvd.
Miami Shores, FL 33138

ETHNIC RESOURCES

AFRICAN-AMERICAN

Afro-American Historical and
Genealogical Society,
Central Florida
P.O. Box 5742
Deltona, FL 32728

HISPANIC

University of Florida
Latin American Collection
Library East, 4th Floor
Gainesville, FL 32611
Phone: (904) 392-0360
Fax: (904) 392-7251

University of Miami
Otto G. Richter Library
Archives and Special Collections
Coral Gables, FL 33124-0320
Phone: (305) 284-3247
Fax: (305) 655-7352

JEWISH

Jewish Genealogical Society of
Orlando
P.O. Box 941332
Maitland, FL 32794-1332

Jewish Genealogical Society of
Palm Beach County, Inc.
c/o Albert M. Silberfeld
6037 Point Regal Circle #205
Delray Beach, FL 33484-4116

GEORGIA

ARCHIVES AND LIBRARIES

National Archives —
Southeast Region

1557 St. Joseph Avenue
East Point, GA 30344
Phone: (404) 763-7477
Fax: (404) 763-7033
e-mail: archives@atlanta.nara.gov
Alabama, Florida, Georgia, Kentucky, Mississippi, North Carolina,
South Carolina, and Tennessee

Georgia Department of Archives
and History
330 Capitol Ave. SE
Atlanta, GA 30334
Phone: (404) 656-2350
Fax: (404) 651-9270

Atlanta-Fulton Public Library
One Margaret Mitchell Sq. NW
Atlanta, GA 30303-1089
Phone: (404) 730-1700
Fax: (404) 730-1990

Washington Memorial Library
Middle Georgia Regional Library
1180 Washington Ave.
Macon, GA 31201-1790
Phone: (912) 744-0841
Fax: (912) 744-0840

GENEALOGICAL SOCIETIES

Carroll County Genealogical
Society
P.O. Box 576
Carrollton, GA 30117

Cobb County Genealogical
Society, Inc.
P.O. Box 1413
Marietta, GA 30061-1413

Family Tree — Ellen Payne Odom
Library
P.O. Box 1110
Moultrie, GA 31776

Friends of the Smyrna Library
100 Village Green Cir.
Smyrna, GA 30080

Georgia Genealogical Society
P.O. Box 38066
Atlanta, GA 30334

Georgia Genealogical Society
P.O. Box 54575
Atlanta, GA 30308-0575
Phone: (404) 475-4404

Middle School Genealogical Society
1144 Seven Springs Cir. NE
Marietta, GA 30068-2661

Northwest Georgia Historical &
Genealogical Society
P.O. Box 2484
Rome, GA 30161

Paulding County Genealogical
Society
P.O. Box 1314
Hiram, GA 30141

HISTORICAL SOCIETIES

Georgia Historical Society Library
501 Whitaker St.
Savannah, GA 31499
Phone: (912) 651-2128

CHURCH RECORDS

BAPTIST

Georgia Baptist Historical
Collection
Eugene W. Stetson Memorial
Library
Mercer University
Macon, GA 31207

METHODIST

United Methodist Museum
P.O. Box 408
St. Simons Island, GA 31522

ROMAN CATHOLIC

Archdiocese of Atlanta
680 W. Peachtree St. NW
Atlanta, GA 30308

Archdiocese of Savannah
P.O. Box 8789
Savannah, GA 31412

ETHNIC RESOURCES

AFRICAN-AMERICAN

Atlanta-Fulton Public Library
Special Collections Department
One Margaret Mitchell Square
Atlanta, GA 30303
Phone: (404) 730-1700
Fax: (404) 730-1989

Atlanta University Center
Robert W. Woodruff Library
Division of Archives and Special
Collections
111 James P. Brawley Dr. SW
Atlanta, GA 30314
Phone: (404) 522-8980
Fax: (404) 577-5158

Sara Hightower Regional Library
Special Collections
205 Riverside Pkwy.
Rome, GA 30161
Phone: (706) 236-4607
Fax: (706) 236-4605

JEWISH

Jewish Genealogical Society of
Georgia
245 Dalrymple Dr.
Atlanta, GA 30328

HAWAII

ARCHIVES AND LIBRARIES

National Archives —
Pacific Sierra Region
1000 Commodore Dr.
San Bruno, CA 94066
Phone: (415) 876-9009
Fax: (415) 876-9233
e-mail: archives@sanbruno.nara.gov
California except southern California, Hawaii, Nevada except Clark County, American Samoa, and Guam

Bishop Museum Library
1525 Bernice St.
Honolulu, HI 96817-0916
Phone: (808) 848-4147
Fax: (808) 841-8968

DAR Memorial Library
1914 Makiki Heights Dr.
Honolulu, HI 96822

Hawaii State Archives
Iolani Palace Grounds
Honolulu, HI 96813
Phone: (808) 586-0329
Fax: (808) 586-0330

Hawaii State Library
465 S. King St.
Honolulu, HI 96813
Phone: (808) 586-3704
Fax: (808) 586-3715

University of Hawaii,
Manoa Campus
Hamilton Library, Hawaii Collection
2550 The Mall
Honolulu, HI 96822
Phone: (808) 956-7203
Fax: (808) 956-5968

Brigham Young University - Hawaii
Joseph F. Smith Library Archives
Library and Academic Support
55-220 Kulanui St. (location)
BYUH Box 1966 (mailing)
Laie, HI 96762

GENEALOGICAL SOCIETIES

Hawaii County Genealogical
Society
P.O. Box 831
Keaau, HI 96749

Sandwich Islands Genealogy
Society
1116 Kealaolu Ave.
Honolulu, HI 96816-5419

HISTORICAL SOCIETIES

Hawaiian Historical Society
560 Kawaiahao St.
Honolulu, HI 96813
Phone: (808) 537-6271

CHURCH RECORDS

CONGREGATIONAL

Congregational Library
14 Beacon St.
Boston, MA 02108

PRESBYTERIAN

Presbyterian Historical Society
United Presbyterian Church
in the U.S.
425 Lombard St.
Philadelphia, PA 19147

ROMAN CATHOLIC

Diocese of Honolulu, Chancery Office
1184 Bishop St.
Honolulu, HI 96813

ETHNIC RESOURCES

ASIAN

Hawaii Chinese History Center
Library
111 N. King St., Suite 410
Honolulu, HI 96817-4703
Phone: (808) 521-5948

Hongwanji Temple Headquarters
1727 Pali Hwy.
Honolulu, HI 96813

Japanese Consulate General
1742 Nuuanu Ave.
Honolulu, HI 96817

Jodo Sect Temples Headquarters
1429 Makki St.
Honolulu, HI 96822

Leward Community College Library
Special Collections
96-045 Ala Ike
Pearl City, HI 96782-0379
Phone: (808)455-0379

University of Hawaii
Hamilton Library
Asia Collection

2550 The Mall
Honolulu, HI 96822
Phone: (808) 956-8116
Fax: (808) 956-5968

University of Hawaii at Manoa
Center for Pacific Island Studies
School of Hawaiian, Asian and Pacific Studies
1890 East-West Rd.
Moore Hall 215
Honolulu, HI 96822
Phone: (808) 956-7700
Fax: (808) 956-7053

IDAHO

ARCHIVES AND LIBRARIES

National Archives —
Pacific Northwest Region
6125 Sand Point Way NE
Seattle, WA 98115
Phone: (206) 526-6507
Fax: (206) 526-4344
e-mail: archives@seattle.nara.gov
Idaho, Oregon, and Washington

Idaho Library and Archives
450 N. Fourth St.
Boise, ID 83702
Phone: (208) 334-3356
Fax: (208) 334-3890

Idaho State Genealogical Library
450 N. 4th St.
Boise, ID 83702
Phone: (208) 334-2305
Fax: (208) 334-3198

Idaho State Library
325 W. State St.
Boise, ID 83702-6072
Phone: (208) 334-2150
Fax: (208) 334-4016

Ricks College Library
Special Collections Area
Rexburg, ID 83460-0405
Phone: (208) 356-2366
Fax: (208) 356-2390

University of Idaho
Special Collections Library
Moscow, ID 83843-4198
Phone: (208) 885-6534
Fax: (208) 885-6817

GENEALOGICAL SOCIETIES

Idaho Genealogical Society, Inc.
4620 Overland Rd. #204
Boise, ID 83705-2867
Phone: (208) 384-0542

Friends of the Idaho Genealogy
Library
Idaho Genealogy Library
459 N. 4th St.
Boise, ID 83702

Predmore Pridemore Pridmore
Prigmore Association
c/o Howard Johnston
545 Jefferson
Kimberly, ID 83341

Idaho State Historical Society
1109 Main St. Ste. 250
Boise, ID 83702
Phone: (208) 334-3890
Fax: (208) 334-3198

HISTORICAL SOCIETIES

Idaho State Historical Society
325 W. State St. (location)
450 N. 4th St. (mailing)
Boise, ID 83702
Phone: (802) 334-3356
Fax: (802) 334-3198

CHURCH RECORDS

ROMAN CATHOLIC

Chancery Office
Diocese of Boise
420 W. Idaho St.
P.O. Box 769
Boise, ID 83701

ILLINOIS

ARCHIVES AND LIBRARIES

National Archives —
Great Lakes Region
7358 S. Pulaski Rd.
Chicago, IL 60629
Phone: (312) 581-7816
Fax: (312) 353-1294
e-mail: archives@chicago.nara.gov
Illinois, Indiana, Michigan, Min-
nesota, Ohio, and Wisconsin

Belleville Public Library
121 E. Washington St.
Belleville, IL 62220-2205
Phone: (618) 234-0441
Fax: (618) 234-9474

Blackhawk Genealogical Library
19th St. and 4th Ave.
Rock Island, IL 61204-3912
Phone: (309) 788-7627

Illinois State Archives
Margaret Cross Norton Building
Archives Building
Springfield, IL 62756
Phone: (217) 782-4682
Fax: (217) 524-3930
www.sos.state.il.us

Newberry Library
60 W. Walton St.
Chicago, IL 60610-3394
Phone: (312) 943-9090
129.231.205.235/isc275

Illinois State Historical Library
Old State Capitol
Springfield, IL 62701
Phone: (217) 524-6358
Fax: (217) 785-6250

Illinois State Library
300 S. Second St.
Springfield, IL 62701
Phone: (217) 782-7596
Fax: (217) 785-4326

GENEALOGICAL SOCIETIES

Bureau County Genealogical
Society
P.O. Box 402
Princeton, IL 61356-0402

Champaign County Genealogical
Society
201 S. Race St.
Urbana, IL 61801

Chicago Genealogical Society
P.O. Box 1160
Chicago, IL 60690-1160

DuPage County Genealogical
Society
P.O. Box 133
Lombard, IL 60148

Edgar County Genealogical Society
P.O. Box 304
Paris, IL 61944

Elgin Genealogical Society
P.O. Box 1418
Elgin, IL 60121-1418

The Genealogical Forum of
Elmhurst
120 E. Park Ave.
Elmhurst, IL 60126

Fox Valley Genealogical Society
705 N. Brainard St.
Naperville, IL 60563

Fulton County Historical and
Genealogical Society
45 N. Park Dr.
Canton, IL 61520-1126

Genealogical Society of Southern
Illinois
John A. Logan College
Route 2 Box 145
Carterville, IL 62918-9599

Illinois State Genealogical Society
P.O. Box 10195
Springfield, IL 62791
Phone: (217) 789-1968

Jacksonville Area Genealogical and
Historical Society
P.O. Box 21
Jacksonville, IL 62651-0021

Lake County Genealogical Society
P.O. Box 721
Libertyville, IL 60048-0721

La Salle County Genealogical Guild
P.O. Box 534
Ottawa, IL 61350

Lithuanian American Genealogy
Society
6500 S. Pulaski Rd.
Chicago, IL 60629

Madison County Genealogical
Society
P.O. Box 631
Edwardsville, IL 62025

McHenry County Genealogical
Society
P.O. Box 184
Crystal Lake, IL 60039-0184

McLean County Genealogical
Society
P.O. Box 488
Normal, IL 61761

North Suburban Genealogical
Society
768 Oak St.
Winnetka, IL 60093

Northwest Suburban Council of
Genealogists
P.O. Box AC
Mount Prospect, IL 60056-9019

O'Fallon/Belleville/St. Clair
Genealogical Society
4259 Sweetgum Ct.
Belleville, IL 62221

South Suburban Genealogical and
Historical Society
P.O. Box 96
South Holland, IL 60473

St. Clair County Genealogical
Society
1046 Oriole Dr.
O'Fallon, IL 62269

Stephenson County Genealogical
Society
P.O. Box 514
Freeport, IL 61032

Tazewell County Genealogical
Society
P.O. Box 312
Pekin, IL 61555-0312

Will/Grundy County Genealogical
Society
P.O. Box 24
Wilmington, IL 60481

Zion Genealogical Society
2400 Gabriel Ave.
Zion, IL 60099

HISTORICAL SOCIETIES

Illinois State Historical Society
Old State Capitol
Springfield, IL 62701
Phone: (217) 782-4836

CHURCH RECORDS

BAPTIST

American Baptist Historical Society
1106 S. Goodman St.
Rochester, NY 14620

LUTHERAN

Archives of the American Lutheran
Church
Wartburg Theological Seminary
333 Wartburg Pl.
Dubuque, IA 52001

METHODIST

Central Illinois Conference
Historical Society
1211 N. Park St.
Bloomington, IL 61701

Garrett Theological Seminary
2121 Sheridan Rd.
Evanston, IL 60201

ROMAN CATHOLIC

Archives of the Archdiocese of
Chicago
St. Mary of the Lake Seminary
Mundelein, IL 60060

ETHNIC RESOURCES

AFRICAN-AMERICAN

Chicago Public Library
Carter G. Woodson Regional
Library
Vivian G. Harsh Research
Collection of Afro-American
History and Literature
9525 S. Halsted St.
Chicago, IL 60628
Phone: (312) 747-6910
Fax: (312) 747-3396

DuSable Museum of African
American History Library
740 E. 56th Pl.
Chicago, IL 60637
Phone: (312) 947-0600
Fax: (312) 947-0677

Afro-American Genealogical and
Historical Society of Chicago
P.O. Box 377651
Chicago, IL 60637

ASIAN

Northern Illinois University
Donn V. Hart Southeast Asia
Collection
Founders Memorial Library
DeKalb, IL 60115
Phone: (815) 753-1808
Fax: (815) 753-2003

JEWISH

Illiana Jewish Genealogical Society
404 Douglas St.
Park Forest, IL 60466

Jewish Genealogical Society of
Illinois
P.O. Box 515
Northbrook, IL 60065-0515

POLISH

Polish Genealogical Society of
America
984 N. Milwaukee Ave.
Chicago, IL 60622

SWEDISH

Swedish-American Historical
Society
Chicago, IL

INDIANA

ARCHIVES AND LIBRARIES

National Archives —
Great Lakes Region
7358 S. Pulaski Rd.
Chicago, IL 60629
Phone: (312) 581-7816
Fax: (312) 353-1294
e-mail: archives@chicago.nara.gov
Illinois, Indiana, Michigan, Minnesota, Ohio, and Wisconsin

Allen County Public Library
Fred J. Reynolds Historical Genealogy Collection
P.O. Box 2270
900 Webster St.
Fort Wayne, IN 46801-2270
Phone: (219) 424-7241
Fax: (219) 422-9688
www.acpl.lib.in.us

Indiana State Archives
Commission on Public Records
State Office Bldg., Rm. W472
Indianapolis, IN 46204-2215
Phone: (317)232-3373
Fax: (317) 232-3154

Indiana State Library
140 N. Senate Ave.
Indianapolis, IN 46204-2296
Phone: (317) 232-3675
Fax: (317) 232-3728
www.statelib.in.us

GENEALOGICAL SOCIETIES

Allen County Genealogical Society
of Indiana
P.O. Box 12003
Fort Wayne, IN 46862

Bartholomew County Genealogical
Society
P.O. Box 2455
Columbus, IN 47202

Blair Society for Genealogical
Research
20 W. College Ave.
Brownsburg, IN 46112

Clinton County Genealogical
Society
c/o Frankfort Public Community
Library

208 W. Clinton St.
Frankfort, IN 46041

Indiana Genealogical Society
P.O. Box 66
Tunnelton, IN 47467

Indiana State Genealogical Society
P.O. Box 10507
Fort Wayne, IN 46852-0507

LaPorte County Indiana
Genealogical Society
904 Indiana Ave.
LaPorte, IN 46350

South Bend Area Genealogical
Society
P.O. Box 1222
South Bend, IN 46624

Southern Indiana Genealogical
Society
P.O. Box 665
New Albany, IN 47151-0665

Sullivan County Historical Society
10 S. Court St.
P.O. Box 326
Sullivan, IN 47882

Tippecanoe County Area
Genealogical Society
909 South St.
Lafayette, IN 47901

Tri-County Genealogical Society
P.O. Box 118
Batesville, IN 47006

Tri-State Genealogical Society
c/o Willard Library
21 First Ave.
Evansville, IN 47710

HISTORICAL SOCIETIES

Indiana Historical Society
Genealogical Section
315 W. Ohio St.
Indianapolis, IN 46202-3299
Phone: (317) 232-1879
Fax: (317) 233-3109

CHURCH RECORDS

BAPTIST

Indiana Baptist Collection
Franklin College Library
Franklin, IN 46131

DISCIPLES OF CHRIST

Christian Theological Seminary
Library
1000 W. 42nd St.
Indianapolis, IN 46208

METHODIST

Archives of DePauw University and
Indiana United Methodism
Roy O. West Library
DePauw University
Greencastle, IN 46135

ROMAN CATHOLIC

University of Notre Dame Archives
P.O. Box 513
Notre Dame, IN 46556

ETHNIC RESOURCES

AFRICAN-AMERICAN

Indiana University
Black Culture Center Library

109 N. Jordan Ave.
Bloomington, IN 47405
Phone: (812) 855-3237

Indiana African American Historical
and Genealogical Society
502 Clover Terrace
Bloomington, IN 47404-1809

IOWA

ARCHIVES AND LIBRARIES

National Archives —
Central Plains Region
2312 E. Bannister Rd.
Kansas City, MO 64131
Phone: (816) 926-6272
Fax: (816) 926-6272
e-mail:
archives@kansascity.nara.gov
Iowa, Kansas, Missouri, and Nebraska

Burlington Public Library
501 N. 4th St.
Burlington, IA 52601-1647
Phone: (319) 753-1647
Fax: (319) 753-5316

State Archives of Iowa
State Historical Society of Iowa
Capitol Complex
600 E. Locust
Des Moines, IA 50319
Phone: (515) 281-8837
Fax: (515) 282-0502

State Library of Iowa
E. 12th and Grand
Des Moines, IA 50319
Phone: (515) 281-4105
Fax: (515) 282-0502

Iowa Genealogical Society Library
6000 Douglas Ave. Ste. 145

Des Moines, IA 50322
Phone: (515) 276-0287

GENEALOGICAL SOCIETIES

American/Schleswig-Holstein
Heritage Society
P.O. Box 313
Davenport, IA 52805-0313

Decorah Genealogy Association
202 Winnebago St.
Decorah, IA 52101

Des Moines County Genealogical
Society
P.O. Box 493
Burlington, IA 52601

Dubuque County-Key City
Genealogical Society
P.O. Box 13
Dubuque, IA 52004-0013

Iowa City Genealogical Society
P.O. Box 822
Iowa City, IA 52244-0822

Iowa Genealogical Society
6000 Douglas St.
P.O. Box 7735
Des Moines, IA 50322

Laurens Genies, Pocahontas
County
13737 410th St.
Laurens, IA 50554-8669

Linn County Heritage Society
P.O. Box 175
Cedar Rapids, IA 52403

Northeast Iowa Genealogical
Society
c/o Grant Museum

503 South St.
Waterloo, IA 50701

Richardson Sloane Genealogical
Library
1019 Mound St., Ste. 301
Davenport, IA 52803

Scott County Iowa Genealogical
Society
P.O. Box 3132
Davenport, IA 52808-3132

HISTORICAL SOCIETIES

Iowa State Historical Department
Division of State Historical Society
of Iowa
402 Iowa Ave.
Iowa City, IA 52240-1806
Phone: (319) 335-3916
Fax: (319) 335-3924

State Historical Society of Iowa
Library/Archives Bureau
State of Iowa Historical Building
600 E. Locust
Des Moines, IA 50319
Phone: (515)281-5111

CHURCH RECORDS

LUTHERAN

Archives, American Lutheran
Church
Wartburg Theological Seminary
333 Wartburg Pl.
Dubuque, IA 52001

METHODIST

Iowa Wesleyan College Library
Mt. Pleasant, IA 52641

ROMAN CATHOLIC

Diocese of Davenport
410 Brady St.
Davenport, IA 52801

Diocese of Sioux City
1821 Jackson St.
Sioux City, IA 51104

Diocese of Des Moines
611 High St.
Des Moines, IA 50309

KANSAS

ARCHIVES AND LIBRARIES

National Archives —
Central Plains Region
2312 E. Bannister Rd.
Kansas City, MO 64131
Phone: (816) 926-6272
Fax: (816) 926-6272
e-mail:
archives@kansascity.nara.gov
Iowa, Kansas, Missouri, and Ne-
braska

Kansas Heritage Center Library
10002 2nd Ave.
Dodge City, KS 67801
Phone: (316) 227-1616
Fax: (316) 227-1695

Kansas State Library
State Capitol Building
Topeka, KS 66612-1593
Phone: (913) 296-3296
Fax: (913) 296-6650

Department of Special Collections
University of Kansas
Spencer Research Library
Lawrence, KS 66045-2800
Phone: (913) 864-4274

GENEALOGICAL SOCIETIES

Atchison County Kansas
Genealogical Society
401 Kansas Ave.
Atchison, KS 66002

Cherokee County (KS)
Genealogical-Historical Society
P.O. Box 33
Columbus, KS 66725-0033

Douglas County Genealogical
Society
P.O. Box 3664-0664
Lawrence, KS 66046

Kansas Council of Genealogical
Societies
P.O. Box 3858
Topeka, KS 66604-6858

Kansas Genealogical Society
Village Square Mall
Lower Level, 2601 Central
P.O. Box 103
Dodge City, KS 67801
Phone: (316) 225-1951

Labette County Genealogical
Society, Inc.
P.O. Box 544
Parsons, KS 67357

Liberal Area Genealogical Society
P.O. Box 1094
Liberal, KS 67905-1094

North Central Kansas Genealogical
Society and Library
P.O. Box 251
Cawker City, KS 67430

Phillips County Genealogical
Society
P.O. Box 114
Phillipsburg, KS 67661-0114

Reno County Genealogical Society
P.O. Box 5
Hutchinson, KS 67504-0005

Riley County Genealogical Society
2005 Claflin Rd.
Manhattan, KS 66502-3415

Topeka Genealogical Society
P.O. Box 4048
Topeka, KS 66604-0048

HISTORICAL SOCIETIES

Kansas State Historical Society
120 W. Tenth St.
Topeka, KS 66612-1291
Phone: (913) 296-3251
Fax: (913) 296-1005

Kansas State Historical Society
Center for Historical Research
6425 SW Sixth Ave.
Topeka, KS 66615-1099
Phone: (913) 272-8681
Fax: (913) 272-8682
history.cc.vkans.edu/heritage/ksh-sl.html

CHURCH RECORDS

MENNONITE

Bethel College
Mennonite Library and Archives
300 E. 27th
North Newton, KS 67117-9989
Phone: (316) 283-2500
Fax: (316) 284-5286

METHODIST

Baker University Library
606 Eighth St.
Baldwin City, KS 66006

Memorial Library
Southwestern College
100 College St.
Winfield, KS 67156

ROMAN CATHOLIC

Archdiocese of Kansas City in
Kansas
Chancery Office
2220 Central Ave.
P.O. Box 2328
Kansas City, KS 66110

KENTUCKY

ARCHIVES AND LIBRARIES

National Archives —
Southeast Region
1557 St. Joseph Ave.
East Point, GA 30344
Phone: (404) 763-7477
Fax: (404)763-7033
e-mail: archives@atlanta.nara.gov
Alabama, Florida, Georgia, Kentucky, Mississippi, North Carolina, South Carolina, and Tennessee

Kentucky Department for Libraries
and Archives
300 Coffee Tree Rd.
Frankfort, KY 40602-0537
Phone: (502) 564-8300
Fax: (502) 564-5773

Western Kentucky University
Kentucky Library
Bowling Green, KY 42101-3576
Phone: (502) 745-6258

University of Kentucky
Margaret I. King Library
Lexington, KY 40506-0039
Phone: (606)257-3801
Fax: (606) 257-8379

GENEALOGICAL SOCIETIES

Bullitt County Genealogical Society
P.O. Box 960
Shepherdsville, KY 40165

Eastern Kentucky Genealogical
Society
P.O. Box 1544
Ashland, KY 41105-1544

Fayette County Genealogical
Society
Lexington, KY

Filson Club
1310 S. Third St.
Louisville, KY 40208

Graves County Genealogical
Society
P.O. Box 245
Mayfield, KY 42066

Kentucky Genealogical Society
P.O. Box H
Frankfort, KY

Kentucky Genealogical Society
P.O. Box 153
Frankfort, KY 40602
Phone: (502) 875-4452

Louisville Genealogical Society
P.O. Box 5164 DGS
Louisville, KY 40255-0164

Marshall County Genealogical and
Historical Society
Benton, KY 42066

McCracken County Genealogical
and Historical Society
Paducah Public Library
555 Washington St.
Paducah, KY 42003

Muhlenberg County Genealogical
Society
N. Main St.
Greenville, KY 42345

Scott County Genealogical Society
c/o Scott County Public Library
230 E. Main St.
Georgetown, KY 40324

Skeleton Closet
P.O. Box 91392
Louisville, KY 40291-0392

Southern Kentucky Genealogical
Society
P.O. Box 1782
Bowling Green, KY 42101

West-Central Kentucky Family
Research Association
P.O. Box 1932
Owensboro, KY 42302

HISTORICAL SOCIETIES

Ancestral Trails Historical
Society, Inc.
P.O. Box 573
Vine Grove, KY 40175-0573

Kentucky Historical Society
300 W. Broadway
P.O. Box H

Frankfort, KY 40602-2108
Phone: (502) 564-3016

CHURCH RECORDS

BAPTIST

Kentucky Baptist Historical Society
10701 Shelbyville Rd.
Middletown, KY 40243-0433

METHODIST

Kentucky Conference Programs
Council Office
P.O. Box 5107
Lexington, KY 40505

PRESBYTERIAN

The Library
Louisville Presbyterian Seminary
1044 Alta Vista Rd.
Louisville, KY 40205

ROMAN CATHOLIC

Diocese of Covington
1140 Madison Ave.
P.O. Box 192
Covington, KY 41017

Archdiocese of Louisville
212 E. College St.
Louisville, KY 40203

LOUISIANA

ARCHIVES AND LIBRARIES

National Archives —
Southwest Region
501 W. Felix St., P.O. Box 6216

Fort Worth, TX 76115
Phone: (817) 334-5525
Fax: (817) 334-5621
e-mail: archives@ftworth.nara.gov
Arkansas, Louisiana, New Mexico,
Oklahoma, and Texas

Division of Archives Records
Management and History
Louisiana Office of the Secretary of
State
3851 Essen Ln.
P.O. Box 94125
Baton Rouge, LA 70804
Phone: (504) 922-1207
Fax: (504) 922-0002

Louisiana State University
Baton Rouge, LA 70803
Phone: (504)388-2217
Fax: (504) 388-6825
www.lib.lsu.edu

Louisiana State Museum/ Louisiana
Historical Center Library
400 Esplanade Ave. (location)
751 Chartres St. (mailing
New Orleans, LA 70176-2448
Phone: (504) 568-8214
Fax: (504) 568-6969

State Library of Louisiana
760 N. 3rd St.
P.O. Box 131
Baton Rouge, LA 70821-0131
Phone: (504) 342-4913
Fax: (504) 342-3547

New Orleans Public Library
Genealogy Section
219 Loyola Ave.
New Orleans, LA 70140-1016
Phone: (504) 596-2602
Fax: (504) 596-2609

GENEALOGICAL SOCIETIES

Baton Rouge Genealogical and
Historical Society
P.O. Box 80565 SE Station
Baton Rouge, LA 70898-0565
Phone: (502)564-3016

Imperial St. Landry Genealogical
and Historical Society
P.O. Box 108
Opelousas, LA 70571-0108

Jefferson Genealogical Society, Inc.
P.O. Box 961
Metairie, LA 70004

LaLourche Genealogical and
Historical Society
Thibodaux, LA 70302

Louisiana Genealogical and
Historical Society
P.O. Box 82060
Baton Rouge, LA 70884-2060

Louisiana Genealogical and
Historical Society
P.O. Box 3454
Baton Rouge, LA 70821
Phone: (504) 766-1555

Terborne Genealogical Society
Houma, LA

HISTORICAL SOCIETIES

Louisiana Historical Association
University of Southwestern
Louisiana
P.O. Box 42808
Lafayette, LA 70504

CHURCH RECORDS

LUTHERAN

University of New Orleans
Earl K. Long Library
Archives and Manuscripts Division
2000 Lakeshore Dr.
New Orleans, LA 70122

METHODIST

Centenary College of Louisiana
Magale Library, Cline Room
Shreveport, LA 71104

ROMAN CATHOLIC

Archdiocese of New Orleans
Archives
1100 Chartres St.
New Orleans, LA 70116
Phone: (504) 529-2651
Fax: (504) 529-2001

Diocese of Alexandria-Shreveport
P.O. Box 7417
Alexandria, LA 71306

Diocese of Baton Rouge Archives
1800 S. Acadian Thruway
P.O. Box 2228
Baton Rouge, LA 708

ETHNIC RESOURCES

AFRICAN-AMERICAN

Tulane University
Howard-Tilton Memorial Library
Louisiana Collection
New Orleans, LA 70118
Phone: (504) 865-5643
Fax: (504) 865-6773

Archives of the Parish of East
Baton Rouge
Genealogy Section
Public Service Department
B1 Governmental Building
222 St. Louis St.
Baton Rouge, LA 70802

JEWISH

Jewish Genealogy Society of
New Orleans
P.O. Box 7811
Metairie, LA 70010

MAINE

ARCHIVES AND LIBRARIES

National Archives —
New England Region
380 Trapelo Rd.
Waltham, MA 02154
Phone:617-647-8100
Fax: (617) 647-8460
e-mail: Archives@waltham.nara.gov
Connecticut, Maine, Massachu-
setts, New Hampshire, Rhode Is-
land, and Vermont

Bangor Public Library
145 Harlow St.
Bangor, ME 04401-1802
Phone: (207) 947-8336
Fax: (207) 945-6694

Maine State Archives
State House-Station House 84
Augusta, ME 04333-0084
Phone: (207) 289-5790
Fax: (207) 287-5739

Maine State Library
State House Station 64
Augusta, ME 04333-0064

Phone: (207) 287-5600
Fax: (207) 287-5615

University of Maine at Orono
Raymond H. Fogler Library
P.O. Box 5729
Orono, ME 04469-5729
Phone: (207) 581-1661
Fax: (207) 581-1653

GENEALOGICAL SOCIETIES

Maine Genealogical Society
P.O. Box 221
Farmington, ME 04938

HISTORICAL SOCIETIES

Maine Historical Society
485 Congress St.
Portland, ME 04101
Phone: (207) 774-1822

CHURCH RECORDS

BAPTIST

American Baptist Historical Society
1106 S. Goodman St.
Rochester, NY 14602

EPISCOPAL

Archives of the Diocesan House
143 State House
Portland, ME 04101

ROMAN CATHOLIC

The Chancery Library of the
Diocese of Portland
510 Ocean Ave.
Portland, ME 04103

MARYLAND

ARCHIVES AND LIBRARIES

National Archives —
Mid Atlantic Region
9th & Market Sts., Room 1350
Philadelphia, PA 19107
Phone: (215) 597-3000
Fax: (215) 597-2303
e-mail: archives@philarch.nara.gov
Delaware, Maryland, Pennsylvania,
Virginia, and West Virginia

Baltimore City Archives
211 E. Pleasant St., Rm. 201
Baltimore, MD 21202

Enoch Pratt Free Library
400 Cathedral St.
Baltimore, MD 21201-4484
Phone: (410) 396-5430
Fax: (410) 396-6856

Johns Hopkins University
Milton S. Eisenhower Library
3400 N. Charles St.
Baltimore, MD 21202
Phone: (410) 516-8325
Fax: (410) 516-5080
milton.mse.jhu.edu:800

Maryland State Law Library
Courts of Appeal Building
361 Rowe Blvd.
Annapolis, MD 21401-1697
Phone: (410) 974-3395
Fax: (410)974-2063

Maryland State Archives
350 Rowe Blvd.
Annapolis, MD 21401
Phone: (410) 974-3915
Fax: (410) 974-3895

McKeldin Library
University of Maryland
College Park, MD 20742
Phone: (301) 405-9128
Fax: (301)314-9408

National Archives and Records
Administration
Washington National Records
Center
4205 Suitland Rd.
Suitland, MD 20746
Phone: (301) 457-7000

Maryland Historical Society Library
201 W. Monument St.
Baltimore, MD 21201
Phone: (410) 685-3750
Fax: (410) 385-2105

GENEALOGICAL SOCIETIES

Anne Arundel Genealogical Society
P.O. Box 221
Pasadena, MD 21122

Baltimore County Genealogical
Society
P.O. Box 10085
Towson, MD 21285-0085

Calvert County Genealogical
Society
P.O. Box 9
Sunderland, MD 20689

Genealogical Council of Maryland
c/o Ann Paxton Brown
12631 Prices Distillery Rd.
Damascus, MD 20872-1520

Genealogical Council of Maryland
c/o Susan Johnston, Secretary
104 Park Dr.
Catonsville, MD 21228

Howard County Genealogical
Society
Box 274
Columbia, MD 21045

The Lower Delmarva Genealogical
Society
P.O. Box 3602
Salisbury, MD 21802-3602

Maryland Genealogical Society
201 W. Monument St.
Baltimore, MD 21201

National Capital Buckeye Chapter
of Genealogical Society
P.O. Box 105
Bladensburg, MD 20710-0105

Prince George's County
Genealogical Society
P.O. Box 819
Bowie, MD 20718-0819

HISTORICAL SOCIETIES

Catonsville Historical Society, Inc.
P.O. Box 9311
Catonsville, MD 21228

Genealogical Club of the
Montgomery
County Historical Society
103 W. Montgomery Ave.
Rockville, MD 20850

Historical Society of Charles
County
P.O. Box 261
Port Tobacco, MD 20677

Maryland Historical Society/
Maryland Genealogical Society
201 W. Monument St.
Baltimore, MD 21201
Phone: (410) 685-3750

Mid-Atlantic Germanic Society
c/o Shirley Forester
P.O. Box 2642
Kensington, MD 20891

CHURCH RECORDS

BAPTIST

Historical Room
Baptist Convention of
Maryland/Delaware
1313 York Rd.
Lutherville, MD 21093

LUTHERAN

Archives of the Maryland Synod
Church in America
7604 York Rd.
Towson, MD 21204

METHODIST

United Methodist Historical
Society
Baltimore Conference
2200 St. Paul St.
Baltimore, MD 21218

ROMAN CATHOLIC

Archives of Archdiocese of
Baltimore
320 Cathedral St.
Baltimore, MD 21201

ETHNIC RESOURCES

AFRICAN-AMERICAN

Afro-American Historical and
Genealogical Society, Baltimore
P.O. Box 66265
Baltimore, MD 21218

Afro-American Historical and
Genealogical Society, Central
Maryland
P.O. Box 2774
Columbia, MD 21045

Black Military History Society
c/o Col. W. A. DeShields
P.O. Box 1134
Ft. Meade, MD

MASSACHUSETTS

ARCHIVES AND LIBRARIES

National Archives —
New England Region
380 Trapelo Rd.
Waltham, MA 02154
Phone:617-647-8100
Fax: (617) 647-8460
e-mail: Archives@waltham.nara.gov
Connecticut, Maine, Massachu-
setts, New Hampshire, Rhode Is-
land, and Vermont

National Archives —
Pittsfield Region
100 Dan Fox Dr.
Pittsfield, MA 01201
Phone: (413) 445-6885
Fax: (413) 445-7599
e-mail: archives@pittsfield.nara.gov

American Antiquarian Society
Library
185 Salisbury St.
Worcester, MA 01609-1634
Phone: (508) 755-5221
Fax: (508) 754-9069

American Congregational Assoc.
Congregational Library
14 Beacon St.
Boston, MA 02108-9999
Phone: (617) 523-0470
Fax: (617) 523-0491

Boston Athenaeum
10½ Beacon St.
Boston, MA 02108-3777
Phone: (617) 227-0270
Fax: (617) 227-5266

Boston Public Library
666 Boylston St.
Boston, MA 02117-0286
Phone: (617) 536-5400
Fax: (617) 236-4306

Connecticut Valley Historical
Museum Library
194 State St.
Springfield, MA 01103
Phone: (413) 732-3080
Fax: (413) 734-6158

Massachusetts Archives
Office of Secretary of State
Boston, MA 02125
Phone: (617) 727-2816
Fax: (617) 727-2826

University of Massachusetts Library
Special Collections and Archives
Amherst, MA 01003
Phone: (413) 545-0284
Fax: (413) 545-6873

Archives of the Commonwealth
Reference Desk
220 Morrissey Blvd.
(Columbia Point)
Boston, MA 02125
Phone: (617) 727-2816
Fax: (617) 727-2816

The Commonwealth of Massachu-
setts State Library
George Fingold Library
State House Rm. 341
Beacon St.
Boston, MA 02133
Phone: (617) 727-2590

Massachusetts Department of
Public Health
Central Library
150 Tremont St.
Boston, MA 02111
Phone: (617) 775-8055

New England Historic Genealogical
Society
101 Newbury St.
Boston, MA 02116
Phone: (617) 536-5740
www.nehgs.org

GENEALOGICAL SOCIETIES

Berkshire Family History
Association, Inc.
P.O. Box 1437
Pittsfield, MA 01201

Central Massachusetts
Genealogical Society
P.O. Box 811
Westminster, MA 01473

Essex Society of Genealogists
P.O. Box 313
Lynnfield, MA 01940

Falmouth Genealogical Society
P.O. Box 2107
Teaticket, MA 02536

The Genealogical Round Table
812 Main St.
Concord, MA 01742

Massachusetts Genealogical
Council
P.O. Box 5393
Cochituate, MA 01778

South Shore Genealogical Society
P.O. Box 396
Norwell, MA 02061

HISTORICAL SOCIETIES

Massachusetts Historical Society
1154 Boylston St.
Boston, MA 02215
Phone: (617) 536-1608

ETHNIC RESOURCES

AFRICAN-AMERICAN

Suffolk University
Mildred F. Sawyer Library
Collection of African-American Lit-
erature
8 Ashburton Place
Boston, MA 02108
Phone: (617) 573-8532

IRISH

Irish Ancestral Research
Association
P.O. Box 619
Sudbury, MA 01776-0619

JEWISH

Jewish Genealogical Society of
Boston
P.O. Box 366
Newton Highlands, MA 02161-0004

MICHIGAN

ARCHIVES AND LIBRARIES

National Archives —
Great Lakes Region
7358 S. Pulaski Rd.
Chicago, IL 60629
Phone: (312) 581-7816
Fax: (312) 353-1294
e-mail: archives@chicago.nara.gov

Illinois, Indiana, Michigan, Minnesota, Ohio, and Wisconsin

Burton Historical Collection/
Detroit Society for Genealogical
Research
Detroit Public Library
5201 Woodward Ave.
Detroit, MI 48202-4007
Phone: (313) 833-1000
Fax: (313) 832-0877

Library of Michigan
717 W. Allegan Ave.
P.O. Box 30007
Lansing, MI 48909
Phone: (517) 373-5866
Fax: (517) 373-9438

Michigan State History Bureau
State Archives
Lansing, MI 48918-1837
Phone: (517) 373-1401
Fax: (517) 373-0851

University of Michigan
Michigan Historical Collections
Bentley Historical Library
1150 Beal Ave.
Ann Arbor, MI 48109-2113
Phone: (313) 764-3482
Fax: (313) 936-1333

Michigan Department of State
Historical Center
State Archives
717 W. Allegan Ave.
Lansing, MI 48918-1837
Phone: (517) 373-1408
Fax: (517) 335-8395

GENEALOGICAL SOCIETIES

Bay County Genealogical Society
P.O. Box 27
Essexville, MI 48732

Calhoun County Genealogical
Society
501 S. Superior St.
Albion, MI 49224

Cheboygan County Genealogical
Society
P.O. Box 51
Cheboygan, MI 49721

Dearborn Genealogical Society
P.O. Box 1112
Dearborn, MI 48121

Detroit Society For Genealogical
Research
5201 Woodward Ave.
Detroit, MI 48202

Downriver Genealogical Society
P.O. Box 476
Lincoln Park, MI 48146

Eaton County Genealogical Society
P.O. Box 337
Charlotte, MI 48813

Flint Genealogical Society
P.O. Box 1217
Flint, MI 48501

Fred Hart Williams Genealogical
Society
DPL Burton Historical Collection
5201 Woodward Ave.
Detroit, MI 48202-4007

French Canadian Heritage Society
of Michigan
P.O. Box 10028
Lansing, MI 48901-0028

Genealogical Society of Washtenaw
County
P.O. Box 7155
Ann Arbor, MI 48107

Grand Traverse Area Genealogical
Society
P.O. Box 2015
Traverse City, MI 49685-2015

Kalamazoo Valley Genealogical
Society
P.O. Box 405
Comstock, MI 49041-0405

Kalkaska Genealogy Society
P.O. Box 353
Kalkaska, MI 49646-0353

Kinseekers
P.O. Box 184
Grawn, MI 499637-0184

Livingston County Genealogical
|Society
P.O. Box 1073
Howell, MI 48844-1073

Marquette County Genealogical
Society
c/o Peter White Public Library
217 N. Front St.
Marquette, MI 49855-4220

Michigan Genealogical Council
P.O. Box 80953
Lansing, MI 48908-0953

Mid-Michigan Genealogical Society
P.O. Box 16033
Lansing, MI 48901-6033

Muskegon County Genealogical
Society
Hackley Public Library
316 W. Webster Ave.
Muskegon, MI 49440

Newaygo County Society of History
and Genealogy
P.O. Box 68
White Cloud, MI 49349

Northville Genealogy Society
Northville, MI

Oakland County Genealogical
Society
P.O. Box 1094
Birmingham, MI 48012

Oceana County Historical Society
114 Dryden St.
Hart, MI 49240

Roseville Historical and
Genealogical Society
c/o Roseville Public Library
29777 Gratiot Ave.
Roseville, MI 48066

Saginaw Genealogical Society
505 Janes
Saginaw, MI 48067

Western Michigan Genealogical
Society
60 Library Plaza
Grand Rapids Public Library
Grand Rapids, MI 49503

Western Wayne County
Genealogical Society
P.O. Box 530063
Livonia, MI 48153-0063

HISTORICAL SOCIETIES

Historical Society of Michigan
2117 Washtenaw Ave.
Ann Arbor, MI 48104

Historical Society of St. Clair
Shores
St. Clair Shores Public Library
22500 Eleven Mile Rd.
St. Clair Shores, MI 48081-1399

Michigan Historical Commission
505 State Office Building
Lansing, MI 48913

CHURCH RECORDS

BAPTIST

Kalamazoo College
Upjohn Library
Thompson & Academy Sts.
Kalamazoo, MI 49007

LUTHERAN

Archives, American Lutheran
Church
Wartburg Theological Seminary
Dubuque, IA 52001

METHODIST

Library Building
Adrian College
Adrian, MI 49221

ROMAN CATHOLIC

Diocese of Marquette
444 S. Fourth St.
P.O. Box 550
Marquette, MI 49855

Diocese of Detroit
1234 Washington Blvd.
Detroit, MI 48226

Diocese of Saginaw
5800 Weiss St.
Saginaw, MI 48603

Diocese of Grand Rapids
660 Burton St. SE
Grand Rapids, MI 49507

Diocese of Lansing
300 W. Ottawa
Lansing, MI 48933

ETHNIC RESOURCES

AFRICAN-AMERICAN

Central Michigan University
Clarke Historical Library
Mt. Pleasant, MI 48859
Phone: (517) 774-3352
Fax: (517) 774-4499

ASIAN

University of Michigan
Asia Library
Hatcher Graduate Library
4th Floor
Ann Arbor, MI 48109-1205
Phone: (313) 764-0406
Fax: (313) 763-5080

POLISH

Polish Genealogical Society of
Michigan
5201 Woodward Ave.
Detroit, MI 48202

MINNESOTA

ARCHIVES AND LIBRARIES

National Archives —
Great Lakes Region
7358 S. Pulaski Rd.
Chicago, IL 60629
Phone: (312) 581-7816
Fax: (312) 353-1294
e-mail: archives@chicago.nara.gov
Illinois, Indiana, Michigan, Min-
nesota, Ohio, and Wisconsin

Minnesota Historical Society
345 Kellogg Blvd. W.
St. Paul, MN 55102-1906
Phone: (612) 296-2143
Fax: (612) 296-7436

GENEALOGICAL SOCIETIES

Douglas County Genealogical
Society
P.O. Box 505
Alexandria, MN 56308

Freeborn County Genealogical
Society
P.O. Box 403
Albert Lea, MN 56007-0403

Germanic Genealogy Society
c/o Mike Haase
3148 Kentucky Ave. So.
St. Louis Park, MN 55426-3471

Minnesota Genealogical Society
P.O. Box 16069
St. Paul, MN 55116-0069

Mower County Genealogical
Society
P.O. Box 145
Austin, MN 55912-0145

Range Genealogical Society
P.O. Box 388
Chisholm, MN 55719

HISTORICAL SOCIETIES

Minnesota Historical Society
Research Center
345 Kellogg Blvd. W.
690 Cedar St.
St. Paul, MN 55101-1906
Phone: (612)296-2143

Minnesota Historical Society
Archives and Manuscripts
Collections
1500 Mississippi St.
St. Paul, MN 55101

CHURCH RECORDS

METHODIST

Minnesota Historical Depository
122 W. Franklin Ave.
Minneapolis, MN 55404

ROMAN CATHOLIC

Archdiocese of St. Paul
226 Summit Ave.
St. Paul, MN 55102

Diocese of New Ulm
1400 Chancery Dr.
New Ulm, MN 56073

Diocese of Duluth
215 W. 4th St.
Duluth, MN 55806

Diocese of St. Cloud
P.O. Box 1248
St. Cloud, MN 56302

Diocese of Winona
P.O. Box 588
Winona, MN 55987

MISSISSIPPI

ARCHIVES AND LIBRARIES

National Archives —
Southeast Region
1557 St. Joseph Ave.
East Point, GA 30344
Phone: (404) 763-7477
Fax: (404)763-7033
e-mail: archives@atlanta.nara.gov
Alabama, Florida, Georgia, Kentucky, Mississippi, North Carolina, South Carolina, and Tennessee

Evans Memorial Library
105 N. Long St.
Aberdeen, MS 39730

Mississippi State Department of
Archives and History
P.O. Box 571
Jackson, MS 39205-0571
Phone: (601) 359-6876
Fax: (601) 359-6946

Mississippi State University
Mitchell Memorial Library
Drawer 9570
Mississippi State, MS 39762
Phone: (601) 325-3061
Fax: (601) 325-4263
www.msstate.edu/library

University of Southern Mississippi
William David McCain Library
P.O. Box 5148
Hattiesburg, MS 39406-5148
Phone: (601) 266-4345
www.lib.asm.edu

GENEALOGICAL SOCIETIES

Mississippi Genealogical Society
P.O. Box 5301
Jackson, MS 39216-5301

Family Research Association of
Mississippi
P.O. Box 13334
Jackson, MS 39236-3334

Jackson County Genealogical
Society
c/o Else J. Martin
6301 Country Ln.
Pascagoula, MS 39581

Mississippi Genealogical Society
P.O. Box 5301
Jackson, MS 39216

Southern Mississippi Genealogical
Society
72 Boggy Hollow Rd.
Purvis, MS 39475

HISTORICAL SOCIETIES

Historical and Genealogical Association of Mississippi
618 Avalon Rd.
Jackson, MS 39206

CHURCH RECORDS

BAPTIST

Mississippi Baptist Historical
Society
Mississippi College Library
P.O. Box 51
Clinton, MS 39056

METHODIST

J. B. Cain Archives of Mississippi
Methodism
Millsaps-Wilson Library
Millsaps College
Jackson, MS 39210

MISSOURI

ARCHIVES AND LIBRARIES

National Archives —
Central Plains Region
2312 E. Bannister Rd.
Kansas City, MO 64131
Phone: (816) 926-6272
Fax: (816) 926-6272
e-mail:
archives@kansascity.nara.gov
Iowa, Kansas, Missouri, and Ne-
braska

American Family Records
Association Library
P.O. Box 15505
Kansas City, MO 64106
Phone: (816) 252-0950
Fax: (816) 252-0950

Kansas City Public Library
311 E. 12th St.
Kansas City, MO 64106-2454
Phone: (816) 221-2685
Fax: (816) 842-6839

St. Louis Public Library
History and Genealogy Department
1301 Olive St.
St. Louis, MO 63103
Phone: (314) 241-2288
Fax: (314) 241-3840

Missouri State Library
600 W. Main
P.O. Box 387
Jefferson City, MO 65102
Phone: (314) 751-3615
Fax: (314) 751-3612
mosl.sos.state.mo.us/lib-ser/lib-
ser.html

Office of the Secretary of State
Missouri State Archives

600 W. Main
P.O. Box 778
Jefferson City, MO 65102
Phone: (314) 751-3280
Fax: (314) 526-7333

GENEALOGICAL SOCIETIES

Genealogical Society of Central
Missouri
P.O. Box 26
Columbia, MO 65205

Heart of America Genealogical
Society and Library, Inc.
c/o Kansas City Public Library
311 E. 12th St.
Kansas City, MO 64106-2412

Jackson County Genealogical
Society
P.O. Box 2145
Independence, MO 64055

Livingston County Genealogical
Society
409 Clay St.
Chillicothe, MO 64601

Magic
c/o Bruce R. Watkins
Cultural Heritage Center
3700 Bleu Pkwy.
Kansas City, MO 64130

Mid-Continent Public Library
15616 E. Highway 24
Independence, MO 64050

Mid-America Computer
Genealogists
P.O. Box 410916
Kansas City, MO 64141-0916

Missouri State Genealogical Society
P.O. Box 833
Columbia, MO 65205-0833

Northwest Missouri Genealogical
Society
P.O. Box 382
St. Joseph, MO 64502-0382

Ozarks Genealogical Society, Inc.
P.O. Box 3494 G.S.
Springfield, MO 65808-3494

Platte County Genealogical Society
P.O. Box 103
Platte City, MO 64079

Ray County Genealogical
Association
901 W. Royle
Richmond, MO 64085

St. Louis Genealogical Society
9011 Manchester Rd., Suite 3
St. Louis, MO 63144-2643

HISTORICAL SOCIETIES

Missouri Historical Society
Research Library and Archives
Jefferson Memorial Building
Forest Park
St. Louis, MO 63112-1099
Phone: (314) 361-1424

State Historical Society of Missouri
Library
1020 Lowrey St.
Columbia, MO 65201-7298
Phone: (573) 882-7083
Fax: (573) 884-4956

CHURCH RECORDS

BAPTIST

Missouri Baptist Historical
Commission
William Jewell College
Liberty, MO 64068

METHODIST

United Methodist Historical
Collection (Missouri West)
Central Methodist College Library
Fayette, MO 65248

Centenary United Methodist
Church (Missouri East)
55 Plaza Square
16th & Pine Sts.
St. Louis, MO 63103

ROMAN CATHOLIC

Archives of the Archdiocese of
St. Louis
4445 Lindell Blvd.
St. Louis, MO 63108a

ETHNIC RESOURCES

AFRICAN-AMERICAN

Western Historical Manuscript
Collection, St. Louis
University of Missouri, St. Louis
Thomas Jefferson Library
8001 Natural Bridge Rd.
St. Louis, MO 63121

Western Historical Manuscript
Collection, Columbia
University of Missouri, Columbia
23 Ellis Library

Columbia, MO 65201
Phone: (314) 882-6028

MONTANA

ARCHIVES AND LIBRARIES

National Archives —
Rocky Mountain Region
Bldg. 48, Denver Federal Center
P.O. Box 25307
Denver, CO 80225
Phone: (303) 236-0817
Fax: (303) 236-9354
e-mail: archives@denver.nara.gov
Colorado, Montana, North Dakota,
South Dakota, Utah, and Wyoming

Montana State University-Bozeman
Renne Library
Bozeman, MT 59717-0332
Phone: (406) 994-3119
Fax: (406) 994-2851

University of Montana
Mansfield Library
Missoula, MT 59812
Phone: (406) 243-6860
Fax: (406) 243-2060

Montana Historical Society
Library and Archives
225 N. Roberts St.
P.O. Box 201201
Helena, MT 59620-1201

Montana State Library
1515 E. Sixth Ave.
Helena, MT 59620-1800
Phone: (406) 444-3115
Fax: (406) 444-5612
nris.msl.mt.gov/library/lib.htm

GENEALOGICAL SOCIETIES

Bitterroot Genealogical Society
Hamilton, MT 59840

Montana State Genealogical Society
P.O. Box 555
Chester, MT 59522

Gallatin Genealogical Society
Bozeman, MT

Great Falls Genealogy Society
Paris Gibson Square
1400 First Ave. N., Rm. 30
Great Falls, MT 59401-3299

Western Montana Genealogical
Society
Missoula, MT 59806

Yellowstone Genealogical Forum
c/o Parmly Billings Library
510 N. Broadway
Billings, MT 59101

HISTORICAL SOCIETIES

Montana Historical Society
225 N. Roberts St.
P.O. Box 201201
Helena, MT 59620
Phone: (406) 444-2681
Fax: (406) 444-2696

CHURCH RECORDS

METHODIST

Montana Methodist Historical
Society
Paul M. Adams Memorial Library
Rocky Mountain College

1511 Poly Dr.
Billings, MT 59102

ROMAN CATHOLIC

Archives of the Diocese of
Great Falls
121 23rd St. S.
P.O. Box 1399
Great Falls, MT 59403

Historian Archivist
Diocese of Helena
515 N. Ewing
P.O. Box 1729
Helena, MT 59624

NEBRASKA

ARCHIVES AND LIBRARIES

Nebraska State Historical Society
Library
Division of Library-Archives
1500 R St.
P.O. Box 82554
Lincoln, NE 68501
Phone: (402) 471-4751
Fax: (402) 471-3100

Nebraska DAR Library
202 W. 4th St.
Alliance, NE 69301

GENEALOGICAL SOCIETIES

National Archives —
Central Plains Region
2312 E. Bannister Rd.
Kansas City, MO 64131
Phone: (816) 926-6272
Fax: (816) 926-6272
e-mail: rchives@kansascity.nara.gov
Iowa, Kansas, Missouri, and Nebraska

Fort Kearny Genealogical Society
P.O. Box 22
Kearney, NE 68847

Greater Omaha Genealogical
Society
P.O. Box 4011
Omaha, NE 68104-0011

Lincoln-Lancaster Genealogical
Society
P.O. Box 30055
Lincoln, NE 68503-0055

Nebraska State Genealogical
Society
P.O. Box 5608
Lincoln, NE 68505
Phone: (402) 371-3468

North Platte Genealogical Society
P.O. Box 1452
North Platte, NE 69103

Prairie Pioneer Genealogical
Society, Inc.
P.O. Box 1122
Grand Island, NE 68802

HISTORICAL SOCIETIES

Nebraska State Historical Society
Department of Reference Resouces
1500 R St.
P.O. Box 82554
Lincoln, NE 68501
Phone: (402) 471-4771
Fax: (402) 471-3100

Mari Sandoz High Plains Heritage
Center
Chadron State College
Chadron, NE 69337
Phone: (308) 432-6361

CHURCH RECORDS

LUTHERAN

Archives of the Nebraska Synod
Ste. 204
124 S. 24th St.
Omaha, NE 68102

METHODIST

Historical Center Nebraska
Conference Depository
Lucas Library Building
Nebraska Wesleyan University
Lincoln, NE 68504

ROMAN CATHOLIC

Chancery Office
Archdiocese of Omaha
100 N. 62 St.
Omaha, NE 68132

ETHNIC RESOURCES

AFRICAN-AMERICAN

Great Plains Black Museum Library
2213 Lake St.
Omaha, NE 68110
Phone: (402) 345-2212

GERMAN

American Historical Society of
Germans from Russia
631 D St.
Lincoln, NE 68502-1199

NEVADA

ARCHIVES AND LIBRARIES

National Archives —
Pacific Southwest Region
24000 Avila Rd.
Laguna Niguel, CA 92677-6719
Phone: (714) 360-2641
Fax: (714) 360-2644
e-mail: archives@laguna.nara.gov
Arizona; southern California; and
Clark County, Nevada

National Archives —
Pacific Sierra Region
1000 Commodore D.
San Bruno, CA 94066
Phone: (415) 876-9009
Fax: (415) 876-9233
e-mail: archives@sanbruno.nara.gov
California except southern California, Hawaii, Nevada except Clark
County, American Samoa, and
Guam

Nevada State Library and Archives
100 Stewart St.
Carson City, NV 89710
Phone: (702) 687-5160
Fax: (702) 687-8311

University of Nevada — Reno
Getchell Library
Reno, NV 89557-0044
Phone: (702)784-6533
Fax: (702) 784-1751

GENEALOGICAL SOCIETIES

Clark County Genealogical Society
P.O. Box 1929
Las Vegas, NV 89125-1929

Nevada State Genealogical Society
P.O. Box 20666
Reno, NV 89515-0066

HISTORICAL SOCIETIES

Nevada Historical Society Library
1650 N. Virginia St.
Reno, NV 89503
Phone: (702) 688-1190
Fax: (702) 688-2917

Nevada State Museum and Historical Society
700 Twin Lakes Dr.
State Mall Complex
Las Vegas, NV 89107
Phone: (702) 486-5205

CHURCH RECORDS

EPISCOPAL

The Nevada Historical Society
1650 N. Virginia St.
Reno, NV 89503

ROMAN CATHOLIC

Diocese of Reno-Las Vegas
Chancery Office
515 Court St.
P.O. Box 1211
Reno, NV 89504

NEW HAMPSHIRE

ARCHIVES AND LIBRARIES

National Archives —
New England Region
380 Trapelo Rd.
Waltham, MA 02154

Phone:617-647-8100
Fax: (617) 647-8460
e-mail: Archives@waltham.nara.gov
Connecticut, Maine, Massachusetts, New Hampshire, Rhode Island, and Vermont

State of New Hampshire
Department of State
New Hampshire Records and
Archives Library
71 S. Fruit St.
Concord, NH 03301-2410
Phone: (603) 271-2236
Fax: (603) 271-2272

New Hampshire State Library
20 Park St.
Concord, NH 03301-6314
Phone: (603) 271-2392
Fax: (603) 271-2205

GENEALOGICAL SOCIETIES

New Hampshire Society of Geneal-
ogists
P.O. Box 633
Exeter, NH 03833
Phone: (603) 432-8137

HISTORICAL SOCIETIES

Association of Historical Societies
of New Hampshire
Maple St.
Plaistow, NH 03865
New Hampshire Historical Society
30 Park St.
Concord, NH 03301
Phone: (603)225-3381

CHURCH RECORDS

BAPTIST

American Baptist Churches of New
Hampshire
89 N. State St.
Concord, NH 03301

CONGREGATIONAL

New Hampshire Congregational
Fellowship
105 Portsmouth Ave., Apt. 29
Exeter, NH 03833

METHODIST

United Methodist Church
Fountain Square
P.O. Box 505
Contoocook, NH 03229

ROMAN CATHOLIC

Chancery Office
Diocese of Manchester
153 Ash St.
P.O. Box 310
Manchester, NH 03105

NEW JERSEY

ARCHIVES AND LIBRARIES

National Archives —
Northeast Region
201 Varick St.
New York, NY 10014
Phone: (212) 337-1300
Fax: (212) 337-1306
e-mail: archives@newyork.nara.gov
New York, New Jersey, Puerto Rico,
and the Virgin Islands

Department of Special Collections
and Archives
Archibald Stevens Alexander Li-
brary
Rutgers University
169 College Ave.
New Brunswick, NJ 08903
Phone: (908) 932-7505
Fax: (908) 932-7637

New Jersey Reference Division
Newark Public Library
5 Washington St.
P.O. Box 630
Newark, NJ 07101-0630
Phone: (201) 733-7800
Fax: (201) 733-5648

New Jersey State Archives
CN 307, 2300 Stuyvesant Ave.
Trenton, NJ 08625
Phone: (609)530-3203
Fax: (609) 530-6121

New Jersey State Library
History and Genealogy Unit
185 W. State St.
CN 520
Trenton, NJ 08625-0520
Phone: (609) 292-6200
Fax: (609) 984-7900

New Jersey State Library
Department of Education
185 W. State St.
Trenton, NJ 08625
Phone: (609) 292-6200 or 6220
Fax: (609) 695-0151

Department of State
New Jersey State Archives
185 W. State St.
Trenton, NJ 08625-0520
Phone: (609) 292-6274

GENEALOGICAL SOCIETIES

Bunker Family Association
9 Somerset Rd.
Turnersville, NJ 08012

Genealogical Society of Bergen
County
P.O. Box 432
Midland Park, NJ 07432

Genealogical Society of New Jersey
P.O. Box 1291
New Brunswick, NJ 08903-1291

Genealogical Society of the West-
fields
550 E. Broad St.
Westfield, NJ 07090

Monmouth County Genealogy Club
Monmouth County Historical Association
70 Court St.
Freehold, NJ 07728

Morris Area Genealogy Society
P.O. Box 105
Convent Station, NJ 07961

The Genealogical Society of
New Jersey
P.O. Box 1291
New Brunswick, NJ 08903-1291

HISTORICAL SOCIETIES

Gloucester County Historical
Society Library
17 Hunter St.
P.O. Box 409
Woodbury, NJ 08096

New Jersey Historical Society
Library
230 Broadway
Newark, NJ 07104
Phone: (201) 483-393

CHURCH RECORDS

DUTCH REFORMED

Commission on History, Reformed
Church in America
New Brunswick Theological Semi-
nary
Gardner A. Sage Library
21 Seminary Place
New Brunswick, NJ 08901

EPISCOPAL

Diocesan House of the Episcopal
Church
808 W. State St.
Trenton, NJ 08618

METHODIST

United Methodist Church
Commission on Archives and
History
Northern New Jersey Conference
Drew University Library
36 Madison Ave.
P.O. Box 127
Madison, NJ 07940
Phone: (201) 822-2787
Fax: (201) 408-3909

United Methodist Church
Commission on Archives and
History
Southern New Jersey Conference
The Meckler Library
Pennington School

112 W. Delaware Ave.
Pennington, NJ 08534

ROMAN CATHOLIC

University Archives
Seton Hall University
South Orange Ave.
South Orange, NJ 07079

ETHNIC RESOURCES

AFRICAN-AMERICAN

Danforth Memorial Library
250 Broadway
Paterson, NJ 07501
Phone: (201) 357-3000
Fax: (201) 881-8338

Afro-American Historical and
Genealogical Society, New Jersey
1841 Kennedy Blvd.
Jersey City, NJ 07305

New Jersey Chapter/Afro-American
Historical and Genealogical Society
c/o Afro-American Historical Society Museum
1841 Kennedy Blvd., 2nd Floor
Jersey City, NJ 07305

JEWISH

Central Jersey Jewish Archives
Jewish Historical Society of Central
Jersey
Central New Jersey Home for the
Aged
380 DeMott Lane
Somerset, NJ 08873

NEW MEXICO

ARCHIVES AND LIBRARIES

National Archives —
Southwest Region
501 W. Felix St., P.O. Box 6216
Fort Worth, TX 76115
Phone: (817) 334-5525
Fax: (817) 334-5621
e-mail: archives@ftworth.nara.gov
Arkansas, Louisiana, New Mexico,
Oklahoma, and Texas

Albuquerque-Bernalillo County
Public Library System
501 Copper Ave. NW
Albuquerque, NM 87102
Phone: (505) 768-5100
Fax: (505) 768-5191

Museum of New Mexico History
Library
110 Washington Ave.
P.O. Box 2087
Santa Fe, NM 87504-2087
Phone: (505) 827-6470
Fax: (505) 827-6427

New Mexico Records and Archives
404 Montezuma Ave.
Santa Fe, NM 87503
Phone: (505) 827-7332
Fax: (505) 827-7331

New Mexico State Library
325 Don Gaspar
Sante Fe, NM 87501-2777
Phone: (505) 827-3800
Fax: (505) 827-3888

University of New Mexico Library
Albuquerque, NM 87131
Phone: (505) 277-4241
Fax: (505) 277-6019

GENEALOGICAL SOCIETIES

Alamogordo Genealogical Society
P.O. Box 246
La Luz, NM 88337

Eddy County Genealogy Society
P.O. Box 803
Carlsbad, NM 88220

Eubank Family History Library
Albuquerque, NM

Genealogy Club of the Albuquerque
Public Library
423 Central Ave. NE
Albuquerque, NM 87102

Los Alamos Family History Society
P.O. Box 900
Los Alamos, NM 87544-0900

New Mexico Genealogical Society
P.O. Box 8283
Albuquerque, NM 87198-8283

Southern New Mexico Genealogical
Society
P.O. Box 2563
Las Cruces, NM 88004-2563

HISTORICAL SOCIETIES

Historical Society of New Mexico
P.O. Box 5819
Santa Fe, NM 87502

Historical Society of New Mexico
P.O. Box 4638
Santa Fe, NM 87501

History Library Museum of New
Mexico
Palace of the Governors
Santa Fe, NM 87501

CHURCH RECORDS

ROMAN CATHOLIC

Archdiocese of Santa Fe
202 Morningside Dr. SE
Albuquerque, NM 87108

Diocese of Gallup
711 S. Puerco Dr.
P.O. Box 1338
Gallup, NM 87301

Diocese of Las Cruces
1280 Med Park
P.O. Box 16318
Las Cruces, NM 88004

ETHNIC RESOURCES

HISPANIC

El Centro de la Familia
2633 Granite NW
Albuquerque, NM 87104

NEW YORK

ARCHIVES AND LIBRARIES

National Archives —
Northeast Region
201 Varick St.
New York, NY 10014
Phone: (212) 337-1300
Fax: (212) 337-1306
e-mail: archives@newyork.nara.gov
New York, New Jersey, Puerto Rico,
and the Virgin Islands

Columbia University
East Asian Library
305 M Kent

New York, NY 10027
Phone: (212) 854-1508

Cornell University Library
201 Olin Library
Ithaca, NY 14853-5301
Phone: (607) 255-4144
Fax: (607) 255-9346

New York City Department of
Records and Information Services
Municipal Archives
Division of Old Records
31 Chambers St., Rm. 103
New York, NY 10007

New York City Public Library
Local History and Genealogy
Division
Fifth Ave. & 42nd St.
New York, NY 10027
Phone: (212) 930-0828
www.nypl.org/research/chss/lhg/ge-
nea.html

The New York State Library
Cultural Education Center
Empire State Plaza
Albany, NY 12230
Phone: (518) 474-5930
Fax: (518) 474-2718

GENEALOGICAL SOCIETIES

Central New York Genealogical
Society
P.O. Box 104, Colvin Station
Syracuse, NY 13205

Chautauqua County Genealogical
Society
P.O. Box 404
Fredonia, NY 14063

Dutchess County Genealogical
Society
P.O. Box 708
Poughkeepsie, NY 12603

Kodak Genealogical Society
Building 28, Kodak Park
Rochester, NY 14652-3211

NASSAU Genealogy Society
c/o Suzanne McVetty
15 Titus Ave.
Carle Place, NY 11514-1325

New York Genealogical and
Biographical Society
122 E. 58th St., 4th Floor
New York, NY 10022-1939
Phone: (212) 755-8532
Fax: (212) 754-4218

New York State Council of
Genealogical Organizations
P.O. Box 2593
Syracuse, NY 13220-2593

Rochester Genealogical Society
1346 Creek St.
Webster, NY 14580-2237

Seeley Genealogical Society
RR 1 Box 314 B Vaughn Rd.
Hudson Falls, NY 12839

Sumner Family Association
62 Sandbury Dr.
Pittsford, NY 14534-2636

Westchester County Genealogical
Society
P.O. Box 518
White Plains, NY 10603

Western New York Genealogical
Society

P.O. Box 338
Hamburg, NY 14075-0338

HISTORICAL SOCIETIES

Brooklyn Historical Society
128 Pierrepont St.
Brooklyn, NY 12201

Greater Ridgewood Historical
Society
1820 Flushing Ave.
Ridgewood, NY 11385-1041

Huntington Historical Society
(Genealogy Workshop)
209 Main St.
Huntington, NY 11743-6993

New York Historical Society
170 Central Park West
New York, NY 10024-5194
Phone: (212)873-3400

CHURCH RECORDS

BAPTIST

American Baptist Historical Society
Samuel Colgate Baptist Historical
Library
Colgate-Rochester Divinity School
Ambrose Swasey Library
1100 Goodman St.
Rochester, NY 14620

DUTCH REFORMED

The Holland Society of New York
Library
122 E. 58th St.
New York, NY 10022

EPISCOPAL

Diocese of New York
1047 Amsterdam Ave.
New York, NY 10025

LUTHERAN

Library of the National Lutheran
Council
50 Madison Ave.
New York, NY 10010

Evangelical Lutheran Church in
America
Metropolitan New York Synod
360 Park Ave. S.
New York, NY 10010

Lutheran Church-Missouri Synod
Atlantic District
315 Park Ave. S., Rm. 1920
New York, NY 10010

ROMAN CATHOLIC

Archdiocese of New York
1011 First Ave.
New York, NY 10022

SOCIETY OF FRIENDS

New York Yearly Meeting Archives
Haviland Records Room
15 Rutherford Place
New York, NY 10003

ETHNIC RESOURCES

AFRICAN-AMERICAN

New York Public Library
The Research Libraries
Schomberg Center for Research in
Black Culture
515 Malcom X Blvd.

New York, NY 10037-1801
Phone: (212) 491-2200
Fax: (212) 491-6760

Staten Island Institute of Arts and
Sciences Archives and Library
75 Stuyvesant Place
Staten Island, NY 10301
Phone: (718) 727-1135
Fax: (718)273-5683

University of Rochester
Government Documents and Mi-
crotext Center
Rush Rhees Library
Rochester, NY 14627
Phone: (716) 275-4484
Fax: (716) 473-1906

African-American Cultural Center
350 Masten Ave.
Buffalo, NY 14209

Afro-American Historical and Ge-
nealogical Society, Greater New
York
P.O. Box 022340
Brooklyn, NY 11202

Afro-American Historical Associa-
tion of the Niagra
P.O. Box 1663
Buffalo, NY 14216

ASIAN

University of Rochester
Asia Library
Rush Rhees Library
River Campus
Rochester, NY 14627
Phone: (716) 275-4489

China Institute in America
125 E. 65th St.
New York, NY 10021

IRISH

The Irish Family History
Forum, Inc.
P.O. Box 351
Rockville Centre, NY 11571-0351

ITALIAN

Italian Genealogical Group of
New York
7 Grayton Dr.
Dix Hills, NY 11746

JEWISH

Jewish Genealogical Society of
Long Island
37 Westcliff Dr.
Dix Hills, NY 11746

Jewish Genealogical Society, Inc.
P.O. Box 6398
New York, NY 10128

Hebrew Immigrant Aid Society
(HIAS)
200 Park Ave. S.
New York, NY 10003

New York City Public Library
Jewish Division
Fifth Ave. at 42nd St.
New York, NY 10018

NATIVE AMERICAN

Huntington Free Library National
Museum of the American Indian
9 Westchester Sq.
Bronx, NY 10461
Phone: (212) 829-7770

NORTH CAROLINA

ARCHIVES AND LIBRARIES

National Archives —
Southeast Region
1557 St. Joseph Ave.
East Point, GA 30344
Phone: (404) 763-7477
Fax: (404)763-7033
e-mail: archives@atlanta.nara.gov
Alabama, Florida, Georgia, Kentucky, Mississippi, North Carolina, South Carolina, and Tennessee

Duke University
William R. Perkins Library
Manuscript Department
Durham, NC 27708-0190
Phone: (919) 660-5800
Fax: (919) 684-2855

North Carolina State Archives
Department of Cultural Resources
109 E. Jones St., Rm. 305
Raleigh, NC 276010-2807
Phone: (919) 733-7305
Fax: (919) 733-5679

State Library of North Carolina
109 E. Jones St.
Raleigh, NC 27601-2807
Phone: (919) 733-2570
Fax: (919) 733-8748

University of North Carolina at Chapel Hill
Walter Royal Davis Library
CB 3900
Chapel Hill, NC 27514-8890
Phone: (919) 962-1301
Fax: (919) 962-4451

GENEALOGICAL SOCIETIES

Council of Genealogy Columnists
c/o Steve Smith, So. Queries
P.O. Box 726
Durham, NC 27702-0726

Durham-Orange Genealogical Society
P.O. Box 4703
Chapel Hill, NC 27515-4703

Forsyth County Genealogical Society
P.O. Box 5715
Winston-Salem, NC 27113-5715

Guilford County Genealogical Society
c/o High Point Public Library
P.O. Box 2530
High Point, NC 27261-2530

Haywood County Genealogical Society, Inc.
P.O. Box 1331
Waynesville, NC 28786

The Heritage Room
(Carolinas Genealogical Society)
P.O. Box 397
Monroe, NC 28111

Johnson County Genealogical Society
c/o Public Library of Johnson County
Smithfield, NC 27577

Kinfolk Trackers Genealogical Society
Route 65 Box 8-A
Arapahoe, NC 28510

North Carolina Genealogical Society

P.O. Box 1492
Raleigh, NC 27602

Old Buncombe County Genealogical Society
Box 2122 Insbruck Mall #22
Asheville, NC 28805

Wake County Genealogical Society
Raleigh, NC

Wilkes Genealogical Society
P.O. Box 1629
North Wilkesboro, NC 28659

HISTORICAL SOCIETIES

North Carolina Society of County and Local Historians
1209 Hill St.
Greensboro, NC 27408

CHURCH RECORDS

BAPTIST

Baptist Historical Collection
Wake Forest University
P.O. Box 7777
Winston-Salem, NC 27109

Free Will Baptist Collections
Moye Library
Mount Olive College
Mount Olive, NC 28365

LUTHERAN

Archives of the North Carolina Synod
P.O. Box 2049
Salisbury, NC 28144

METHODIST

Western NC Conference Depository
Shamrock Dr., Box 12005
Charlotte, NC 28205

MORAVIAN

Moravian Archives
Drawer M, Salem Station
Winston-Salem, NC 27108

PRESBYTERIAN

Presbyterian Historical Foundation
P.O. Box 847
Montreat, NC 27410

SOCIETY OF FRIENDS

Quaker Collections
Guilford College Library
Greensboro, NC 27410

ETHNIC RESOURCES

AFRICAN-AMERICAN

Livingstone College
Andrew Carnegie Library
701 W. Monroe St.
Salisbury, NC 28144
Phone: (704) 638-5630
Fax: (704) 638-5646

Afro-American Genealogical
Society, North Carolina
P.O. Box 26785
Raleigh, NC 27611-6785

North Carolina African-American
Heritage Society
P.O. Box 26334
Raleigh, NC 27611

NORTH DAKOTA

ARCHIVES AND LIBRARIES

National Archives —
Rocky Mountain Region
Building 48, Denver Federal Center
P.O. Box 25307
Denver, CO 80225
Phone: (303) 236-0817
Fax: (303) 236-9354
e-mail: archives@denver.nara.gov
Colorado, Montana, North Dakota,
South Dakota, Utah, and Wyoming

North Dakota State University Library
1301 12th Ave. N.
P.O. Box 5599

University of North Dakota
Chester Fritz Library
Box 9000
Grand Forks, ND 58202-9000
Phone: (701) 777-2617
Fax: (701) 777-3319

State Historical Society of North
Dakota
State Archives and Historical
Research Library
Heritage Center
Capitol Grounds
612 E. Boulevard Ave.
Bismarck, ND 58505

North Dakota State Library
Liberty Memorial Building
604 E. Boulevard Ave.
Bismarck, ND 58505-0800
Phone: (701) 328-2490
Fax: (701) 328-2040

GENEALOGICAL SOCIETIES

Bismarck-Mandan Historical and
Genealogical Society, Inc.
P.O. Box 485
Bismark, ND 58502-0485

Red River Valley Genealogical
Society
P.O. Box 9284
Fargo, ND 58106

Williams County Genealogical
Society
c/o Fay Lufkin Halvorsen
906 16th Ave. W.
Williston, ND 58801

HISTORICAL SOCIETIES

State Historical Society of North
Dakota
North Dakota Heritage Center
612 E. Boulevard Ave.
Bismarck, ND 58505-0830
Phone: (701) 224-2668
Fax: (701) 224-3000

CHURCH RECORDS

LUTHERAN

North Dakota State University
Library
North Dakota Institute for Regional
Studies
Fargo, ND 58102

METHODIST

United Methodist Church
North Dakota Conference
Wesley United Methodist Church
1600 4th Ave. N.
Grand Forks, ND 58201

ROMAN CATHOLIC

Diocese of Bismarck Archives
Box 1137
Bismarck, ND 58502

Diocese of Fargo Archives
1310 Broadway
Box 1750
Fargo, ND 58107

ETHNIC RESOURCES

GERMAN

Germans from Russia Heritage
Society
1008 E. Central Ave.
Bismarck, ND 58501

OHIO

ARCHIVES AND LIBRARIES

National Archives —
Great Lakes Region
7358 S. Pulaski Rd.
Chicago, IL 60629
Phone: (312) 581-7816
Fax: (312) 353-1294
e-mail: archives@chicago.nara.gov
Illinois, Indiana, Michigan, Minnesota, Ohio, and Wisconsin

Cleveland Public Library
325 Superior Ave.
Cleveland, OH 44114-1271
Phone: (216) 623-2800
Fax: (216) 623-7015

State Library of Ohio
Genealogical Division
65 S. Front St., Rm. 510
Columbus, OH 43215-4163

Phone: (614) 644-7061
Fax: (614) 466-3584

GENEALOGICAL SOCIETIES

Cuyahoga Valley Chapter-OGS
Brecksville, OH 44141

East Cuyahoga County
Genealogical Society
c/o Jim Walton
2696 Edgehill Rd.
Cleveland Heights, OH 44106

Franklin County Genealogical
Society
560 W. Brood St.
Columbus, OH

Franklin County Historical Society
Ohio State Library
Front St.
Columbus, OH

Ganst Museum
Greenville, OH 45331
Genealogy by Computer Society
c/o Ralph Trease, Sr.
11 Bronson Place
Toledo, OH 43608

Greater Cleveland Genealogical
Society
P.O. Box 40254
Cleveland, OH 44140-0254

Hamilton County Chapter of OGS
P.O. Box 15851
Cincinnati, OH 45215

Lorain County Chapter of Ohio
Genealogical Society
P.O. Box 865
Elyria, OH 44036-0865

Lucas County Chapter-OGS
325 N. Michigan St.
Toledo, OH 43624-1614

Mahoning County Chapter-OGS
P.O. Box 9333
Youngstown, OH 44513-9333

Ohio Genealogical Society
34 Sturges Ave.
P.O. Box 2625
Mansfield, OH 44906-0625
Phone: (419) 522-9077
Fax: (419) 522-0224

Pinkham Family History Society
1867 Bedford Rd.
Columbus, OH 43212

Washington County Chapter-OGS
P.O. Box 2174
Marietta, OH 45750

HISTORICAL SOCIETIES

Ohio Historical Society
Archives Library
Columbus, OH 43211-2497
Phone: (614) 297-2510
Fax: (614) 297-2546

Western Reserve Historical Society
10825 E. Boulevard
Cleveland, OH 44106

CHURCH RECORDS

METHODIST

Methodist Historical Commission
Ohio Wesleyan University
Delaware, OH 43015

United Methodist Church
601 W. Riverview Ave.
Dayton, OH 45406

ROMAN CATHOLIC

Archdiocese of Cincinnati
Chancery Office
100 E. Eighth St.
Cincinnati, OH 45202

Diocese of Columbus
Chancery Office
198 E. Broad St.
Columbus, OH 43215

Diocese of Cleveland
Chancery Building
1027 Superior Ave.
Cleveland, OH 44114

Diocese of Steubenville
422 Washington St.
P.O. Box 969
Steubenville, OH 43952

Diocese of Toledo
Chancery
2544 Parkwood Ave.
Toledo, OH 43610

Diocese of Youngstown
Chancery Office
144 W. Wood St.
Youngstown, OH 44503

SOCIETY OF FRIENDS

Historical Committee of the Yearly
Meeting
Route 2
Barnesville, OH 43713

ETHNIC RESOURCES

AFRICAN-AMERICAN

Afro-American Genealogical
Society, Cleveland

P.O. Box 200382
Cleveland, OH 44120

Afro-American Family History
Association
8716 Harkness Rd.
Cleveland, OH 44106

Cleveland Public Library
History and Geography Department
325 Superior Ave.
Cleveland, OH 44114-1271
Phone: (216) 623-2864

Ohio State University
Black Studies Library
1858 Neil Ave. Mall
Columbus, OH 43210-1286
Phone: (614) 292-2393
Fax: (614) 292-7859

Western Reserve Historical Society
Library
10825 E. Boulevard
Cleveland, OH 44106
Phone: (216) 721-5722
Fax: (216) 721-0645

Wilberforce University
Rembert Stokes Learning Center
Archives and Special Collections
Wilberforce, OH 45384-1003
Phone: (513) 376-2911

HISPANIC

Fabela Lozano Solis Villanueva
Genealogy Record
7747 Wildwood Rd.
Findlay, OH 45840-9538
Phone: (419) 422-1733

JEWISH

Jewish Genealogy Society of
Cleveland

996 Eastlawn Dr.
Highland Heights, OH 44143

OKLAHOMA

ARCHIVES AND LIBRARIES

National Archives —
Southwest Region
501 W. Felix St., P.O. Box 6216
Fort Worth, TX 76115
Phone: (817) 334-5525
Fax: (817) 334-5621
e-mail: archives@ftworth.nara.gov
Arkansas, Louisiana, New Mexico,
Oklahoma, and Texas

Oklahoma Department of Libraries
200 NE 18th St.
Oklahoma City, OK 73105-3298
Phone: (405) 521-2502
Fax: (405) 525-7804

University of Oklahoma-University
Libraries
401 W. Brooks
Norman, OK 73019
Phone: (405) 325-2611
Fax: (405) 325-7550

GENEALOGICAL SOCIETIES

Canadian County Genealogical
Society
P.O. Box 866
El Reno, OK 73036

Oklahoma Genealogical Society
P.O. Box 12986
Oklahoma City, OK 73157-2986

Oklahoma Genealogical Society
P.O. Box 314
Oklahoma City, OK 73101

Ottawa County Oklahoma
Genealogical Society
P.O. Box 1383
Miami, OK 74354

Southwest Oklahoma Genealogical
Society
P.O. Box 148
Lawton, OK 73502-0148

Tulsa Genealogy Society
Tulsa, OK

HISTORICAL SOCIETIES

Oklahoma Historical Society
Archives and Manuscript Division
Historical Building
2100 N. Lincoln Blvd.
Oklahoma City, OK 73105-4997
Phone: (405) 522-5209
Fax: (405) 521-2492

Thomas Gilcrease Institute of
American History and Art
1400 Gilcrease Museum Rd.
Tulsa, OK 74127
Phone: (918) 596-2700
Fax: (918) 596-2770

Museum of the Great Plains
601 Ferris
P.O. Box 68
Lawton, OK 73502
Phone: (405) 581-3460
Fax: (405) 581-3460

CHURCH RECORDS

METHODIST

United Methodist Church
Box 1138
Briston, OK 74010

ROMAN CATHOLIC

Chancery Office
1521 N. Hudson
Oklahoma City, OK 63103

ETHNIC RESOURCES

AFRICAN-AMERICAN

Langston University
Melvin B. Tolson Black Heritage
Center
Langston, OK 73050

OREGON

ARCHIVES AND LIBRARIES

National Archives —
Pacific Northwest Region
6125 Sand Point Way NE
Seattle, WA 98115
Phone: (206) 526-6507
Fax: (206) 526-4344
e-mail: archives@seattle.nara.gov
Idaho, Oregon, and Washington

Oregon State Archives
800 Summer St. NE
Salem, OR 97310
Phone: (503) 373-0701
Fax: (503) 373-0659

Oregon State Library
State Library Building
250 Winter St. NE
Salem, OR 97310-0640
Phone: (503) 378-4243
Fax: (503) 588-7119

University of Oregon Library
Eugene, OR 97403-1299
Phone: (503) 346-1567
Fax: (503) 346-3056

GENEALOGICAL SOCIETIES

The Belgian Researchers
62073 Fruitdale Lane
Le Grande, OR 97850-5312

Bend Genealogical Society
P.O. Box 8254
Bend, OR 97708

Columbia Gorge Genealogical
Society
c/o The Dalles Public Library
722 Court St.
The Dalles, OR 97058

Coos County Genealogical Society
Coos Bay, OR

Cottage Grove Genealogical Society
P.O. Box 388
Cottage Grove, OR 97424

Genealogical Council of Oregon,
Inc.
P.O. Box 15169
Portland, OR 97215

Genealogical Forum of Oregon,
Inc.
2130 SW 5th Ave. #220
Portland, OR 97201-4934

Genealogical Forum of Portland,
Oregon, Inc.
1410 SW Morrison St., Rm. 812
Portland, OR 97205
Phone: (503) 227-2398

Grants Pass Genealogical Society
P.O. Box 1834
Grants Pass, OR 97526
Lebanon Genealogical Society
626 2nd St.
Lebanon, OR 97355-2624

Oregon Genealogical Society
P.O. Box 10306
Eugene, OR 97440-2306
Phone: (503) 746-7924

Rogue Valley Genealogical Society
113 S. Central
Medford, OR 97501

Willamette Valley Genealogical
Society
P.O. Box 2083
Salem, OR

HISTORICAL SOCIETIES

Oregon Historical Society
1230 SW Park Ave.
Portland, OR 97205
Phone: (503) 222-1741

CHURCH RECORDS

BAPTIST

Linfield College Library
McMinnville, OR 97158

ROMAN CATHOLIC

Archdiocese of Portland in Oregon
Chancery Office
P.O. Box 351
Portland, OR 97207

PENNSYLVANIA

ARCHIVES AND LIBRARIES

National Archives—
Mid Atlantic Region
9th & Market Sts., Rm. 1350
Philadelphia, PA 19107
Phone: (215) 597-3000
Fax: (215) 597-2303
e-mail: archives@philarch.nara.gov
Delaware, Maryland, Pennsylvania,
Virginia, and West Virginia

State Library of Pennsylvania
Walnut St. & Commonwealth Ave.
P.O. Box 1601
Harrisburg, PA 17105
Phone: (717) 787-4440
Fax: (717) 783-2070

Pennsylvania State Archives
Third & Forster Sts.
P.O. Box 1026
Harrisburg, PA 17108-1026
Phone: (717) 787-2891
call or write before visiting

GENEALOGICAL SOCIETIES

Blair County Genealogical Society
P.O. Box 855
Altoona, PA 16603

Centre County Genealogical
Society
P.O. Box 1135
State College, PA 16804-1135

Cornerstone Genealogical Society
P.O. Box 547
Waynesburg, PA 15370

Genealogy Society of Pennsylvania
1300 Locust St.
Philadelphia, PA 19107

Lycoming County Genealogical
Society
P.O. Box 3625
Williamsport, PA 17701

North Hills Genealogists
c/o Northland Public Library
300 Cumberland Rd.
Pittsburgh, PA 15237-5455

South Central Pennsylvania
Genealogical Society, Inc.
P.O. Box 1824
York, PA 17405-1824

Warren County Genealogical
Society
6 Main St.
North Warren, PA 16365-4616

Western Pennsylvania Genealogical
Society
c/o Carnegie Library/Oakland
4400 Forbes Ave.
Pittsburgh, PA 15213

HISTORICAL SOCIETIES

Heritage Society of Pennsylvania
P.O. Box 146
Laughlintown, PA 15655

Historical Society of Pennsylvania
1300 Locust St.
Philadelphia, PA 19107
Phone: (215)545-0391

Historical Society of Pennsylvania/
Genealogical Society of
Pennsylvania
4338 Bigelow Blvd.
Pittsburgh, PA 15213

Historical Society of Western Pennsylvania and Western Pennsylvania Genealogical Society
4338 Bigelow Blvd.
P.O. Box 8530
Pittsburgh, PA 15220-0530

Pennsylvania Historical and Museum Commission
Bureau of Archives and History
P.O. Box 1026
Harrisburg, PA 17108-1026
Phone: (717) 783-3281

CHURCH RECORDS

BAPTIST

American Baptist Historical Society Archives
Box 851
Valley Forge, PA 19482-0851
Phone: (215) 768-2378

The Baptist Theological Seminary
City Line and Lancaster Ave.
Philadelphia, PA 19151

EPISCOPAL

Diocese of Pennsylvania
The History Committee
202 W. Rittenhouse Square
Philadelphia, PA 19103

LUTHERAN

A. R. Wentz Library
Lutheran Theological Seminary
Gettysburg, PA 17325

Lutheran Church Archives
Krauth Memorial Library
7301 Germantown Ave.
Philadelphia, PA 19119

METHODIST

The Historical Society of the Philadelphia Annual Conference
326 New St.
Philadelphia, PA 19106

PRESBYTERIAN

Presbyterian Church Department of History Library
425 Lombard St.
Philadelphia, PA 19147
Phone: (215) 627-1852
Fax: (215) 627-0509

Presbyterian Historical Society
United Presbyterian Church in the U.S.
425 Lombard St.
Philadelphia, PA 19147

REFORMED

Philip Schaff Library
Evangelical and Reformed Historical Library
555 W. James St.
Lancaster, PA 17603

ROMAN CATHOLIC

Archives of the American Catholic Historical Society of Philadelphia
St. Charles Borromeo Seminary
Overbrook
Philadelphia, PA 19151

SOCIETY OF FRIENDS

Friends Historical Library of Swarthmore College
Swarthmore College
Swarthmore, PA 19081

Quaker Collection
Haverford College Library
Haverford, PA 19041

ETHNIC RESOURCES

AFRICAN-AMERICAN

Historical Society of Pennsylvania Library
1300 Locust St.
Philadelphia, PA 19107
Phone: (215) 732-6201
Fax: (215) 732-2680

Leigh County Historical Society
Scott Andrew Trexler II Memorial Library
Old Court House
Fifth & Hamilton Sts.
Box 1548
Allentown, PA 18105
Phone: (610) 435-1072
Fax: (610) 435-9812

Lincoln University
Langston Hughes Memorial Library
Special Collections
Lincoln University, PA 19352-0999
Phone: (215) 932-8300
Fax: (215) 932-8317

Library Company of Philadelphia
1314 Locust St.
Philadelphia, PA 19107
Phone: (215) 546-3181
Fax: (215) 546-5167

Temple University
Charles L. Blockson Afro-American Historical Collection
Sullivan Hall, 1st Floor
Philadelphia, PA 19122
Phone: (215) 787-6632
Fax: (215) 204-5197

Afro-American Genealogical
Society, Western Pennsylvania
1307 Point View St.
Pittsburgh, PA 15206

African American Genealogy Group
P.O. Box 1798
Philadelphia, PA 19107
Phone: (215) 572-6063
Fax: (215) 885-7244

JEWISH

Jewish Genealogical Society of
Philadelphia
332 Harrison Ave.
Elkins Park, PA 19027-2662

Jewish Genealogical Society of
Pittsburgh
2131 Fifth Ave.
Pittsburgh, PA 15219

RHODE ISLAND

ARCHIVES AND LIBRARIES

National Archives —
New England Region
380 Trapelo Rd.
Waltham, MA 02154
Phone:617-647-8100
Fax: (617) 647-8460
e-mail: Archives@waltham.nara.gov
Connecticut, Maine, Massachu-
setts, New Hampshire, Rhode Is-
land, and Vermont

Rhode Island State Archives
337 Westminister St.
Providence, RI 02903-3302
Phone: (401) 277-2353
Fax: (401) 277-3199

Rhode Island State Library
State House
Room 208
Providence, RI 02903
Phone: (401) 277-2473
Fax: (401) 331-6430

GENEALOGICAL SOCIETIES

Rhode Island Genealogical Society
507 Clark's Row
Bristol, RI 02809-1481

Rhode Island Genealogical Society
P.O. Box 7618
Warwick, RI 02887-7618

HISTORICAL SOCIETIES

Rhode Island State Historical
Society
121 Hope St.
Providence, RI 02909
Phone: (401)331-8575

CHURCH RECORDS

ROMAN CATHOLIC

Diocese of Providence
Chancery Office
34 Fenner St.
Providence, RI 02903

SOCIETY OF FRIENDS

Archives of the New England Yearly
Meeting of Friends
Rhode Island Historical Society
121 Hope St.
Providence, RI 02906

ETHNIC RESOURCES

AFRICAN-AMERICAN

Rhode Island Black Heritage
Society
46 Aborn St.
Providence, RI 02903

ITALIAN

Italian Genealogical Society of
America
P.O. Box 8571
Cranston, RI 02920-8571

SOUTH CAROLINA

ARCHIVES AND LIBRARIES

National Archives —
Southeast Region
1557 St. Joseph Ave.
East Point, GA 30344
Phone: (404) 763-7477
Fax: (404)763-7033
e-mail: archives@atlanta.nara.gov
Alabama, Florida, Georgia, Ken-
tucky, Mississippi, North Carolina,
South Carolina, and Tennessee

South Carolina Department of
Archives and History
Capitol Station
P.O. Box 11669
Columbia, SC 29211-1669
Phone: (803) 734-8577
Fax: (803) 734-8820

South Carolina State Library
1500 Senate St.
P.O. Box 11469
Columbia, SC 29211
Phone: (803) 734-8666
Fax: (803) 734-8676

GENEALOGICAL SOCIETIES

Charleston Chapter SCGS
200 Ferry St.
Mt. Pleasant, SC 29464

Chester District Genealogical
Society
P.O. Box 336
Richburg, SC 29729

Laurens District Chapter SCGS
P.O. Box 1217
Laurens, SC 29360

Pinckney District Chapter SCGS
385 S. Spring St.
Spartanburg, SC 29301

The Orangeburg German-Swiss
Genealogical Society
P.O. Box 964
Orangeburg, SC 29116

River Hills Genealogists
74 Honeysuckle Woods
Lake Wylie, SC 29710

South Carolina Genealogical
Society
P.O. Box 16355
Greenville, SC 29606

South Carolina Genealogical
Society
P.O. Box 20266
Charleston, SC 294113-0266
Phone: (803) 766-1667

HISTORICAL SOCIETIES

Historical Center of York County
212 E. Jefferson St.
York, SC 29745

South Carolina Historical Society
100 Meeting St.
Charleston, SC 29401
Phone: (803) 723-3225

CHURCH RECORDS

BAPTIST

South Carolina Baptist Historical
Collection
James B. Duke Library
Poinsett Highway
Furman University
Greenville, SC 29613

METHODIST

South Carolina Methodist
Conference Archives
Sandor Teszler Library
Wofford College
N. Church St.
Spartanburg, SC 29301

ROMAN CATHOLIC

Charleston Diocesan Archives
119 Broad St.
P.O. Box 818
Charleston, SC 29402

SOUTH DAKOTA

ARCHIVES AND LIBRARIES

National Archives —
Rocky Mountain Region
Bldg. 48, Denver Federal Center
P.O. Box 25307
Denver, CO 80225
Phone: (303) 236-0817
Fax: (303) 236-9354
e-mail: archives@denver.nara.gov
Colorado, Montana, North Dakota,
South Dakota, Utah, and Wyoming

South Dakota Archives
Cultural Heritage Center
900 Governors Dr.
Pierre, SD 57501-2217
Phone: (605) 773-3804

South Dakota State Library
800 Governors Dr.
Pierre, SD 57501
Phone: (605) 773-3131
Fax: (605) 773-4950

GENEALOGICAL SOCIETIES

Sioux Valley Genealogical Society
200 W. Sixth St.
Sioux Falls, SD 57102-0302

South Dakota Genealogical Society
P.O. Box 490
Winner, SD 57580

South Dakota Genealogical Society
P.O. Box 1101
Pierre, SD 57501

HISTORICAL SOCIETIES

South Dakota Historical
Society/State Archives
900 Governors Dr.
Pierre, SD 57501-2217
Phone: (605) 773-3458
Fax: (605) 773-6041

South Dakota State Historical
Society
State Archives
900 Governors Dr.
Pierre, SD 57501-2217
Phone: (605) 773-3616
Fax: (605) 773-6041

CHURCH RECORDS

METHODIST

Historical Committee, SD
Conference
Dakota Wesleyan University
Mitchell, SD 57301

ROMAN CATHOLIC

Diocese of Rapid City
Chancery Office
606 Cathedral Dr.
P.O. Box 678
Rapid City, SD 57709

Diocese of Sioux Falls Archives
Catholic Chancery Office
423 N. Duluth Ave.
Box 5033
Sioux Falls, SD 57717

TENNESSEE

ARCHIVES AND LIBRARIES

National Archives —
Southeast Region
1557 St. Joseph Ave.
East Point, GA 30344
Phone: (404) 763-7477
Fax: (404)763-7033
e-mail: archives@atlanta.nara.gov
Alabama, Florida, Georgia, Kentucky, Mississippi, North Carolina,
South Carolina, and Tennessee

Tennessee State Library and
Archives
403 Seventh Ave. N.
Nashville, TN 37243-0312
Phone: (615) 741-2451
Fax: (615) 741-6471

GENEALOGICAL SOCIETIES

AAGHS of Tennessee
P.O. Box 17684
Nashville, TN 37217

Clan Dunbar, Inc.
224 Riverview Rd.
Townsend, TN 37882

East Tennessee User's Group
Genealogy SIG
c/o Dale Smelser
1211 Lindsey Dr.
Sevierville, TN 37876

Middle Tennessee Genealogical
Society
P.O. Box 190625
Nashville, TN 37219-0625

Tennessee Genealogical Society
P.O. Box 111249
Memphis, TN 38111-1249

Tennessee Genealogical Society
P.O. Box 12124
Memphis, TN 38112

HISTORICAL SOCIETIES

Dickson County Historical Society
County Courthouse
Charlotte, TN 37036

East Tennessee Historical Society
P.O. Box 1629
Knoxville, TN 37901

Tennessee Historical Commission
Conservation Department
701 Brdwy.
Nashville, TN 37203
Phone: (615)742-6717

Tennessee Historical Society
Ground Floor
War Memorial Building
300 Capital Blvd.
Nashville, TN 37243-0084
Phone: (615)242-1796

CHURCH RECORDS

BAPTIST

Southern Baptist Historical Library
and Archives
901 Commerce, Suite 200
Nashville, TN 37203

DISCIPLES OF CHRIST

Disciples of Christ Historical
Society
1101 Nineteenth Ave. S.
Nashville, TN 37212

METHODIST

Memphis Conference United
Methodist Archives
Luther L. Gobbel Library
Lambuth College
Lambuth Blvd.
Jackson, TN 38301

ETHNIC RESOURCES

AFRICAN-AMERICAN

Center for Southern Folklore
Archives
130 Beale St.
P.O. Box 226
Memphis, TN 38101
Phone: (901) 525-36A5
Fax: (901) 525-3945

Fisk University
Special Collections Department
Seventeenth at Jackson St.
Nashville, TN 37203
Phone: (615) 329-8646
Fax: (615) 329-9761

TEXAS

ARCHIVES AND LIBRARIES

National Archives —
Southwest Region
501 W. Felix St., P.O. Box 6216
Fort Worth, TX 76115
Phone: (817) 334-5525
Fax: (817) 334-5621
e-mail: archives@ftworth.nara.gov
Arkansas, Louisiana, New Mexico,
Oklahoma, and Texas

Texas State Archives Division
Lorenzo de Zavala State Archives

and Library Building
P.O. Box 12927
Austin, TX 78711-2927
Phone: (512) 463-5480
Fax: (512) 463-5436

Texas State Library
1201 Brazos
P.O. Box 12927
Austin, TX 78711
Phone: (512) 463-5460
Fax: (512) 463-5436

GENEALOGICAL SOCIETIES

Austin Genealogical Society
3101 Sweet Gum Cove
Austin, TX 78735

Bay Area Genealogy Study Club
914 Forest Lake
Seabrook, TX 77586

Baytown Genealogical Society
P.O. Box 2486
Baytown, TX 77522

Brazos Genealogical Society
c/o Janis Hunt
2605 Todd
Bryan, TX 77802

Clayton Library Friends
P.O. Box 271078
Houston, TX 77277-1078

Collin County Genealogical Society
P.O. Box 865052
Plano, TX 75086-5052

Dallas Genealogical Society
P.O. Box 12648
Dallas, TX 75225-0648

Denison Library Historical and Ge-

nealogical Society
RR Box 273C
Denison, TX 75020

East Texas Genealogical Society
Tyler Public Library
201 S. College
Tyler, TX 75702

El Paso Genealogical Society
501 N. Oregon St.
El Paso, TX 79901

Galveston County Genealogical So-
ciety
P.O. Box 1141
Galveston, TX 77550-1141

Garland Genealogical Society
P.O. Box 461882
Garland, TX 76046

Genealogical Institute of Texas, Inc.
P.O. Box 832856
Richardson, TX 75083-2856

Gentech, Inc.
P.O. Box 28021
Dallas, TX 75228-0021

Guadalupe County Genealogical
Society
707 E. College St.
Seguin, TX 78155

Hinchman Heritage Society
3883 Turtle Creek Blvd., Suite 1618
Dallas, TX 75319-4431

Hopkins County Genealogical Soci-
ety
P.O. Box 624
Sulphur Springs, TX 75483-0624

Houston Genealogical Forum
P.O. Box 271466

Houston, TX 77277-1466

Irving Genealogical Society
Irving, TX

Johnson County Genealogical
Society
P.O. Box 1256
Cleburne, TX 76033-1256

Kidwell Family Association
c/o Billy Dan Kidwell
2616 Janice Lane
Fort Worth, TX 76112

McAllen Genealogical Society
P.O. Box 4714
McAllen, TX 78502

Montgomery Genealogical and
Historical Society, Inc.
P.O. Box 867
Conroe, TX 77305-0867

NARFE Chapter 1320 Genealogy
Group
11327 Chaco Canyon
San Antonio, TX 78245-2808

NT/BNR Genealogy Club
MS D-311
P.O. Box 833871
Richardson, TX 75083-3871

Rockwall County Genealogical
Society
P.O. Box 471
Rockwall, TX 75087

San Antonio Genealogical and
Historical Society
P.O. Box 17461
San Antonio, TX 78217-0461

South Plains Genealogical Society
P.O. Box 6607
Lubbock, TX 79493

Texas Research Ramblers
c/o Mary Collin Cooper
740 Garden Acres
Bryan, TX 77802-4005

Texas State Genealogical Society
2507 Tannehill
Houston, TX 77008-3052

Texas State Genealogical Society
Route 4 Box 56
Sulphur Springs, TX 75482

Tip-O'-Texas Genealogical Society
Harlingen Public Library
410 76 Dr.
Harlingen, TX 78550

HISTORICAL SOCIETIES

Texas State Historical Association
2.306 SRH, University Station
Austin, TX 78712

CHURCH RECORDS

BAPTIST

Southwestern Baptist Theological
Seminary
A. Webb Roberts Library
Box 22000-2E
Fort Worth, TX 76122

Baylor University
Tidwell Bible Library
Box 6307
Waco, TX 76703

DISCIPLES OF CHRIST

Brite Divinity School Collection
Mary Couts Burnett Library
Texas Christian University
Fort Worth, TX 76129

METHODIST

Center for Methodist Studies
United Methodist Historical
Collection
Bridwell Library
Southern Methodist University
Dallas, TX 75275

ROMAN CATHOLIC

Catholic Archives of Texas
N. Congress & W. 16th
Capitol Station P.O. Box 13327
Austin, TX 78711

ETHNIC RESOURCES

AFRICAN-AMERICAN

African American Genealogical and
Historical Society
P.O. Box 200784
San Antonio, TX 78220

Afro-American Historical and
Genealogical Society, Texas
P.O. Box 670045
Houston, TX 77267-0034

Black Genealogy
P.O. Box 6825
Lubbock, TX 79493-6825

Tarrant County Black Historical
and Genealogical Society, Inc.
1020 E. Humbolt
Fort Worth, TX 76104
Phone: (817) 332-6049

HISPANIC

University of Texas at Austin
Benson Latin American Collection
General Libraries, Sid Richardson
Hall 1.108
Austin, TX 78712-7330
Phone: (512) 495-4520
Fax: (512) 495-4568

University of Texas at El Paso
Library
Special Collections
El Paso, TX 79968-0582
Phone: (915) 747-5697
Fax: (915) 747-5327

Hidalgos of New Mexico
3310 Tyrone
El Paso, TX 79925
Phone: (915) 594-1648

Hispanic Genealogical Society
P.O. Box 1792
Houston, TX 77251-1792

Las Porciones Genealogical Society
P.O. Box 3323
Edinburg, TX 78450-0392

Los Bexarenos Genealogical Society
P.O. Box 1935
San Antonio, TX 78297

Spanish American Genealogical
Association
P.O. Box 5407
Corpus Christi, TX 78405

POLISH

Polish Genealogical Society
17811 Theisswood Lane
Spring, TX 77379

UTAH

ARCHIVES AND LIBRARIES

National Archives —
Rocky Mountain Region
Bldg. 48, Denver Federal Center
P.O. Box 25307
Denver, CO 80225
Phone: (303) 236-0817
Fax: (303) 236-9354
e-mail: archives@denver.nara.gov
Colorado, Montana, North Dakota,
South Dakota, Utah, and Wyoming

Brigham Young University
Provo, UT 84602
Harold B. Lee Library
Phone: (801) 378-2905
Fax: (801) 378-3221

Family History Library
35 North West Temple
Salt Lake City, UT 84150
Phone: (801) 240-2331
Fax: (801) 240-5551

Utah State Archives
Archives Building, Capitol Hill
Salt Lake City, UT 84114
Phone: (801) 538-3013
Fax: (801) 538-3354

Utah State Library
2150 S. 300 W., Ste. 16
Salt Lake City, UT 84115
Phone: (801) 466-5888
Fax: (801) 533-4657

GENEALOGICAL SOCIETIES

Alice's Ancestral Nostalgia
P.O. Box 510092
Salt Lake City, UT 84151

American Research Bureau, Inc.
2386 E. Heritage Way
Salt Lake City, UT 84109-1865

Association of One-Name Studies
57 West South Temple, Suite 300
Salt Lake City, UT 84101

Automated Research, Inc.
327 E. 1200 S., Suite #8
Orem, UT 84058

Brigham City Family History Center
10 S. 400 E.
Brigham City, UT 84302

Family Heritage Resources
178 E. 600 S.
Kaysville, UT 84307-2589

GeneSys
c/o Betty Walling
400 Dynix Dr.
Provo, UT 84604-5650

Genealogical Society of Utah
35 North West Temple
Salt Lake City, UT 84150
Phone: (801) 240-2331
Fax: (801) 240-5551

International Society for British
Genealogy
and Family History
P.O. Box 3115
Salt Lake City, UT 84110-3115

Rogers of Delphi Falls
9547 High Meadow Dr.
South Jordan, UT 84095

Utah Genealogical Association
P.O. Box 1144
Salt Lake City, UT 84110-1144

HISTORICAL SOCIETIES

Historical Department
Church of Jesus Christ of Latter-
day Saints
50 East North Temple
Salt Lake City, UT 84150

Utah State Historical Society
Library
300 Rio Grande
Salt Lake City, UT 84101-1182
Phone: (801) 533-3536
Fax: (801) 533-3053

CHURCH RECORDS

EPISCOPAL

Episcopal Diocese of Utah
231 E. 100 S.
Salt Lake City, UT 84111

LATTER-DAY SAINTS
(MORMONS)

LDS Church Archives
Historical Department
50 East North Temple
Salt Lake City, UT 84150

PRESBYTERIAN

Presbytery of Utah
3500 S. Main, Suite 100
Salt Lake City, UT 84115

ROMAN CATHOLIC

Pastoral Center
Diocese of Salt Lake City
27 C St.
Salt Lake City, UT 84103

ETHNIC RESOURCES

AFRICAN-AMERICAN

Registry of Black American
Ancestry
P.O. Box 417
Salt Lake City, UT 84110

HISPANIC

Cuban Genealogical Society
2552 Tamara Dr.
P.O. Box 2650
Salt Lake City, UT 84110-2650

Hispanic American Genealogical
Association
P.O. Box 2650
Salt Lake City, UT 84110

Institute of Genealogy and History
for Latin America
316 W. 500 N.
St. George, UT 84770

VERMONT

ARCHIVES AND LIBRARIES

National Archives —
New England Region
380 Trapelo Rd.
Waltham, MA 02154
Phone:617-647-8100
Fax: (617) 647-8460
e-mail: Archives@waltham.nara.gov
Connecticut, Maine, Massachu-
setts, New Hampshire, Rhode Is-
land, and Vermont

Vermont Department of Libraries
109 State St.
Montpelier, VT 05609
Phone: (802) 828-3261
Fax: (802) 828-2199

State of Vermont Archives
Office of Secretary of State
26 Terrace St.
Montpelier, VT 05609-1103
Phone: (802) 828-2362
Fax: (802) 828-2496

Vermont Historical Library
Pavillion Building
109 State St.
Montpelier, VT 05602
Phone: (802) 828-2291
Fax: (802) 8282-3638

GENEALOGICAL SOCIETIES

Vermont Genealogical Society
P.O. Box 422
Pittsford, VT 05763

HISTORICAL SOCIETIES

Vermont Historical Society
Pavillion Building
109 State St.
Montpelier, VT 05602
Phone: (802) 828-2291
Fax: (802) 828-3638

CHURCH RECORDS

BAPTIST

Bailey-Howe Memorial Library
University of Vermont
Burlington, VT 05405

EPISCOPAL

Episcopal Diocesan Center
Rock Point
Burlington, VT 05405

METHODIST

Green Mountain College Library
Poultney, VT 05764

ROMAN CATHOLIC

Archives of the Roman Catholic
Diocese of Burlington
351 North Ave.
Burlington, VT 05401

VIRGINIA

ARCHIVES AND LIBRARIES

National Archives —
Mid Atlantic Region
9th & Market Sts., Rm. 1350
Philadelphia, PA 19107
Phone: (215) 597-3000
Fax: (215) 597-2303
e-mail: archives@philarch.nara.gov
Delaware, Maryland, Pennsylvania,
Virginia, and West Virginia

University of Virginia
Alderman Library
Charlottesville, VA 22903-2498
Phone: (804) 924-3026
Fax: (804) 924-1431

National Genealogical Society
Library
4527 17th St. N.
Arlington, VA 22207-2399
Phone: (703) 525-0050
Fax: (703) 525-0052
www.genealogy.org/NGS

Virginia State Library and Archives
11th St. at Capitol Square
Richmond, VA 23219-3491
Phone: (804) 786-8929
Fax: (804) 786-5855

GENEALOGICAL SOCIETIES

Alleghany Highlands Genealogical
Society
1011 N. Rockbridge Ave.
Covington, VA 24426

Arlington County Historical Society
Arlington, VA

Central Virginia Genealogical
Association
P.O. Box 5583
Charlottesville, VA 22905-5583

Fairfax Genealogical Society
P.O. Box 2290
Merrifield, VA 22116-2290

Fredericksburg Regional
Genealogical Association
P.O. Box 42013
Fredericksburg, VA 22404

Genealogical Research Institute of
Virginia
P.O. Box 29178
Richmond, VA 23242-0178

Genealogical Society of the
Northern Neck of Virginia
P.O. Box 221
Heathsville, VA 22473

Loridous County Genealogical
Society
Loisburg, VA

Mt. Vernon Genealogical Society
Fairfax, VA

National Genealogical Society
4527 17th St. N.
Arlington, VA 22207-2399

New River Valley Genealogical
Society
Roanoke, VA

New Sweden, Iowa Descendants
c/o Bernice Wilson Munsey
3623 N. 37th St.
Arlington, VA 22207

Prince William County
Genealogical Society
P.O. Box 2019
Manassas, VA 22110-0812

The Scott One-Name Study
39475 Tollhouse Rd.
Lovettsville, VA 22080-9703

Tidewater Virginia Genealogical
Society
P.O. Box 7650
Hampton, VA 23666

Virginia Beach Genealogical Society
P.O. Box 62901
Virginia Beach, VA 23466-2901

Virginia Genealogical Society
5001 W. Broad St., Ste. 115
Richmond, VA 23230-3023

Virginia Genealogical Society
P.O. Box 7469
Richmond, VA 23221

HISTORICAL SOCIETIES

Grayson County Historical Society
Independence, VA

Virginia Historical Society
428 North Blvd.
P.O. Box 7311
Richmond, VA 23211
Phone: (804)342-9677

CHURCH RECORDS

BAPTIST

Virginia Baptist Historical Society
Boatwright Memorial Library
P.O. Box 34
University of Richmond
Richmond, VA 23173

METHODIST

Virginia United Methodist
Historical Society
Randolph Macon College
Walter Hines Page Library
Ashland, VA 23005

PRESBYTERIAN

Presbyterian Church Archives
Union Theological Seminary in
Virginia
3401 Brook Rd.
Richmond, VA 23227

ETHNIC RESOURCES

AFRICAN-AMERICAN

Hampton University
William R. and Norma B. Harvey
Library
130 E. Tyler St.
Hampton, VA 23668
Phone: (804) 727-5371
Fax: (804) 727-5084

Virginia Union University
William J. Clark Library
Special Collections
1500 N. Lombardy St.
Richmond, VA 23220
Phone: (804) 257-5820
Fax: (804) 257-5818

Afro-American Historical and
Genealogical Society,
Hampton Roads
P.O. Box 2448
Newport News, VA 23609-2448

JEWISH

Jewish Genealogical Society of
Greater Washington
c/o Rita Margolis
P.O. Box 412
Vienna, VA 22180

WASHINGTON

ARCHIVES AND LIBRARIES

National Archives —
Pacific Northwest Region
6125 Sand Point Way NE
Seattle, WA 98115
Phone: (206) 526-6507
Fax: (206) 526-4344
e-mail: archives@seattle.nara.gov
Idaho, Oregon, and Washington

Washington State Office of
Secretary of State
Division of Archives and Records
Management
1120 Washington St. SE
P.O. Box 40238
Olympia, WA 98504-0238
Phone: (206) 586-1492
Fax: (206) 586-9137

Washington State Archives
1120 Washington St. (location)
P.O. Box 40238 (mailing)
Olympia, WA 98504-0238
Phone: (360) 753-5485
Fax: (360) 664-8814

Washington State Library
P.O. Box 42460
Olympia, WA 98504-2460
Phone: (206) 753-5590
Fax: (206) 586-7575

GENEALOGICAL SOCIETIES

Callam County Genealogical
Society
223 E. Fourth St.
Port Angeles, WA 98362-3098

Clark County Genealogical Society
c/o Sharon Wodtke
12918 NE Seventh Ave.
Vancouver, WA 98685-2659

Eastern Washington Genealogical
Society
P.O. Box 1826
Spokane, WA 99210-1826

Eastside Genealogical Society
P.O. Box 374
Bellevue, WA 98009-0374

Grays Harbor Genealogy
P.O. Box 867
Cosmopolis, WA 98537

Heritage Archives
P.O. Box 10427
Seattle, WA 98110

Kittatas County Genealogical
Society
P.O. Box 1342
Ellensburg, WA 98926

Northeast Washington Genealogical
Society
c/o Colville Public Library
195 S. Oak
Colville, WA 99114

Puget Sound Genealogical Society
P.O. Box 601
Tracyton, WA 98393

Seattle Genealogical Society
P.O. Box 1708
Seattle, WA 98111

Skagit Valley Genealogical Society
P.O. Box 715
Conway, WA 98238-0715

Sno-Isle Genealogical Society
P.O. Box 63
Edmonds, WA 98020

Tacoma-Pierce County
Genealogical Society
P.O. Box 1952
Tacoma, WA 98401

Washington State Genealogical
Society
P.O. Box 1422
Olympia, WA 98507
Phone: (206) 352-0595

Wenatchee Area Genealogical
Society
P.O. Box 5280
Wenatchee, WA 98807-5280

Whidbey Island Genealogical
Searchers
P.O. Box 627
Oak Harbor, WA 98277

Whitman County Genealogical
Society
P.O. Box 393
Pullman, WA 99163

HISTORICAL SOCIETIES

Washington State Historical Society
Hewitt Library
State Historical Building
315 N. Stadium Way
Tacoma, WA 98403
Phone: (206) 593-2830

CHURCH RECORDS

METHODIST

Pacific Northwest Conference
Depository
United Methodist Church
Collins Memorial Library
1500 N. Warner
Tacoma, WA 98416

ROMAN CATHOLIC

Archdiocese of Seattle
Chancery Office
910 Marion St.
Seattle, WA 98104

ETHNIC RESOURCES

ASIAN

University of Washington
East Asia Library
322 Gowen Hall, DO-27
Seattle, WA 98195
Phone: (206) 543-4490
Fax: (206) 685-8049

Wing Luke Asian Museum
407 Seventh Ave. S
Seattle, WA 98507
Phone: (206) 623-5124
Fax: (206) 623-4559

GERMAN

Galizien German Descendants
c/o Evelyn R. Wolfer
12367 SE 214th St.
Kent, WA 98031-2215

WEST VIRGINIA

ARCHIVES AND LIBRARIES

National Archives —
Mid Atlantic Region
9th & Market Sts., Rm. 1350
Philadelphia, PA 19107
Phone: (215) 597-3000
Fax: (215) 597-2303
e-mail: archives@philarch.nara.gov
Delaware, Maryland, Pennsylvania,
Virginia, and West Virginia

West Virginia Archives and History
Division Library
1900 Kanawha Blvd. E.
Charleston, WV 25305-0300
Phone: (304) 558-0230
Fax: (304) 558-2779

West Virginia University Library
West Virginia and Regional History
Collection
Colson Hall
P.O. Box 6464
Morgantown, WV 26506
Phone: (304) 293-3536

GENEALOGICAL SOCIETIES

West Virginia Genealogical Society
P.O. Box 172
Elkview, WV 25017

West Virginia Genealogical Society, Inc.
P.O. Box 249
Elkview, WV 25071

HISTORICAL SOCIETIES

West Virginia Historical Society
Department of Culture and History
The Cultural Center
Capitol Complex
Charleston, WV 25305

CHURCH RECORDS

BAPTIST

West Virginia Baptist Historical Society
P.O. Box 1019
Parkersburg, WV 26101

METHODIST

Methodist Historical Society
West Virginia Wesleyan College
Annie M. Pfeiffer Library
College Ave.
Buckhannon, WV 26201

EPISCOPAL

Episcopal Diocese of West Virginia
1608 Virginia St. E.
Charleston, WV 25311

ROMAN CATHOLIC

Diocese of Wheeling-Charleston
1300 Bryan St.
P.O. Box 230
Wheeling, WV 26003

WISCONSIN

ARCHIVES AND LIBRARIES

National Archives —
Great Lakes Region
7358 S. Pulaski Rd.
Chicago, IL 60629
Phone: (312) 581-7816
Fax: (312) 353-1294
e-mail: archives@chicago.nara.gov
Illinois, Indiana, Michigan, Minnesota, Ohio, and Wisconsin

GENEALOGICAL SOCIETIES

Chippewa County Genealogical Society
403 Franklin St.
Stanley, WI 54768

Fox Valley Genealogical Society
P.O. Box 1592
Appleton, WI 54913-1592

Heart O' Wisconsin Genealogical Society
490 E. Grand Ave.
Wisconsin Rapids, WI 54494-4876

Lost in Canada?
Joy Reisinger, C.G.R.S.
1020 Central Ave.
Sparta, WI 54656

Marathon County Genealogical Society
Wausau, WI 54401

Milwaukee County Genealogical Society
P.O. Box 27326
Milwaukee, WI 53227-0326

Monroe, Juneau, Jackson Genealogical Workshop
Route 3 Box 253
Black River Falls, WI 54615-9405

Northwoods Genealogical Society
P.O. Box 1132
Rhinelander, WI 54501

Sheboygan County Genealogical Society
518 Water St.
Sheboygan Falls, WI 53085-1455

South Central Chapter WSGS
Route 2, 529 Keito Valley Rd.
Brooklyn, WI 53521

State Historical Society of Wisconsin
816 State St.
Madison, WI 53706-1488

Wisconsin Genealogical Council, Inc.
6083 Co. Trk S.
Wisconsin Rapids, WI 54495-9212

Wisconsin Genealogical Council, Inc.
Route 3, Box 253
Black River Falls, WI 54615-9405
Phone: (608) 378-4388
Fax: (608) 378-3006

Wisconsin State Genealogical Society, Inc.
P.O. Box 5106
Madison, WI 53705

Wisconsin State Genealogical Society
2109 Twentieth Ave.
Monroe, WI 53566-3426
Phone: (608) 325-2609

HISTORICAL SOCIETIES

State Historical Society of
Wisconsin
816 State St.
Madison, WI 53706
Phone: (608) 264-6450
Fax: (608) 264-6472

CHURCH RECORDS

METHODIST

Historical Library
Methodist Manor
Box 2828
West Allis, WI 27018

ROMAN CATHOLIC

Archdiocese of Milwaukee
2000 W. Wisconsin Ave.
Milwaukee, WI 53403

Diocese of Green Bay
1910 S. Webster Ave.
P.O. Box 66
Green Bay, WI 54301

Diocese of La Crosse
421 Main St.
P.O. Box 982
La Crosse, WI 54601

Diocese of Madison
15 E. Wilson St.
Madison, WI 53703

Diocese of Superior
1201 Hughitt Ave.
Superior, WI 54880

ETHNIC RESOURCES

AFRICAN-AMERICAN

State Historical Society of
Wisconsin Library
816 State St.
Madison, WI 53706-1482
Phone: (608) 264-6534
Fax: (608) 264-6520

WYOMING

ARCHIVES AND LIBRARIES

National Archives —
Rocky Mountain Region
Building 48, Denver Federal Center
P.O. Box 25307
Denver, CO 80225
Phone: (303) 236-0817
Fax: (303) 236-9354
e-mail: archives@denver.nara.gov
Colorado, Montana, North Dakota,
South Dakota, Utah, and Wyoming

University of Wyoming
University Station
P.O. Box 3334
Laramie, WY 82071-3334
Phone: (307) 766-3279
Fax: (307) 766-3062

Wyoming State Archives
Barrett Building
6101 Yellowstone Rd.
Cheyenne, WY 82002-0013
Phone: (307) 777-7016
Fax: (307) 777-7044

Wyoming State Library
2301 Capitol Ave.
Cheyenne, WY 82002-0006
Phone: (307) 777-7281
Fax: (307) 777-6289

GENEALOGICAL SOCIETIES

Fremont County Genealogical
Society
Riverton Branch Library
1330 W. Park Ave.
Riverton, WY 82501

CHURCH RECORDS

ROMAN CATHOLIC

Diocese of Cheyenne
Box 426
Cheyenne, WY 82003

Before you send for vital records, call ahead for the price of the copy. If you know the city or county where the record was created, try finding the record there first. Copies at the local level are often less expensive than at the state level. If you are unsuccessful at the local level, then try the state level.

PLACE OF EVENT	ADDRESS	REMARKS
ALABAMA		
Birth or Death	Center for Health Statistics State Department of Public Health P.O. Box 5625 Montgomery, AL 36103-5625	State office has had records since January 1908. Call (205) 242-5033 for current fees.
Marriage	Same as Birth or Death See remarks	State office has had records since August 1936. Probate Judge in county where license was issued.
Divorce	Same as Birth or Death See remarks	State office has had records since January 1950. Clerk or Register of Court of Equity in county where divorce was granted.
ALASKA		
Birth or Death	Department of Health and Social Services Bureau of Vital Statistics P.O. Box H-02G Juneau, AK 99811-0675	State office has had records since January 1913. Call (907) 465-3391 for current fees. This is a recorded message.
Marriage	Same as Birth or Death	State office has had records since 1913.
Divorce	Same as Birth or Death See Remarks	State office has had records since 1950. Clerk of Superior Court in judicial district where divorce was granted. Juneau and Ketchikan (First District), Nome (Second District), Anchorage (Third District), Fairbanks (Fourth District).
AMERICAN SAMOA		
Birth or Death	Registrar of Vital Statistics, Vital Statistics Section Government of American Samoa Pago Pago, AS 96799	Registrar has had records since 1900. Call (684) 633-1222, ext. 214 for current fees. Personal identification is required before a record will be sent.
Marriage	Same as Birth or Death	
Divorce	High Court of American Samoa Tutuila, AS 96799	

ARIZONA

Place of event	Address	Remarks
Birth (long form)	Vital Records Section Arizona Department of Health Services P.O. Box 3887 Phoenix, AZ 85030	State office has had records sine July 1909 and abstracts of records filed in counties before then. Call (602) 255-3260 for current fees. This is a recorded message. Applicants must submit a copy of picture identification or have their request notarized.
Birth (short form)	Same as Birth (long form)	Same as Birth (long form)
Marriage	See remarks	Clerk of Superior Court in county where license was issued.
Divorce	See remarks	Clerk of Superior Court in county where divorce was granted.

ARKANSAS

Place of event	Address	Remarks
Birth	Division of Vital Records Arkansas Department of Health 4815 West Markham Street Little Rock, AR 72201	State office has had records since February 1914 and some original Little Rock and Fort Smith records from 1881. Call (501) 661-2336 for current fees. This is a recorded message.
Death	Same as Birth	Same as Birth
Marriage	Same as Birth or Death See remarks	Coupons since 1917. Full certified copy may be obtained from County Clerk in county where license was issued.
Divorce	Same as Birth or Death See remarks	Coupons since 1923. Full certified copy may be obtained from Circuit or Chancery Clerk in county where divorce was granted.

CALIFORNIA

Place of event	Address	Remarks
Birth	Vital Statistics Section Department of Health Services P.O. Box 730241 Sacramento, CA 94244-0241	State office has had records since July 1905. For earlier records, write to County Recorder in county where event occurred. Call (916) 445-2684 for current fees.
Death	Same as Birth	Same as Birth
Heirloom Birth	Not available until further notice	Decorative birth certificate (11" × 14") suitable for framing.
Marriage	Same as Birth or Death	State office has had records since July 1905. For earlier records, write to County Recorder in county where event occurred.
Divorce	Same as Birth or Death See remarks	Fee for search and identification of county where certified copy can be obtained. Certified copies are not available from State Health Department. Clerk of Superior Court in county where divorce was granted.

CANAL ZONE

Place of event	Address	Remarks
Birth or Death	Panama Canal Commission Vital Statistics Clerk APOAA 34011	Records available from May 1904 to September 1979.
Marriage	Same as Birth or Death	Records available from May 1904 to September 1979.
Divorce	Same as Birth or Death	Records available from May 1904 to September 1979.

COLORADO

Place of event	Address	Remarks
Birth or Death	Vital Records Section Colorado Department of Health	State office has had death records since 1910. State office also has birth records for some counties for years before 1910. Call (303) 756-

PLACE OF EVENT	ADDRESS	REMARKS
	4300 Cherry Creek Drive South Denver, CO 80222-1530	4464 for current fees. This is a recorded message.
Marriage	Same as Birth or Death	Certified copies are not available from State Health Department. Statewide index of records for 1900-39 and 1975 to present. Fee for verification.
Divorce	Same as Birth or Death	Certified copies are not available from State Health Department. Statewide index of records for 1900-39 and 1968 is present. Fee for verification. Copies available from Clerk of District Court in county where divorce was granted.

CONNECTICUT

PLACE OF EVENT	ADDRESS	REMARKS
Birth or Death	Vital Records Department of Health Services 150 Washington Street Hartford, CT 06106	State office has had records since July 1897. For earlier records, write to Registrar of Vital Statistics in town or city where event occurred. Fax requests are not accepted. Request must have original signature. Call (203) 566-2334 for current fees. This is a recorded message.
Marriage	Same as Birth or Death	Records since July 1897 at State Registry. For older records, contact Clerk of Superior Court where marriage occurred.
Divorce	See remarks	Applicant must contact Clerk of Superior Court where divorce was granted. State office does not have divorce decrees and cannot issue certified copies.

DELAWARE

PLACE OF EVENT	ADDRESS	REMARKS
Birth or Death	Office of Vital Statistics Division of Public Health P.O. Box 637 Dover, DE 19903	State office has death records since 1930 and birth records since 1920. Call (302) 739-4721 for current fees.
Marriage	Same as Birth or Death	Records since 1930.
Divorce	Same as Birth or Death	Records since 1935. Inquiries will be forwarded to appropriate office. Certified copies are not available from state office.
	See remarks	Prothonotary in county where divorce was granted up to 1975. For divorces granted after 1975 the parties concerned should contact Family Court in county where divorce was granted.

DISTRICT OF COLUMBIA

PLACE OF EVENT	ADDRESS	REMARKS
Birth or Death	Vital Records Branch Room 3009 425 I Street, NW Washington, DC 20001	Office has had death records since 1855 and birth records since 1874, but no death records were filed during the Civil War. Call (202) 727-9281 for current fees.
Marriage	Marriage Bureau 515 5th Street, NW Washington, DC 20001	
Divorce	Clerk, Superior Court for the District of Columbia, Family Division 500 Indiana Avenue, NW Washington, DC 20001	Records since 16 September 1956.
	Clerk, U.S. District Court for the District of Columbia Washington, DC 20001	Records before 16 September 1956.

FLORIDA

PLACE OF EVENT	ADDRESS	REMARKS
Birth or Death	Department of Health and Rehabilitative Services Office of Vital Statistics P.O. Box 210 1217 Pearl Street Jacksonville, FL 32231	State office has some birth records dating back to April 1865 and some death records dating back to August 1877. The majority of records date from January 1917. (If the exact date is unknown, there is a fee for the first year searched and another fee for each additional year. Fee includes one copy of record if found or certified statement stating record not on file.) Call (904) 359-6900 for current fees. This is a recorded message.
Marriage	Same as Birth or Death	Records since 6 June 1927. (If the exact date is unknown, there is a fee for the first year searched and another fee for each additional year. Fee includes one copy of record if found or certified statement stating record not on file.)
Divorce	Same as Birth or Death	Records since 6 June 1927. (If the exact date is unknown, there is a fee for the first year searched and another fee for each additional year. Fee includes one copy of record if found or certified statement stating record not on file.)

GEORGIA

PLACE OF EVENT	ADDRESS	REMARKS
Birth or Death	Georgia Department of Human Resources Vital Records Unit Room 217-H 47 Trinity Avenue, SW Atlanta, GA 30334	State office has had records since January 1919. For earlier records in Atlanta or Savannah, write to County Health Department in county where event occurred. Call (404) 656-4900 for current fees. This is a recorded message.
Marriage	Same as Birth or Death	Centralized state records since 9 June 1952. Certified copies are not issued at state office. Inquiries about marriages occurring before 9 June 1952 will be forwarded to appropriate Probate Judge in county where license was issued.
Divorce	See remarks	Probate Judge in county where license issued.
	See remarks	Centralized state records since 9 June 1952. Certified copies are not issued at state office. Inquiries will be forwarded to appropriate Clerk of Superior Court in county where divorce was granted.
	See remarks	Clerk of Superior Court in county where divorce was granted.

GUAM

PLACE OF EVENT	ADDRESS	REMARKS
Birth or Death	Office of Vital Statistics Department of Public Health and Social Services Government of Guam P.O. Box 2816 Agana, GU, M.I. 96910	Office has had records since 16 October 1901. Call (671) 734-4589 for current fees.
Marriage	Same as Birth or Death	
Divorce	Clerk, Superior Court of Guam Agana, GU, M.I. 96910	

HAWAII

PLACE OF EVENT	ADDRESS	REMARKS
Birth or Death	Office of Health Status Monitoring State Department of Health P.O. Box 2816 Agana, GU, M.I., 96910	State office has had records since 1853. Call (808) 586-4533 for current fees. This is a recorded message.

PLACE OF EVENT	ADDRESS	REMARKS
Marriage	Same as Birth or Death	
Divorce	Same as Birth or Death	Records since July 1951.
	See remarks	Circuit Court in county where divorce was granted.

IDAHO

PLACE OF EVENT	ADDRESS	REMARKS
Birth	Vital Statistics Unit Idaho Department of Health and Welfare P.O. Box 83720 Boise, ID 83720-0036	State office has had records since July 1911. For records from 1907 to 1911, write to County Recorder in county where event occurred.
Wallet card	Same as Birth	
Death	Same as Birth	
Heirloom Birth	Same as Birth or Death	Decorative birth certificates (8 1/2" × 11" and 5" × 7") are suitable for framing. Call (208) 334-5988 for current fees. This is a recorded message.
Marriage	Same as Birth or Death	Records since May 1947. Earlier records are with County Recorder in county where license was issued.
	See remarks	County Recorder in county where license was issued.
Divorce	Same as Birth or Death	Records since May 1947. Earlier records are with County Recorder in county where divorce was granted.
	See remarks	County records in county where divorce was granted.

ILLINOIS

PLACE OF EVENT	ADDRESS	REMARKS
Birth or Death	Division of Vital Records Illinois Department of Public Health 605 West Jefferson Street Springfield, IL 62702-5097	State office has had records since January 1916. For earlier records and for copies of state records since January 1916, write to County Clerk in county where event occurred. Call (217) 782-6553 for current fees. This is a recorded message.
Marriage	Same as Birth or Death	Marriage index since January 1962. Selected items may be verified. Certified copies are not available from state office. For certified copies, write to the County Clerk in county where license was issued.
Divorce	Same as Birth or Death	Divorce index since January 1962. Selected items may be verified. Certified copies are not available from the state office. For certified copies, write to the Clerk of Circuit Court in county where divorce was granted.

INDIANA

PLACE OF EVENT	ADDRESS	REMARKS
Birth	Vital Records Section State Department of Health 1330 West Michigan Street P.O. Box 1964 Indianapolis, IN 46206-1964	State office has had birth records since October 1907 and death records since 1900. For earlier records, write to Health Officer in city or county where event occurred. Call (317) 633-0274 for current fees.
Death	Same as Birth	
Marriage	Same as Birth or Death	Marriage index since 1958. Certified copies are not available from State Health Department.
	See remarks	Clerk of Circuit Court or Clerk of Superior Court in county where license was issued.

PLACE OF EVENT	ADDRESS	REMARKS
Divorce	See remarks	County Clerk in county where divorce was granted.

IOWA

Birth or Death	Iowa Department of Public Health Vital Records Section Lucas Office Building 321 East 12th Street Des Moines, IA 50319-0075	State office has had records since July 1880. Call (515) 281-4944 for current fees. This is a recorded message.
Marriage	Same as Birth or Death	State office has had records since July 1880.
Divorce	Same as Birth or Death	Brief statistical record only since 1906. Inquiries will be forwarded to appropriate office. Certified copies are not available from State Health Department. Clerk of District Court in county where divorce was granted.

KANSAS

Birth	Office of Vital Statistics Kansas State Department of Health and Environment 900 Jackson Street Topeka, KS 66612-1290	State office has had records since July 1911. For earlier records, write to County Clerk in county where event occurred. Call (913) 296-1400 for current fees. This is a recorded message.
Death	Same as Birth	
Marriage	Same as Birth or Death See remarks	State office has had records since May 1913. District Judge in county where license was issued.
Divorce	Same as Birth or Death See remarks	State office has had records since July 1951. Clerk of District Court in county where divorce was granted.

KENTUCKY

Birth	Office of Vital Statistics Department for Health Services 275 East Main Street Frankfort, KY 40621	State office has had records since January 1911 and some records for the cities of Louisville, Lexington, Covington, and Newport before then. Call (502) 564-4212 for current fees.
Death	Same as Birth	
Marriage	Same as Birth or Death See remarks	Records since June 1958. Clerk of County Court in county where license was issued.
Divorce	Same as Birth or Death See remarks	Records since June 1958. Clerk of Circuit Court in count where decree was issued.

LOUISIANA

Birth (long form)	Vital Records Registry Office of Public Health 325 Loyola Avenue New Orleans, LA 70112	State office has had records since July 1914. Birth records for City of New Orleans are available from 1892. Death records are available since 1942. Older birth, death, and marriage records are available through the Louisiana State Archives, P.O. Box 94125, Baton Rouge, LA 70804. Call (504) 568-5152 for current fees.
Birth (short form)	Same as Birth (long form)	Same as Birth (long form)
Death	Same as Birth	Same as Birth
Marriage Orleans Parish	Same as Birth or Death	

PLACE OF EVENT	ADDRESS	REMARKS
Marriage Other Parishes	See remarks	Certified copies are issued by Clerk of Court in parish where license was issued.
Divorce	See remarks	Clerk of Court in parish where divorce was granted.

MAINE

Birth or Death	Office of Vital Statistics Maine Department of Human Services State House Station 11 Augusta, ME 04333-0011	State office has had records since 1892. Records for 1892–1922 are available at the Maine State Archives. For earlier records, write to the municipality where the event occurred. Call (207) 289-3184 for current fees.
Marriage	Same as Birth or Death	Same as Birth or Death
Divorce	Same as Birth or Death See remarks	Same as Birth or Death. Clerk of District Court in judicial division where divorce was granted.

MARYLAND

Birth or Death	Division of Vital Records Department of Health and Mental Hygiene Metro Executive Building 4201 Paterson Avenue P.O. Box 68760 Baltimore, MD 21215-0020	State office has had records since August 1898. Records for City of Baltimore are available from January 1875. Will not do research for genealogical studies. Must apply to State of Maryland Archives, 350 Robe Blvd., Annapolis, MD 21401, (301) 974-3914. Call (301) 225-5988 for current fees. This is a recorded message.
Marriage	Same as Birth or Death See remarks	Records since June 1951. Clerk of Circuit Court in county where license was issued or Clerk of Court of Common Pleas of Baltimore City (for licenses issued in City of Baltimore).
Divorce Verification only	Same as Birth or Death See remarks	Records since January 1961. Certified copies are not available from state office. Some items may be verified. Clerk of Circuit Court in county where divorce was granted.

MASSACHUSETTS

Birth or Death	Registry of Vital Records and Statistics 150 Tremont Street, Room B-3 Boston, MA 02111	State office has records since 1901. For earlier records, write to the Massachusetts Archives at Columbia Point, 220 Morrissey Boulevard, Boston, MA 02125, (617) 727-2816. Call (617) 727-7388 for current fees. This is a recorded message.
Marriage	Same as Birth or Death	Records since 1901
Divorce	Same as Birth or Death See remarks	Index only since 1952. Inquirer will be directed where to send request. Certified copies are not available from state office. Registrar of Probate Court in county where divorce was granted

MICHIGAN

Birth or Death	Office of the State Registrar and Center for Health Statistics Michigan Department of Public Health 3423 North Laguna Street Lansing, MI 48909	State office has had records since 1867. Copies of most records since 1867 may also be obtained from County Clerk in county where event occurred. Fees vary from county to county. Detroit records may be obtained from the City of Detroit Health Department for births occurring since 1893 and for deaths since 1897. Call (517) 335-8655 for current fees. This is a recorded message.
Marriage	Same as Birth or Death See remarks	Records since April 1867. County Clerk in county where license was issued.

PLACE OF EVENT	ADDRESS	REMARKS
Divorce	Same as Birth or Death	Records since 1897
	See remarks	County Clerk in county where divorce was granted.

MINNESOTA

Birth	Minnesota Department of Health Section of Vital Statistics 717 Delaware Street, SE P.O. Box 9441 Minneapolis, MN 55440	State office has had records since January 1908. Copies of earlier records may be obtained from Local Registrar in county where event occurred or for the St. Paul City Health Department if the event occurred in St. Paul. Call (612) 623-5121 for current fees.
Death	Same as Birth	Same as Birth
Marriage	Same as Birth or Death	Statewide index since January 1958. Inquiries will be forwarded to appropriate office. Certified copies are not available from State Department of Health.
	See remarks	Local Registrar in county where license was issued.
Divorce	Same as Birth or Death	Index since January 1970. Certified copies are not available from state office.
	See remarks	Local Registrar in county where divorce was granted.

MISSISSIPPI

Birth	Vital Records State Department of Health 2423 North State Street Jackson, MI 39216	State office has had records since 1912. Call (601) 960-7981 for current fees. A recorded message may be reached at (601) 960-7450.
Birth (short form)	Same as Birth	
Death	Same as Birth	
Marriage	Same as Birth or Death	Statistical records only from January 1926 to 1 July 1938, and since January 1942.
	See remarks	Circuit Clerk in county where license was issued.
Divorce	Same as Birth or Death	Records since January 1926. Certified copies are not available from state office. Index search is available for each 5-year increment. Book and page number for county record provided.
	See remarks	Chancery Clerk in county where divorce was granted.

MISSOURI

Birth or Death	Missouri Department of Health Bureau of Vital Records 1730 East Elm P.O. Box 570 Jefferson City, MO 65102-0570	State office has had records since January 1910. If event occurred in St. Louis (City), St. Louis County, or Kansas City before 1910, write to the City or County Health Department. Call (314) 751-6400 for current fees.
Marriage	Same as Birth or Death	Indexes since July 1948. Correspondents will be referred to appropriate Recorder of Deeds in county where license was issued.
	See remarks	Recorder of Deeds in county where license was issued.
Divorce	Same as Birth or Death	Indexes since July 1948. Certified copies are not available from State Health Department. Inquiries will be forwarded to appropriate office.
	See remarks	Clerk of Circuit Court in county where divorce was granted.

MONTANA

Birth or Death	Bureau of Records and Statistics State Department of Health and	State office has had records since late 1907. Call (406) 444-2614 for current fees.

PLACE OF EVENT	ADDRESS	REMARKS
	Environmental Sciences Helena, MT 59620	
Marriage	Same as Birth or Death	Records since July 1943. Some items may be verified. Inquiries will be forwarded to appropriate office. Apply to county where license was issued if known. Certified copies are not available from state office.
	See remarks	Clerk of District Court in county where license was issued.
Divorce	Same as Birth or Death	Records since July 1943. Some items may be verified. Inquiries will be forwarded to appropriate office. Apply to court where divorce was granted if known. Certified copies are not available from state office.
	See remarks	Clerk of District Court in county where divorce was granted.

NEBRASKA

PLACE OF EVENT	ADDRESS	REMARKS
Birth	Bureau of Vital Statistics State Department of Health 301 Centennial Mall South P.O. Box 95007 Lincoln, NE 68509-5007	State office has had records since late 1904. If birth occurred before then, write the state office for information. Call (402) 471-2871 for current fees. This is a recorded message.
Death	Same as Birth	Same as Birth
Marriage	Same as Birth or Death See remarks	Records since January 1909. County Court in county where license was issued.
Divorce	Same as Birth or Death See remarks	Records since January 1909. Clerk of District Court in county where divorce was granted.

NEVADA

PLACE OF EVENT	ADDRESS	REMARKS
Birth	Division of Health-Vital Statistics Capitol Complex 505 East King Street #102 Carson City, NV 89710	State office has records since July 1911. For earlier records, write to County Recorder in county where event occurred. Call (702) 687-4480 for current fees.
Death	Same as Birth	Same as Birth
Marriage	Same as Birth or Death	Indexes since January 1968. Certified copies are not available from State Health Department. Inquiries will be forwarded to appropriate office.
	See remarks	County Recorder in county where license was issued.
Divorce	Same as Birth or Death	Indexes since January 1968. Certified copies are not available from State Health Department. Inquiries will be forwarded to appropriate office.
	See remarks	County Clerk in county where divorce was granted.

NEW HAMPSHIRE

PLACE OF EVENT	ADDRESS	REMARKS
Birth or Death	Bureau of Vital Records Health and Welfare Building 6 Hazen Drive Concord, NH 03301	State office has had records since 1640. Copies of records may be obtained from state office or from City or Town Clerk in place where event occurred. Call (603) 271-4654 for current fees. This is a recorded message.
Marriage	Same as Birth or Death See remarks	Records since 1640. Town Clerk in town where license was issued.
Divorce	Same as Birth or Death See remarks	Records since 1808. Clerk of Superior Court where divorce was granted.

New Jersey

Birth or Death	State Department of Health Bureau of Vital Statistics South Warren and Market Streets CN 370 Trenton, NJ 08625	State office has had records since June 1878.
	Archives and History Bureau State Library Division State Department of Education Trenton, NJ 08625	For records from May 1848 to May 1878. Call (609) 292-4087 for current fees. This is a recorded message.
Marriage	Same as Birth or Death	
	Archives and History Bureau State Library Division State Department of Education Trenton, NJ 08625	For records from May 1848 to May 1878.
Divorce	Public Information Center CN 967 Trenton, NJ 08625	The fee is for a certified Blue Seal copy.

New Mexico

Birth	Vital Statistics New Mexico Health Services Division P.O. Box 26110 Santa Fe, NM 87502	State office has had records since 1880. Call (505) 827-2338 for current fees. This is a recorded message.
Death	Same as Birth	Same as Birth
Marriage	See remarks	County Clerk in county where license was issued.
Divorce	See remarks	Clerk of Superior Court where divorce was granted.

New York
(except New York City)

Birth or Death	Vital Records Section State Department of Health Empire State Building Tower Building Albany, NY 12237-0023	State office has had records since 1880. For records before 1914 in Albany, Buffalo, and Yonkers, or before 1880 in any other city, write to Registrar of Vital Statistics in city where event occurred. For the rest of the state, except New York City, write to state office. Call (518) 474-3075 for current fees. This is a recorded message.
Marriage	Same as Birth or Death See remarks	Records from 1880 to present. For records from 1880-1907 and licenses issued in the cities of Albany: City Clerk, City Hall, Albany, NY 12207; Buffalo: City Clerk, City Hall, Buffalo, NY 14202; Yonkers: Registrar of Vital Statistics, Health Center Building, Yonkers, NY 10701.
Divorce	Same as Birth or Death See remarks	Records since January 1963. County Clerk in county where divorce was granted.

New York City

Birth or Death	Division of Vital Records New York City Department of Health	Office has birth records since 1910 and death records since 1949 for those occurring in the boroughs of Manhattan, Brooklyn, Bronx, Queens, and Staten Island. For birth records prior to 1910 and death

PLACE OF EVENT	ADDRESS	REMARKS
	P.O. Box 3776 New York, NY 10007	records prior to 1949, write to Archives Division, Department of Records and Information Services, 31 Chambers Street, New York, NY 10007. Call (212) 619-4530 or (212) 693-4637 for current fees. These are recorded messages.
Marriage		
Bronx Borough	City Clerk's Office 1780 Grand Concourse Bronx, NY 10457	Records from 1847 to 1865. Archives Division, Department of Records and Information Services, 31 Chambers Street, New York, NY 1007, except Brooklyn records for this period, which are filed with County Clerk's Office, Kings County, Supreme Court Building, Brooklyn, NY 11201. Records from 1866 to 1907. City Clerk's Office in borough where marriage was performed. Records from 1908 to 12 May 1943. New York City residents write to City Clerk's Office in the borough of the bride's residence; nonresidents write to City Clerk's Office in borough where license was obtained. Records since 13 May 1943. City Clerk's Office in borough where license was issued.
Brooklyn Borough	City Clerk's Office Municipal Building Brooklyn, NY 11201	
Manhattan Borough	City Clerk's Office Municipal Building New York, NY 10007	
Queen's Borough	City Clerk's Office 120-55 Queen's Boulevard Kew Gardens, NY 11424	
Staten Island Borough (no longer called Richmond)	City Clerk's Office Staten Island Borough Hall Staten Island, NY 10301	
Divorce		See New York State

NORTH CAROLINA

PLACE OF EVENT	ADDRESS	REMARKS
Birth or Death	Department of Environment, Health and Natural Resources Division of Epidemiology Vital Records Section 225 North McDowell Street P.O. Box 29537 Raleigh, NC 27626-0537	State office has had records since October 1913 and death records since 1 January 1946. Death records from 1913 through 1945 are available from Archives and Records Section, 109 East Jones Street, Raleigh, NC 27611. Call (919) 733-3526 for current fees.
Marriage	Same as Birth or Death See remarks	Records since January 1962. Registrar of Deeds in county where marriage was performed.
Divorce	Same as Birth or Death See remarks	Records since January 1958. Clerk of Superior Court where divorce was granted.

NORTH DAKOTA

PLACE OF EVENT	ADDRESS	REMARKS
Birth	Division of Vital Records State Capitol 600 East Boulevard Avenue Bismarck, ND 58505	State office has had some records since July 1893. Years from 1894 to 1920 are incomplete. Call (701) 224-2360 for current fees.
Death	Same as Birth	Same as Birth
Marriage	Same as Birth	Records since July 1925. Requests for earlier records will be forwarded to appropriate office.
	See remarks	County Judge in county where license was issued.
Divorce	Same as Birth	Index of records since July 1949. Some items may be verified. Certified copies are not available from State Health Department. Inquiries will be forwarded to appropriate office.
	See remarks	Clerk of District Court in county where divorce was granted.

PLACE OF EVENT	ADDRESS	REMARKS
NORTHERN MARIAN ISLANDS		
Birth or Death	Superior Court Vital Records Section P.O. Box 307 Saipan, MP 96950	Office has had records for birth and death since 1945 and records for marriage since 1954. Years from 1945 to 1950 are incomplete.
Marriage	Same as Birth or Death	Call (670) 234-6401, ext. 15 for current fees.
Divorce	Same as Birth or Death	Office has had records for divorce since 1960.
OHIO		
Birth or Death	Bureau of Vital Statistics Ohio Department of Health P.O. Box 15098 Columbus, OH 43215-0098	State office has had birth records since December 20, 1908. For earlier birth and death records, write to the Probate Court in the county where the event occurred. The state office has death records for deaths since 31 December 1936. Death records for deaths 20 December 1908–31 December 1936 can be obtained from the Ohio Historical Society, Archives Library Division, 1985 Velma Avenue, Columbus, OH 43211-2497. Call (614) 466-2531 for current fees. This is a recorded message.
Marriage	Same as Birth or Death	Records since September 1949. All items may be verified. Certified copies are not available from State Health Department. Inquiries will be referred to appropriate office.
	See remarks	Probate Judge in county where license was issued.
Divorce	Same as Birth or Death	Records since September 1949. All items may be verified. Certified copies are not available for State Health Department. Inquiries will be forwarded to appropriate office.
	See remarks	Clerk of Court of Common Pleas in county where divorce was granted.
OREGON		
Birth or Death	Oregon Health Division Vital Statistics Section P.O. Box 14050 Portland, OR 97214-0050	State office has had records since January 1903. Some earlier records for the City of Portland since approximately 1880 are available from the Oregon State Archives, 1005 Broadway, NE, Salem, OR 97310.
Heirloom Birth	Same as Birth or Death	Presentation style calligraphy certificate suitable for framing. Call (503) 731-4095 for current fees. This is a recorded message.
Marriage	Same as Birth or Death See remarks	Records since January 1906. County Clerk in county where license was issued. County Clerks also have some records before 1906.
Divorce	Same as Birth or Death See remarks	Records since 1925. County Circuit Court Clerk where divorce was granted. County Clerks also have some records before 1925.
PENNSYLVANIA		
Birth	Division of Vital Records State Department of Health Central Building 101 South Mercer Street P.O. Box 1528 New Castle, PA 16103	State office has had records since January 1906. For earlier records, write to Register of Wills, Orphans Court, in county seat of county where event occurred. Persons born in Pittsburgh from 1870 to 1905 or in Allegheny City, now part of Pittsburgh, from 1882 to 1905 should write to Office of Biostatistics, Pittsburgh, PA

PLACE OF EVENT	ADDRESS	REMARKS
		15219. For events occurring in City of Philadelphia from 1860 to 1915, write Vital Statistics, Philadelphia Department of Public Health, 401 North Broad Street, Room 942, Philadelphia, PA 19108. Call (412) 656-3100 for current fees.
Death	Same as Birth	Same as Birth
Marriage	See remarks	Make application to the Marriage License Clerks, County Court House, in county where license was issued.
Divorce	See remarks	Make application to the Prothonotary Court House, in county seat of county where divorce was granted.

PUERTO RICO

PLACE OF EVENT	ADDRESS	REMARKS
Birth or Death	Department of Health Demographic Registry P.O. Box 11854 Fernandez Juncos Station San Juan, PR 00910	Central office has had records since 22 July 1931. Copies of earlier records may be obtained by writing to local Registrar (Registrador Demografico) in municipality where event occurred or by writing to central office for information. Call (809) 728-7980 for current fees.
Marriage	Same as Birth or Death	
Divorce	Same as Birth or Death See remarks	Superior Court where divorce was granted.

RHODE ISLAND

PLACE OF EVENT	ADDRESS	REMARKS
Birth or Death	Division of Vital Records Rhode Island Department of Health Room 201, Cannon Building 3 Capitol Hill Providence, RI 02908-5097	State office has had records since 1853. For earlier records, write to Town Clerk in town where event occurred. Call (401) 277-2811 for current fees. This is a recorded message.
Marriage	Same as Birth or Death	Records since January 1853.
Divorce	Clerk of Family Court 1 Dorrance Plaza Providence, RI 02903	

SOUTH CAROLINA

PLACE OF EVENT	ADDRESS	REMARKS
Birth or Death	Office of Vital Records and Public Health Statistics South Carolina Department of Health and Environmental Control 2600 Bull Street Columbia, SC 29201	State office has had records since January 1915. City of Charleston births from 1877 and deaths from 1821 are on file at Charleston County Health Department. Ledger entries of Florence City births and deaths from 1895 to 1914 are on file at Florence County Health Department. Ledger entries of Newberry City births and deaths from the late 1800s are on file at Newberry County Health Department. These are the only early records obtainable. Call (803) 734-4830 for current fees.
Marriage	Same as Birth or Death See remarks	Records since July 1950. Records since July 1911. Probate Judge in county where license was issued.
Divorce	Same as Birth or Death See remarks	Records since July 1962. Records since April 1949. Clerk of county where petition was filed.

SOUTH DAKOTA

PLACE OF EVENT	ADDRESS	REMARKS
Birth or Death	State Department of Health Center for Health Policy and Statistics	State office has had records since July 1905 and access to other records for some events that occurred before then. Call (605) 773-3355 for cur-

PLACE OF EVENT	ADDRESS	REMARKS
	Vital Records 523 East Capitol Pierre, SD 57501	rent fees. This is a recorded message.
Marriage	Same as Birth or Death See remarks	Records since July 1905. County Treasury in county where license was issued.
Divorce	Same as Birth or Death See remarks	Records since July 1905 Clerk of Court in county where divorce was granted.

TENNESSEE

Birth (long form)	Tennessee Vital Records Department of Health Cordell Hull Building Nashville, TN 37247-0350	State office has had birth records for entire state since January 1914, for Nashville since June 1881, for Knoxville since July 1881, and for Chattanooga since January 1882. State office has had death records for entire state since January 1914, for Nashville since July 1874, for Knoxville since July 1887, and for Chattanooga since 6 March 1872. Birth and death enumeration records by school district are available for July 1908 through June 1912. Vital Records Office keeps death records for 50 years; older records are maintained by Tennessee Library and Archives, Archives Division, Nashville, TN 37243-0312. For Memphis birth records from April 1874 through December 1887 and November 1898 to 1 January 1914, and for Memphis death records from May 1848 to 1 January 1914, write to Memphis-Shelby County Health Department, Division of Vital Records, Memphis, TN 38105. Call (615) 741-1763 for current fees.
Birth (short form)	Same as Birth (long form)	Same as Birth (long form)
Death	Same as Birth	Same as Birth
Marriage	Same as Birth See remarks	Records since July 1945. Varies/County Clerk in county where license was issued.
Divorce	Same as Birth or Death See remarks	Records since July 1945. Clerk of Court in county where divorce was granted.

TEXAS

Birth	Bureau of Vital Statistics Texas Department of Health 1100 West 49th Street Austin, TX 78756-3191	State office has had records since 1903. Call (512) 458-7111 for current fees. This is a recorded message.
Death	Same as Birth	Same as Birth
Marriage		Records since January 1966. Certified copies are not available from state office.
	See remarks	County Clerk is county where license was issued.
Divorce		Records since January 1968. Certified copies are not available from state office.
	See remarks	Clerk of District Court in county where divorce was granted.

UTAH

Birth	Bureau of Vital Records Utah Department of Health 288 North 1460 West P.O. Box 16700 Salt Lake City, UT 84116-0700	State office has had records since 1905. If event occurred from 1890 to 1904 in Salt Lake City or Ogden, write to City Board of Health. For records elsewhere in the state from 1898 to 1904, write to County Clerk in county where event occurred. Call (801) 538-6105 for current fees. This is a recorded message.

PLACE OF EVENT	ADDRESS	REMARKS
Death	Same as Birth	Same as Birth
Marriage	Same as Birth or Death	State office has had records since 1978. Only short form certified copies are available.
	See remarks	County Clerk in county where license was issued.
Divorce	Same as Birth or Death	State office has had records since 1978. Only short form certified copies are available.
	See remarks	County Clerk where divorce was granted.

VERMONT

PLACE OF EVENT	ADDRESS	REMARKS
Birth or Death	Vermont Department of Health Vital Records Section Box 70 60 Main Street Burlington, VT 05402	State office has had records since 1981. Call (802) 863-7275 for current fees.
Birth, Death or Marriage	Division of Public Records US Route 2-Middlesex 133 State Street Montpelier, VT 05633	Records prior to 1981. Call (802) 828-3286 for current fees. Town or City Clerk of town where birth or death occurred.
Marriage	Same as Birth or Death See remarks	State office has had records since 1981. Town Clerk in town where license was issued.
Divorce	Same as Birth or Death See remarks	State office has had records since 1981. Town Clerk in town where divorce was granted.

VIRGINIA

PLACE OF EVENT	ADDRESS	REMARKS
Birth or Death	Division of Vital Records State Health Department P.O. Box 1000 Richmond, VA 23208-1000	State office has had records from January 1853 to December 1896 and since 14 June 1912. Only the cities of Hampton, Newport News, Norfolk, and Richmond have records between 1896 and 14 June 1912. Call (804) 786-6228 for current fees. This is a recorded message.
Marriage	Same as Birth or Death See remarks	Records since January 1853. Clerk of Court in county or city where license was issued.
Divorce	Same as Birth or Death See remarks	Records since January 1918. Clerk of Court in county or city where divorce was granted.

VIRGIN ISLANDS

PLACE OF EVENT	ADDRESS	REMARKS
Birth or Death St. Croix	Registrar of Vital Statistics Charles Harwood Memorial Hospital Christiansted St. Croix, VI 00820	Registrar has had birth and death records on file since 1840.
St. Thomas and St. John	Registrar of Vital Statistics Knud Hansen Complex Hospital Ground Charlotte Amalie St. Thomas, VI 00802	Registrar has had birth records on file since July 1906 and death records since January 1906. Call (809) 774-9000 ext. 4621 or 4623 for current fees.
Marriage	Bureau of Vital Records and Statistical Services Virgin Islands Department of Health Charlotte Amalie St. Thomas, VI 00801	Certified copies are not available. Inquiries will be forwarded to the appropriate office.

PLACE OF EVENT	ADDRESS	REMARKS
Divorce	Same as Marriage	Certified copies are not available. Inquiries will be forwarded to appropriate office.
St. Croix	Same as Marriage	
St. Thomas and St. John	Same as Marriage	Same as Marriage

WASHINGTON

Birth or Death	Department of Health Center for Health Statistics P.O. Box 9709 Olympia, WA 98507-9709	State office has had records since July 1907. For King, Pierce, and Spokane counties copies may also be obtained from county health departments. County Auditor of county of birth has registered births prior to July 1907. Call (206) 753-5936 for current fees.
Marriage	Same as Birth or Death See remarks	State office has had records since January 1968. County Auditor in county where license was issued.
Divorce	Same as Birth or Death See remarks	State office has had records since January 1968. County Clerk in county where divorce was granted.

WEST VIRGINIA

Birth or Death	Vital Registration Office Division of Health State Capitol Complex Bldg. 3 Charleston, WV 25305	State office has had records since January 1917. For earlier records, write to Clerk of County Court in county where event occurred. Call (304) 558-2931 for current fees.
Marriage	Same as Birth or Death See remarks	Records since 1921. Certified copies available from 1964. County Clerk in county where license was issued.
Divorce	Same as Birth or Death See remarks	Index since 1968. Some items may be verified. Certified copies are not available from state office. Clerk of Circuit Court, Chancery Side, in county where divorce was granted.

WISCONSIN

Birth	Vital Records 1 West Wilson Street P.O. Box 309 Madison, WI 53701	State office has scattered records earlier than 1857. Records before 1 October 1907 are very incomplete. Call (608) 266-1371 for current fees.
Death	Same as Birth	Same as Birth
Marriage	Same as Birth	Records since April 1836. Records before 1 October 1907, are incomplete.
Divorce	Same as Birth	Records since October 1907.

WYOMING

Birth	Vital Records Services Hathaway Building Cheyenne, WY 82002	State office has had records since July 1909. Call (307) 777-7591 for current fees.
Death	Same as Birth	Same as Birth
Marriage	Same as Birth See remarks	Records since May 1941. County Clerk in county where license was issued.
Divorce	Same as Birth See remarks	Records since May 1941. Clerk of District Court where divorce took place.

Used by permission of Ancestry, Inc.

CHAPTER NOTES
AND SUGGESTED READING

INTRODUCTION:
GETTING STARTED

1. Jennifer Fulkerson, "Climbing the Family Tree," *American Demographics,* December 1995, 42–50.

Victor's research led him to write two books about his family history. Victor Villasenor, *Rain of Gold* (New York: Dell, 1992) and *Wild Steps of Heaven* (New York: Dell, 1995).

SUGGESTED READING

Frazier, Ian. *Family.* New York: Harper Perennial, 1994.

CHAPTER ONE:
THE PEDIGREE CHART

A comprehensive and interesting study of kinship and the relationship it has on society can be found in Alex Shoumatoff, *The Mountain of Names* (New York: Vintage Books, 1990).

SUGGESTED READING

Goodwin, Doris Kearns. *The Fitzgeralds and the Kennedys: An American Saga.* New York: Simon and Schuster, 1988.

Rachin, Harvey. *The Kennedys: A Chronological History.* New York: Ballantine Books, 1986.

Szucs, Loretto D., and Sandra Hargreaves Luebking. *The Source: A Guidebook of American Genealogy.* Revised edition. Salt Lake City, Utah: Ancestry, Inc., 1997. *The Source* is widely recognized as an excellent reference for American genealogy. It makes a good addition to any family historian's library.

CHAPTER TWO:
LOOKING AT HOME

Shannon Applegate's story of her family history is complete in the award-winning and critically acclaimed Shannon Applegate, *Skookum: An Oregon Pioneer Family's History and Lore* (New York: William Morrow, 1988).

SUGGESTED READING

Weitzman, David. *My Backyard History Book.* New York: Little, Brown and Company, 1975. Children love searching through attics and old boxes for family history treasures. This is a great source for getting children hooked on family history.

Wolfman, Ira. *Do People Grow on Family Trees? Genealogy for Kids and Other Beginners.* New York: NY Workman Publishing Company, 1991. Another good book for children.

CHAPTER THREE:
GATHERING FAMILY STORIES

The quote on page 26 is taken from the transcript of a video of Alex Haley that was shot at the beginning of the *Ancestors* project before his death.

Bill Zimmerman, *How to Tape Instant Oral Biographies* (New York: Guarionex Press, 1992). This book makes a wonderful gift for anyone interested in taping oral biographies of family members.

SUGGESTED READING

Ritchie, Donald A. *Doing Oral History*. New York: Maxwell Macmillan International, 1995.

CHAPTER FOUR:
THE PAPER TRAIL

Szucs, Loretto D., and Sandra Hargreaves Luebking. *The Source: A Guidebook of American Genealogy*. Revised edition. (Salt Lake City, Utah: Ancestry, Inc., 1997).

AGLL Genealogical Services. P.O. Box 329, Bountiful, Utah 84011-0329. (801) 298-5446 www.xmission.com/~agll/. AGLL has more than 200,000 titles of government records on microfilm and many other products that members may borrow. Their holdings include census, military, vital, church records, and many other types of records.

Brent H. Holcomb, *Passenger Arrivals at the Port of Charleston, 1820–1829* (Baltimore: Genealogical Publishing Company, Inc., 1994).

Betty Couch Wiltshire, *Marriages and Deaths*

from Mississippi Newspapers, Vol. 4: 1850–1861 (Bowie, Maryland: Heritage Books, Inc., 1987).

Alice Morse Earles, *Home Life in Colonial Days* (Stockbridge, Massachusetts: Berkshire House Publishers, 1993). Originally published in 1898.

Harvey Green, *The Uncertainty of Everyday Life*, 1915–1945 (New York: Harper Perennial, 1992).

SUGGESTED READING

Coletta, John Phillip, Ph.D. *They Came in Ships: A Guide to Finding Your Immigrant Ancestor's Arrival Record*. Salt Lake City, Utah: Ancestry, Inc., 1989.

CHAPTER FIVE:
LIBRARIES AND ARCHIVES

R.R Bowker, *American Library Directory* (New Providence, New Jersey: R.R. Bowker, 1996).

For information on local resources for genealogists, refer to:

Bentley, Elizabeth Petty. *The Genealogists Address Book*. Baltimore: Genealogical Publishing Company, Inc., 1993.

Eichholz, Alice, Ph.D.,C.G., maps by William Dollarhide. *Ancestry's Red Book: American State, County and Town Sources*. Salt Lake City, Utah: Ancestry, Inc. Revised edition, 1992.

For information on genealogical sources availiable in major research libraries consult:

Cerny, Johni, and Wendy Elliott, eds. *The Library: A Guide to the LDS Family History Library*. Salt Lake City, Utah: Ancestry, Inc., 1988.

Neagles, James C. *The Library of Congress: A Guide to Genealogical and Historical Research.* Salt Lake City, Utah: Ancestry, Inc., 1990.

Szucs, Loretto D., and Sandra Hargreaves Luebking. *The Archives: A Guide to the National Archives Field Branches.* Salt Lake City, Utah: Ancestry, Inc., 1988.

CHAPTER SIX: CENSUS AND MILITARY RECORDS

For a comprehensive survey of military records for the genealogist, consult: James C. Neagles, *U. S. Military Records: A Guide to Federal and State Sources, Colonial America to the Present* (Salt Lake City, Utah: Ancestry, Inc., 1994).

A useful handbook for locating information on military personnel is Lt. Col. Richard S. Johnson, *How to Locate Anyone Who Is or Has Been in the Military: Armed Forces Locator Directory* (San Antonio, Texas: MIE Publishing, 1996).

A helpful publication to use when researching collections of diaries is *American Diaries: An Annotated Bibliography of Published American Diaries and Journals, 1492–1980* (Detroit: Gale Research, 1983).

To help narrrow a search of federal census records, use E. Kay Kirkham, *A Handy Guide to Record-Searching in the Larger Cities of the United States* (Logan, Utah: Everton Publisher, Inc., 1974).

For information on questions asked by census takers, consult *Twenty Censuses, Population and Housing Questions 1790–1980* (Washington, D.C.: United States Department of Commerce, 1979).

To help locate specific censuses, use the *Periodical Source Index* (Fort Wayne, Indiana: Allen County Public Library, 1987).

The Family History Library publishes a pamphlet that's useful when researching military records. To order the pamphlet, *U.S. Military Records,* contact Family History Library, 35 North West Temple, Salt Lake City, UT 84150, phone (801) 240-2331, fax (801) 240-5551.

CHAPTER SEVEN: AFRICAN-AMERICAN RESEARCH

1. Arlene Eakle and Johni Cerny, *The Source: A Guidebook of American Genealogy* (Salt Lake City, Utah: Ancestry, Inc., 1984), page 579.

2. Paula K. Byers, ed. *African American Genealogical Sourcebook* (Detroit: Gale Reserach Inc., 1995).

3. Eakle and Cerny, page 579.

Ralph Ginsburg, ed. *100 Years of Lynching* (Baltimore: Black Classic Press, 1988).

George P. Rawick, *The American Slave: A Composite Autobiography.* Forty-one volumes. (Westport, Connecticut: Greenwood Press, 1972).

SUGGESTED READING

For ethnic groups with specific research challenges in U.S. research:

Byers, Paula K., ed. *Asian American Genealogical Sourcebook.* Detroit: Gale Research Inc., 1995.

Byers, Paula K., ed. *Hispanic American Genealogical Sourcebook*. Detroit: Gale Research Inc., 1995.

Byers, Paula K., ed. *Native American Genealogical Sourcebook*. Detroit: Gale Research Inc., 1995.

CHAPTER EIGHT: YOUR MEDICAL HERITAGE

1. Nelson-Anderson, Danette L., R.N., B.S.N., and Cynthia V. Water. *Genetic Connections: A Guide to Documenting Your Individual and Family Health History*. Washington, Missouri: Sonters Publishing, 1995, page 7.

2. Krause, Carol. *How Healthy Is Your Family Tree?* New York: Fireside Books, 1995. Carol Krause has written about her experience and has provided practical advice on creating a medical family history.

Arlene Eakle and Johni Cerny, *The Source: A Guidebook of American Genealogy* (Salt Lake City, Utah: Ancestry, Inc., 1984).

CHAPTER NINE: HIGH-TECH HELP

SUGGESTED READING

Crowe, Elizabeth Powell. *Genealogy Online: Researching Your Roots*. New York: Windcrest/McGraw-Hill, 1995.

Eastman, Richard. *Your Roots: Total Genealogical Planning on Your Computer*. Emeryville, California: Ziff-Davis Press, 1995.

CHAPTER TEN: LEAVING A LEGACY

Hannibal Lakumbe's recording *African Portraits* explores the evolution of African-American culture and is available on compact disc through Atlantic Classics.

SUGGESTED READING

Burdick, Nancilu B. *Legacy: The Story of Talula Bottoms and Her Quilts*. Nashville: Rutledge Hill Press, 1988.

Eastman Kodak Company. *Conservation of Photographs*. Rochester, New York: 1985.

Reilly, James M. *Care and Identification of Nineteenth Century Photographic Prints*. Rochester, New York: Eastman Kodak Company, 1986.

Tuttle, Craig. *An Ounce of Preservation: A Guide to the Care of Papers and Photographs*. Highland City, Florida: Rainbow Books, 1995.

PEDIGREE CHART

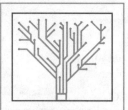

ANCESTORS™

8
FATHER (of no. 4)
Born
Place
Married
Place
Died
Place

4
FATHER (of no. 2)
Born
Place
Married
Place
Died
Place

9
MOTHER (of no. 4)
Born
Place
Married
Place

2
FATHER (of no. 1)
Born
Place
Married
Place
Died
Place

10
FATHER (of no. 5)
Born
Place
Married
Place
Died
Place

5
MOTHER (of no. 2)
Born
Place
Married
Place

11
MOTHER (of no. 5)
Born
Place
Married
Place

1
YOU
Born
Place
Married
Place

12
FATHER (of no. 6)
Born
Place
Married
Place
Died
Place

SPOUSE (of no. 1)

6
FATHER (of no. 3)
Born
Place
Married
Place
Died
Place

13
MOTHER (of no. 6)
Born
Place
Married
Place

3
MOTHER (of no. 1)
Born
Place
Married
Place

14
FATHER (of no. 7)
Born
Place
Married
Place
Died
Place

7
MOTHER (of no. 3)
Born
Place
Married
Place

15
MOTHER (of no. 7)
Born
Place
Married
Place

Person 1 on this chart is the same as person ___ on chart ___.

This page may be duplicated for personal use.

ANCESTORS™

FAMILY GROUP
RECORD

Husband's name

Born		Place	
Mar.		Place	
Died		Place	
Father			Mother

Wife's name

Born		Place	
Mar.		Place	
Died		Place	
Father			Mother

Children (In order of birth)

1 Sex   Name   Spouse

Born		Place	
Mar.		Place	
Died		Place	

2 Sex   Name   Spouse

Born		Place	
Mar.		Place	
Died		Place	

3 Sex   Name   Spouse

Born		Place	
Mar.		Place	
Died		Place	

4 Sex   Name   Spouse

Born		Place	
Mar.		Place	
Died		Place	

This page may be duplicated for personal use.

Additional Children (In order of birth)

5	Sex	Name	Spouse
Born		Place
Mar.		Place
Died		Place

6 | Sex | Name | Spouse
Born | | Place
Mar. | | Place
Died | | Place

7 | Sex | Name | Spouse
Born | | Place
Mar. | | Place
Died | | Place

8 | Sex | Name | Spouse
Born | | Place
Mar. | | Place:
Died | | Place

9 | Sex | Name | Spouse
Born | | Place
Mar. | | Place
Died | | Place

OTHER MARRIAGES:

SOURCES:

This page may be duplicated for personal use.

ANCESTORS 209

ANCESTORS™

RESEARCH LOG

Ancestor's name

Objective(s)	Locality
Birth, Marriage, Death	

Date of search	Location/ call number	Description of source (Author, title, year, pages)	Comments (Purpose of search, results, years, and names searched)	Doc. number

This page may be duplicated for personal use.

Date of search	Location/ call number	Description of source (Author, title, year, pages)	Comments (Purpose of search, results, years, and names searched)	Doc. number

This page may be duplicated for personal use.